An Emptyful Chair

JOURNEYING INTO GOD'S MYSTICAL PRESENCE

SECOND EDITION

Andrew Harnack

Library of Congress Control Number		2019945002
ISBN	Softcover	978-1-950955-25-1
	Hardcover	978-1-950955-26-8
	Ebook	978-1-950955-27-5

Printed in the United States of America.

Book Vine Press
2516 Highland Dr.
Palatine, IL 60067

"Andy insightfully and lovingly invites you
to experience the deep mystical presence of God
that contemplative prayer offers to everyone."

—Richard Rohr

This book is dedicated to Ringo.

Acknowledgments

I wish to extend my deepest appreciation to Kara Beth Brunner of Brunner Studios in Berea, Kentucky, for permission to reproduce and include photographs of my daughter Chelsea and me in Chapter 3. To Bill and Elaine Hallada at Village Photography in Barnesville, GA, my profound gratitude for creating and editing the many composite images that grace the pages of *An Emptyful Chair*. Your professionalism and hospitality is admired by all. All other photographs in *An Emptyful Chair* were taken either by me or members of my family. My uncle George Harnack, took the 1945 photograph of my father standing in the pulpit of his church in York, Pennsylvania. My heartfelt appreciation to Kay Pedrotti, dear parish friend, whose wonderful editorial advice helped me put the finishing touches on the manuscript, fifteen years in the making. For the cartoons in Chapter 5, I laughingly thank David Hayward for the remarkable insights he provides in an art form blessed by honesty, abundant spiritual criticism, and pastoral concern for the life of the church. And thanks to my wife, June, for putting Ringo in my lap and taking our picture for the dedication page. And thank you, Ringo, for going with me on our morning and evening walks!

Can you imagine! Two days before I was to send in my manuscript to Book Vine Press, my computer unexpectedly would not let me open the final text of this book. I thought I had lost everything. But technical advisor Georgia Diaz-Raines of Bakersfield, CA, came to my rescue. After spending hours with me on the phone and screen, all was saved so that I could send *An Emptyful Chair* to Eric Mason at BVP in Palatine, Illinois, for publication. With everything now on printed paper with an attractive book cover, my high fives go to everyone on the BVP Press editorial team who so thoughtfully and professionally gave me the best encouragements and advice possible. Finally, to all in my family who said, "Go ahead, Dad!" and "Get it done, Grandpa!" so that I might include their memories, letters, poems, and jottings in this book, you have my eternal gratitude and love.

Contents

Preface to the Second Edition

This second edition of *An Emptyful Chair* is about three-quarters the size of the first edition because it does not contain the exceptionally detailed information about my life and family, written primarily for my children, grandchildren, neighbors, close associates, and friends in the first edition. Much of that information has been greatly reduced; moreover, this second edition contains fewer family photographs printed in the first edition. There are, however, some textual additions in this edition that I trust will prove helpful. Whenever possible, I've updated bibliographical entries, articles and books more recently published. That said, the basic structure, my theological convictions, and steady appreciation for mystical prayer and contemplative living remain faithful to their expression in the first edition. The subtitle of this edition of *An Emptyful Chair* is now "Journeying into God's Mystical Presence." If you wish take a look at or read the first edition of *An Emptyful Chair: Journeying into the Mystical Presence of God*, it is available at www.amazon.com.

For more information about the concerns of this book, visit

www.andrewharnack.com.

ALL NET PROCEEDS FROM THE SALE OF THIS BOOK WILL BE GIVEN TO GRACE MISSIONS, INC. FOR THE SUPPORT OF *CHEZ MOI*, AN ORPHANAGE FOR GIRLS IN PORT-AU-PRINCE, HAITI.

www.gracemissionsinc.org

Introduction

As a gift to my family, friends, and you, this book briefly tells the story of my life. Late in life and now more than eighty years old, I'm not the same Andy I used to be as a young man. My story is like that of a tadpole who has changed into a frog. Or like a moth's tale about becoming a butterfly. Or that of a new moon turning into a full moon. While the number on my Social Security remains the same, the Andrew in this book is not what he used to be.

But, of course, that may be—or will be!--true for you too. We all are born, grow up, pass through adolescence, enter adulthood, and get older in one way or another. Yet my observations tell me that my personal maturing has been quite different from the experience of many others. At least that's what some of my friends tell me. It's what I know to be true.

Writing about myself has been a challenge. For a long time, this question has loomed large in my life: Is it really possible to chart the circuitous meanderings of one's life? Many people have tried to chart lives like mine. Some say they see five, six, seven, or eight life stages; others say there are basically only three or four phases.[1] After long

---

1 Bruce Powers's *Growing Faith* (Nashville: Broadman, 1982) maps out five phases; although interesting, it doesn't quite fit me. James Fowler's *Weaving the New Creation* (New York: HarperCollins, 1991) gives us seven stages. More accurately reflecting my journey, it's too detailed for our purposes here. M. Scott Peck's four-stage presentation in *Further Along the Road Less Travelled* (New York: Simon and Schuster, 1993) is excellent and fits me to a tee. If choose I must, however, I have come to prefer Richard Rohr's *Falling Upward: A Spirituality for the Two Halves of Life* (San Francisco, CA: Jossey-Bass, 2011). As you will see in *An Emptyful Chair*, it's my guiding template.

musings, lots of journal keeping, dream-haunted nights, and lots of reading, I've decided to tell you about my life journey as one having three basic stages:

1. Life with an inherited faith
2. Life with disappointments, failures, and questions
3. Life renewed in contemplative spirituality

As you read my story, you'll see that as a child I inherited the faith of my parents, their community of friends, their church—their heritage. I treasured my inherited faith for a long time, well into my mid-twenties, even when I began seminary studies.

As strange as it sounds, after my ordination as a Lutheran pastor, I entered a life-changing transitional phase in my spiritual journey, a time of serious questionings. Over a period of about twenty years, I investigated the roots of my inherited thinking. I investigated what I had been taught and probed the crevices of my convictions. Slowly but surely I began to doubt the validity of much that I had been taught. I began to discard a lot of ideas that did not stand up to the light of serious research and reading. I emptied myself of considerable nineteenth-century Lutheran theology, the "faith of my fathers."

Eventually I left the church in which I was raised because much of its dogma was inadequate and injurious to authentic, God-pleasing living. To my dismay, I discovered that certain Christian convictions actually lead to prejudice, spiritual aloofness, harsh judgments, a sense of enormous superiority, and well-disguised violent thoughts toward people living in different faith traditions. I saw my inherited faith for what it was—a tribal version of Christianity. In other words, I saw the *dark* side of an institution I had once known as the "church." In short, I saw the belly of a fire-breathing dragon, masquerading itself as God's organization set up to safeguard morality and guarantee the world's salvation.

I also encountered failure. As outwardly successful as I was, I experienced crippling personal disappointments, a loss of who I was, a collapse of spirit. I went into darkness.

But in all my missteps, moral bankruptcy, and messiness of life, things were not so utterly dark that I could not see faint glimmers of light and hope. Marvelously God opened previously unknown doors for a new and more wholesome journey. Some call this third phase of spiritual development a movement toward "holistic faith," an "enlightened return," "a second journey," "unitive consciousness," and "the miracle of spiritual evolution," among a host of other descriptive terms. I simply call it my entrance into inner awareness and contemplative living. It's a vision and way of life that sees God radically present and working everywhere, in everyone, even in me. After undergoing what some call "post traumatic church syndrome," I gradually returned to a Spirit-filled life. I am now keenly aware that God beyond the three-letter word "God," whoever s/he may be, is quite unfathomable, beyond language, largely unknowable. In this epical age of the Holy Spirit, God is encouraging us to reimagine his judgmental bearings, even encouraging a familiarization of his mythic past. Shocking? Yes, but wonderfully liberating, endorsed with scholarly sobriety, a new awareness shared by many pilgrims and blessed by the witness of Christians in earlier centuries, especially contemplatives and mystics like the Desert Fathers and Mothers, Gregory of Nyssa, Evagrius Ponticus, and Meister Eckhart, to mention but a few.

My life is but one example of how it all happens. As you read, you'll be introduced to those who have guided me. Some simply came out of the woodwork. The road to others was paved by bloggers and conference speakers. More than one helpful bibliography entry required the purchase of a book, and a dozen or so placed me in their prayers and hearts as together we learned to walk a new way, hand in hand.

My three-stage story has fourteen chapters. In chapters 1–4 you'll observe the first half of my life, characterized by an inherited faith, God's goodness, and my ups and downs. In chapters 5 and 6, I tell you about my dark realizations as the first foundation began to crumble and undergo inner earthquakes. In time God helped me climb out of the rubble as the Spirit "crossed" me over to a different way of thinking and living. In chapters 7-14, I show you what it's like to live within what Richard Rohr calls "a second simplicity," "a bright sadness," and "the shadowlands."[2] It's a life of awareness within an ecumenical, worldwide, all-inclusive, and all-embracing life of faith. It's the way I live, believe, and love now. It's a contemplative life. It's life within the mystical presence of God.

When I began working on *An Emptyful Chair*, my expectations as to what might be accomplished were modest. They still are. Having kept books of jottings, journal entries, scattered notes, photographs, and assorted papers in lots of boxes, file drawers, and notebooks, I assumed I could piece things together in some kind of narrative, a wee memoir of sorts. Little did I know how difficult that would be. To help gather up memories and recollect things, I've spent hours and sometimes days fingering through old scribblings, notes, and diary entries, which I hoped would provide some grounding and assistance. Scattered piles of calendars, old archived manuscripts, newspaper clippings, photographs, and coffee-stained scratchings have more than once seemed too disorganized to manage. Much has been thrown into the waste can. Lots saved.

My awareness of the difficulties eventually became acute when I read what Wendell Berry, Kentucky's poet laureate, has said as he described the shocking truth about what we think we remember as we look back on our lives:

> We know almost nothing of our history as it was actually lived. We know little of the lives even of our parents. We have forgotten almost everything that has happened to ourselves. The easy assumption that we have remembered the most important people and events and have preserved the most valuable evidence is immediately trumped by our inability to know what we have forgotten.[3]

---

2 These designations are the headings for chapters describing the grace-filled second half of life in Rohr, *Falling Upward*, v.

3 Wendell Berry, *The Way of Ignorance and Other Essays* (Berkeley, CA: Counterpoint, 2005), 54.

Wendell Berry well describes my own not-knowings, and I can only promise that I've now scratched out and gathered up things as best I can—despite extensive disrememberings.

Some things, of course, I remember well but have decided that they best stay unrecorded. As Will Campbell puts it, "We are all bastards, but God loves us." So you will (by God's grace), forgive me if I let many dark, bastardly shadows of my life stay unrecorded, known for the most part only to God. Simply assume the worst. Here and there may be intimations, but nothing so revealing as to cast me into whatever hell many imagine. I prefer to underscore God's grace rather than my indiscretions, unseemly foibles, and errant trajectories. I trust you understand.

While working on this book, I ran across these opening words to Richard Lischer's "Writing the Christian Life: The Essence of Spiritual Memoir":

> A sparrow flutters through the window into a banquet hall filled with light, music, and feasting. Then, just as quickly, the bird flies away again into the darkness. The flight of the bird is our life—brief, dramatic, and framed by two immense darknesses. Where has it come from? From what primordial past? Where is it going? Into what unknowable future?
>
> The ancient parable suggests a religious dimension to the telling of any life. It begins in mystery and ends in faith. So compelling is the mystery that it must be puzzled over and prayed out and finally written down.[4]

In writing *An Emptyful Chair*, I've puzzled over much and prayed over each page. That said, I have enjoyed delving into my past because life has given me so much joy, undeserved happiness,

4 Richard Lischer, "Writing the Christian Life: The Essence of Spiritual Memoir," *Christian Century* (August 24, 2015), 22; available at https://www.christiancentury.org/article/2015-08/writing-christian-life.

good luck, a wonderful assortment of friends, cherished wives, and children who have been God's blessings to me, year after year. If anyone or anything could be more worthy of praise and gratitude, it would be only this: God's gift of my living contemplatively as a Christian. As you turn the pages, I hope you'll come to know what I mean.

And just who will turn these pages? Many years ago Pastor Robert Blythe of First Baptist Church in Richmond, Kentucky, asked me if I'd write a book for pastors who have experienced divorce. This is such a book, written for pastors, ministers, and priests whose lives have been disrupted by separation, divorce, the breaking of a marriage vow, and the sense of failure that often accompanies such a tragedy. If such an undoing has been a part of your life's journey, this book may be for you a voice of healing, hope, and renewing spiritual health. I write for you.

An Emptyful Chair?

The title of this little book may seem strange, perhaps odd, or even off-putting. If so, good! For several years I thought that the adjective "emptyful" was my very own neologism, a new word I invented, never used in the English language before. But I was wrong. "Emptyful" is actually the name of a tall thirty-five-foot glass flask-like sculpture filled with shifting lights, cascading and boiling water, and cool fog, designed by Bill Pechet and installed at the Millennium Library Plaza in Winnipeg, Canada, in June 2012. As Pechet tells us, this monumental work of art gives artistic expression to the idea that something can be empty and full at the same time. Good for Pechet! Using his neologism, my book tries paradoxically to say exactly that! But with a difference.

I welcome you to the image of a chair. Like you, I have sat on many chairs. Mom and Dad fed me as a baby in a high chair (I still have it sitting near the breakfast table). As a student I sat at many desks. On Sundays I frequently sat in uncomfortable church pews. With Dad I watched the Syracuse Chiefs play baseball in a chair ten rows up behind third base. In my mid-thirties I once sat at "high table" in the refectory of Trinity College, Oxford, England. When a beach bum, I sat on the sand just inches from the lapping waves on the shores of Cape Cod. As a teacher I sat in a university office grading papers. For most of my life, I've been a "chaired" person, sitting as teacher, pastor, TV watcher, bus and bike rider, car driver, and a writer.

As a contemplative Christian, I now sit in an old Windsor with its saddle-shaped seat carved for comfort. I bought that chair years ago at the Antiques on Atlanta in Barnesville, Georgia, for seventy-five dollars. It's the chair in which I now practice what's known as "centering prayer," a form of prayer that provides me with deep inner emptiness that is also paradoxically full of God's presence. This book will help you understand how, why, when, where, with, and to whom that emptying and filling happen. As you turn the pages of this gift to you, please know that you are invited to sit in your own emptyful chair, becoming simultaneously empty and full.

As a teacher, Jesus also spent a lot of time sitting in chairs. Following Rabbinic custom, he liked to teach and tell puzzling and enigmatic stories while sitting. Just as Luke reminds us:

> When Jesus came to Nazareth, where he had been brought up, he went to the synagogue on the Sabbath day, as was his custom. He stood up to read, and the scroll of the prophet Isaiah was given to him. He unrolled the scroll and found the place where it was written: "The Spirit of the Lord is upon me, because he has anointed me to bring good news to the poor." And he rolled up the scroll, gave it back to the attendant, and sat down. The eyes of all in the synagogue were fixed on him. (4:16–20)

One time, Matthew says, when he had some difficulty finding a beach bench, Jesus used a seat in a boat as his teaching chair:

> That same day Jesus went out of the house and sat beside the sea. Such great crowds gathered around him that he got into a boat and sat there, while the whole crowd stood on the beach. And he told them many things in parables. (3:1–3)

Today the Apostles' Creed encourages us to imagine Jesus "seated at the right hand of the Father" on a throne in glory. Such sitting asks us to remember that in the Hebrew Scriptures it is said that God "sits" on the "mercy seat" on the Ark of the Covenant between the cherubs. We, of course, mustn't take all this sitting too literally. Nevertheless, the image of a divinely favored chair urges us to take seriously the importance of sitting in our own lives. Like God we too are sitters, often sitting in silence, quietly allowing the mystery of God's presence to ease us away from the preoccupations of a feverish pace of living. One of the creation stories tells that God rested on the seventh day as He observed the Sabbath. We too are to slow down, read, rest, pray, and be compassionate like our creative God and compassionate Jesus.

It's for these reasons that I choose to photograph my favorite chair for this book's cover. It's the chair I use in my Barnesville, Georgia, home to reinforce contemplative prayer and open myself to a quiet way of living. Yes, it's scratched, chipped, and well-worn, but it does its work without complaint.

This book is written for you and my children and family. They know a lot about me, but not everything. I hope *An Emptyful Chair* will help them understand me as their father, grandfather, great-grandfather, and maybe "Abba" for generations to come.[5]

---

5 "Abba" is a transliteration of the Aramaic "abba." It appears three times in the Greek New Testament of the Bible (Mark 14:36; Rom. 8:15; Gal. 4:6), and in each case is followed by its Greek equivalent, "pater," translated as "father." As a term expressing warm affection and filial confidence, *Abba* has no perfect equivalent in our English language. Some say that the words *Da-da* or *Daddy* comes about as close as we can get. It's one of the first words a baby learns to say when he or she and his or her father look into each other's eyes; it's a word revealing a wonderful relationship. In the last chapter of this book, you'll see why *Abba* is the word I quietly but silently murmur when I wish to be closest to God, within the Divine Presence.

I'd like that your reading of this story becomes for you a life-changing experience, similar perhaps to my own unfolding and transformation. Wherever you are on the trajectory of your life, I'm hoping that *An Emptyful Chair* will give you the surprise of welcoming emptiness, new ways of letting go, wonderful unexpected fullness, and above all, "the mind of Christ," the Emptyful One of God.

About the footnotes

I have a tendency to use documentary evidence in footnotes. I've inserted them sparingly and only when I think you might want to look something up to make sure I'm on track. Maybe like me, you too may appreciate hunting down sources to allusions and quotations, more books to read, and pleasant trips to the library. Returning, of course, to your own emptyful chair.

You have nothing to fear.

I fully realize this book may introduce you to ideas and ways of seeing life that are perhaps new and possibly uncomfortable for you. If in reading this book, you find yourself wary and perhaps even terrified at the mention of meditation, contemplation, and maybe worse, the word "mysticism," please know that as I have been writing this book, I've been listening to St. Teresa's advice on how to work with and guide people who cannot and will not explore the possibility of Christian meditation, contemplation, and silent prayer. Here is what St. Teresa has been whispering to me:

> Let us now return to speak of those souls I have mentioned who cannot practice recollection or tie down their minds to mental prayer or make a meditation. We must not talk to them of either of those two things—they will not hear of them; as a matter of fact, there are a great many people who

> seem terrified at the very name of contemplation or mental prayer.[6]

Commenting on her words of wisdom, Carl McColman underscores St. Teresa's concern: "Whether we like it or not, talking about contemplation (and meditation) to those who either aren't called to it, or not yet called to it, or actively resisting such a call, could simply stimulate a response of fear." Surely I don't want to say things that will scare you. There is no point in anyone's having to deal with fear, so often expressed as hostility. In writing this book and when teaching others about contemplation and Christian mysticism, I try always to be aware of how my brothers and sisters, especially if they are Christians, respond to what I write and say. And, dear reader, that goes for you too. If, on the one hand, you think you will fearfully read my book, allow me to put *An Emptyful Chair* down for you and simply hold you in love. If, on the other hand, you can read without fear, I write for you.

If you are even slightly interested in exploring the possibility of living a contemplative life, this book is for you. As you open this book, I will sit beside you, give you a bookmark, and turn the pages as together we make our way through *An Emptyful Chair*. May the Divine Presence bless my writing and your reading, enfolding us in his Sabbath, silence, centering grace, and spacious love.

6 Quoted by Carl McColman, "St. Teresa's Advice for Dealing with People Who Cannot or Will Not Engage in Christian Contemplation," *A Contemplative Faith* (December 22, 2016), http://www.patheos.com/blogs/carlmccolman/2016/12/st-teresas-advice-dealing-people-cannot--will-not-engage-christian-contemplation.

Chapter 1

THE JOURNEY BEGINS

The two most important days in your life
are the day you are born
and the day you find out why.
—Mark Twain

If you accept the belief that baptism
incorporates us into the mystical body of Christ,
into the divine DNA, then you might say that
the Holy Spirit is present in each of us,
and thus we have the capacity for the fullness
of redemption, of transformation.
—Thomas Keating

Entering light

Sometime in late February 1937 (was it the night of February 21?), with the help of the Divine Presence, my mom and dad made love and I was conceived. It was a nice idea for God, Mom, and Dad to make love, and I hope they enjoyed everything as I was given life. Nine months later, as their firstborn, I met the world on October 21,

1937, when my mother, Helen Gertrude Harnack, gave birth to me in the Harrisburg Polyclinic Hospital.

Mom once told me that I was born well after sunset, sometime on a Thursday around 9:30 p.m. So while I didn't enter the world under a blazing noonday sun, after I opened my little eyes for the first time, I managed to see some old-fashioned electrical lights in the delivery room as Mom gave birth to me, and Dr. Stine, her obstetrician, handed me into her welcoming arms. Nakedly I entered life, light, and love.

And more. Like everybody else, from day one I inherited an original identity at birth. I started to hear my name. During the next several years, Mom and Dad told me who I was and who I should be. The vast majority of parents—Protestants, Catholics, Jews, Taoists, atheists and agnostics, Muslims, Hindus, Seventh-day Adventists, Buddhists, nones, secularists, whatever—also give original identities to their newborn offspring. It's like Jesus once said, "That which born of flesh is flesh" (John 3:6). Our parents not only pass on our physical DNA (the color of our eyes and hair), but they also imprint on us our ethnic, tribal, cultural, and communal DNA (where we live and how we learn). If raised in a Methodist family, a Methodist boy or girl is infused with some sort of Methodism. If raised in a black family, one gets to know what ebony is all about.

I was born into a family with distinct beliefs within a religious tradition, into a nation with a particular culture, and into a social class with a shared consciousness. Yes, I eventually came to lose some of that identity, but I can never escape the fact that I was born Caucasian, Pennsylvanian, middle class with educational opportunities, and Christian in faith and tradition. From day one I found out that my religious identity was Lutheran. And for all that, I'm grateful.

Even though one's original identity is deeply imprinted on the psyche, mind, and soul, new awakenings and realizations may eventually help one create a second identity, perhaps (and perhaps not) more profound than the first. Take Martin Luther, for example. His mother, Margaret, and father, Hans Luder, (derived from "Lothar") changed their peasant names to "Luther" when Hans became a prosperous copper-mining industrialist in Eisleben. Born

"Martinus Luther," the great Reformer loved to brag about his peasant roots ("Ich bin ein Bauern Sohn!"; "I am the son of peasants!"). However, after a radical reorientation, Luther later signed his name as "Eleutherios" (Greek for "a free man") to advertise his new identity as a Reformer. Like Luther, I was born "Lutheran." And like Luther, I too have changed my sense of identity.

More light

I was baptized a month or so later. In a journal entry dated November 30, 2009 (seventy-two years later), I thought about my baptism and described it to myself this way:

> My baptism reminds me of a scene in the movie *Blind Side*. It's the story of Michael Oher, a homeless African-American youngster from a broken home, taken in by the Touhys, a well-to-do white family who helped him fulfill his potential. While I don't know the details of the story, this short conversation between Michael and Leigh Anne Touhy, the woman who brought Michael into her family's home, nearly says it all:
>
> Leigh Anne: Would you like to be a member of our family?
>
> Michael: I thought I already was.

Now that's a conversation about grace. When Leigh Anne brought Michael into her family and home, she gave Michael a brand-new identity. After she introduced Michael to the family, she showed him his new bedroom and served him food at the family table. Michael was "hooked." That is, he could only think of himself as a "Touhy," an "adopted" but permanent member of a wonderful family. When Leigh Anne asks, "Would you like to be in our family?" Michael is astonished at the question and can only tell the truth, "I thought I already was!" Yes, Michael already was!

That's exactly the way I grew up. Ever since I can remember, I've said to myself, "Andy, you're a Christian." I've known no other identity ever since God took me by holy baptism into his family, the church, the Body of Christ. Oh yes, I had to learn how to live by faith as a Christian, what sort of manners we Christians observe, how we love one another and other people, how we worship our adoptive Father, Son, and Spirit. All that came naturally and spiritually as the Holy Spirit of God led me on my journey and cultivated my growing faith and trust in the mercy of God.

My wonderful Mother, Father, and Dr. Stine gave me my first birth. Some forty days later I was "born from above"[7] and adopted by God into his family and presented to the Body of Christ, the church. This time God took me into his trifold Name, lifted me to the cross of Christ and, as St. Paul says, "immersed me into the death and resurrection of Christ" (Rom. 6). How wonderful always to know that. Like any child adopted into a good family, I was delighted at being a Christian. I learned to pray, clean my room, read Scriptures, do my homework, ride a bike, manage a newspaper route in the sixth grade, and let Jesus meet me Sunday after Sunday in Holy Communion. I learned what forgiveness, grace, and mercy are all about—beginning in infancy.

---

[7] Yes, I know that many (but not all) of my Baptist friends say that they are "born again." However, Lutherans, along with Episcopalians, Roman Catholics, Presbyterians, most Methodists, and Eastern Orthodox Christians, prefer describing the baptized as "born from above." That's the English idiom many scholars and recent translations (e.g., NRSV) now prefer when translating the original Greek text into English. Jesus compares my second birth to my first birth. Like a mother, Jesus says, our Mother God gives birth to us "from above." God as our mother delivers and births us. And when we come from the divine womb for a second birth ("born from above"), like that first birth into this world, our response is simply to breathe in his Spirit, his Pneuma ("breath" or "wind" as the Greek puts it). By "birthing" me in Holy Baptism, God plunged me into the whirlpool of Jesus's death and resurrection (Rom. 6:1). In both births I'm the blessed recipient of life-giving grace, first earthly and then heavenly or spiritually. In both deliveries all I do is enter a world of the parental and divine love, love so wonderfully and generously given that it'll take me a while (maybe a lifetime) to breathe it all in and appreciate the miracle. That's why I'm put into a family of brothers and sisters, the community of the church, so I can learn who (and Whose!) I am as a baptized child of God. For an excellent short essay on how best to read the story of Jesus talking to Nicodemus about somehow being "born again" and/or "from above," read Gene Veith's "Born Again & Born from Above" at http://www.patheos.com/blogs/geneveith/2018/10/born-again-born-from-above/

Mother and me / Dad in the pulpit of Good Shepherd Lutheran Church, York, Pennsylvania

Dad, Art, me, Gordon, and Mom sometime in the early 1940s

What a life God has given me! I wouldn't have it any other way. Thank you, Mom and Dad, for bringing me to the baptismal font. Thank you, Church, for welcoming me into your blessed family. And thank You, Most Holy Trinity, for baptizing me into your name, the best name I ever was given and will always have--Christian. Now, some eighty years later, I remember my baptism at the beginning of worship almost every Sunday.[8]

Be that as it may, I know I was baptized as Harvey Andrew Harnack on Saint Andrew's Day and Saint Andrew has long been my patron saint. A Greek icon of Saint Andrew now hangs next to my bed so that I see him every morning and evening. Although the icon itself displays Saint Andrew as a rather dour-looking fellow (I am, of course, dour at times myself), I like to look at the icon appreciatively

---

8 Lutherans are encouraged to remember their baptisms daily and especially on Sundays. Whenever I make the sign of the cross (usually privately, for example, after getting out of bed), I remember my baptism into the death and resurrection of Christ. Often on Sundays everyone in my parish faces the baptismal font at the entrance of the sanctuary as our pastor encourages us to give thanks for our baptisms with this prayer:

> Blessed be the holy Trinity, one God, the fountain of living water, the rock who gave us birth, our light and our salvation. All: Amen.

As we hear the sound of splashing water poured from a large pitcher into the baptismal font, our pastor continues to pray like this:

> Joined to Christ in the waters of baptism, we are clothed with God's mercy and forgiveness. Let us give thanks for the gift of baptism.
>
> We give you thanks, O God, for in the beginning your Spirit moved over the waters and by your Word you created the world, calling forth life in which you took delight.
>
> Through the waters of the flood you delivered Noah and his family. Through the sea you led your people Israel from slavery into freedom. At the river your Son was baptized by John and anointed with the Holy Spirit. By water and your Word, you claim us as daughters and sons, making us heirs of your promise and servants of all.
>
> We praise you for the gift of water that sustains life, and above all, we praise you for the gift of new life in Jesus Christ. Shower us with your Spirit, and renew our lives with your forgiveness, grace and love. To you be given honor and praise through Jesus Christ our Lord in the unity of the Holy Spirit, now and forever. All: Amen.
>
> Speaking of "showers," during the Easter Vigil our pastor dips an evergreen branch into water and "showers" us with water so that, dripping with water, we're sure to remember our most holy baptisms!

for at least two reasons. First, it was to Andrew that Jesus said clearly, "You did not choose me; I chose you!" And second, in Scripture it is Saint Andrew who likes to introduce people to Jesus. He is, after all, the disciple who introduced Peter to Jesus. All of this reminds me that I am Andy only by the grace of God and that one of my jobs is to introduce as many people to Christ as I possibly can.

One request: please call me "Andy." I never did like "Harvey," my first name. Here's why. When I was thirteen years old, I went to a local theater in Syracuse, New York, and saw *Harvey*, a movie starring Jimmy Stewart. The story is about a man whose best friend is a six-foot, three-and-a-half-inch tall invisible rabbit, whom he refers to as a *pooka*, named Harvey. The movie was incredibly popular, but I thought it a real fruitcake of a film. As a 110-pound adolescent, I didn't want anybody associating me with an invisible rabbit, no matter how tall. So to this day, I avoid the name "Harvey." Yes, it's on my passport, but only there.

Richard Rohr has reminded me that Eric Fromm in *The Art of Loving* tells us that the spiritually healthiest people he has known are "those who received from their two parents and early authority figures a combination of unconditional and spiritual love."[9] My brothers—Gordon and Art--and I were the recipients of such parental loving.

In the early years of the first half of my life, I was certainly blessed in so many ways. Born into the Harnack family, baptized and born again from above, and answering to my nickname "Andy," I grew up a very disciplined but happy boy with two terrific brothers, a pastoring father, and a wonderful mother. I certainly had no identity problems. I knew who I was. Loved and Lutheran. Thoroughly grounded, my identity was established. I lived in a middle-class home with disciplining and doting parents. I was secure. My little ego developed nicely. As authority figures, my parents taught me how to obey rules. Although Santa Claus was real and a wee bit intimidating, I liked him. I liked God, my brothers, and school. It was even okay to be left-handed. Everybody loved me. I was off to a good start.

I had inherited an identity. Wonderful!

---

9 Rohr, *Falling Upward: A Spirituality for the Two Halves of Life* (San Francisco: CA: Jossey-Bass, 2011), 32.

A first naïveté

But let's be honest. As good as all this inherited identity was and is, in truth it is simply first and foremost a "first naïveté." The word "naïveté" comes from the Latin *natus*; it's the past participle of *nasci* meaning "to be born." Coined by Paul Ricoeur,[10] the phrase "first naïveté" refers to that stage in life when we live as newborns, perhaps for a long time! Such a person is often said to be as "simple and credulous" like a child. The designation "first naïveté" alerts us to a way of seeing, feeling, and believing, which we receive as infants, toddlers, first graders, eighth graders, and so on until perhaps we experience a "second naïveté." Within one's "first naïveté," one simply accepts what Mom, Dad, teachers, pastors, and other cultural authorities say is true. It's also what many people still continue to accept as a way of life as adults. Living in their first naïveties, such adults continue to believe everything about their religion, nation, and social class as it was first given to them. One can, in fact, live in her or his "first naïveté" for a very long time, naïvely accepting the world into which she or he was born. Such a person has a lot to learn and unlearn. Like me: disciplined, loved, happy, and naïve.

A Reflection on Beginnings

Looking back, pondering the meaning of my beginnings, I can't help but realize that you too, whoever you are, started your life with an inherited identity, a knowing about yourself to which you fell heir. Like Jesus who was taken to the temple to officially become a Jewish boy, each of us was taken to a Bethlehem or Jerusalem to become our first self. We received a name, a family of some kind, and a community in which to live. It all came as something of a gift.

10 Paul Ricoeur was a French philosopher best known for his preoccupation with the question as to how does one interpret one's self, who one is. Captured during World War II, he used his five years in captivity to work out his observations, answers, and suggestions. He taught and lectured in France through 1956 and then in the United States. His most widely read works are *The Rule of Metaphor*, *From Text to Action*, and *Oneself as Another*.

Some of us are given a single parent. Others are adopted. Many are hospitalized with disabilities. A few are raised in wealthy families. Lots arrive in middle-income families. Twenty percent in the United States are raised in poverty and cared for by grandparents, aunts, and uncles. Whatever the circumstances, we entered this world and inherited an initial identity without knowing much about it all until later. If we're lucky and blessed, we received parental love (hopefully unconditional). Then too, our entrance into the world may have been marked with hardships, child abuse, and governmental interventions. However we begin the first half of our lives, it's necessary that each of us becomes acquainted with who we first were (and still perhaps are) in the beginning and shortly thereafter.

All of us need to realize, however, that whether our received identity is good, sad, or bad, it need not be our only or lasting identity. We may change names, meet new caregivers, discover new kinds of love, and even move to the other side of the world, physically and spiritually. We can assume new and different ways of seeing ourselves. Yes, we may stay in the quiet valley or noisy city of our birth. Or we may not. What's important is that we learn to appreciate both the blessings and the baggage originally given to us, realizing that there may well be a second half of life, the possibility of another life transcending our first, a life enlarging our sense of self. Ultimately within that second half of life, whenever it makes its appearance, you may become aware of your truest identity. You may be introduced by a second naïveté to a full realization of your True Self.

Chapter 2

SCHOOLINGS

Without education, we are
in a horrible and deadly danger
of taking educated people seriously.
—G. K. Chesterton

Educating the mind without educating
the heart is no education at all.
—Aristotle

Only Lutheran

Once I had my parent-given Lutheran identity imprinted on my emerging consciousness, Mom and Dad (mostly Dad) made sure that it got stamped like a notary public seal on my realizations about life. They took me to church services every Sunday, enrolled me in parochial school, sent me to Saturday confirmation classes for three years, and gave me a Lutheran high-school and college education. As a consequence, for many years I only knew myself as a Lutheran Christian. I was not someone else. Not "big-C" Catholic. Heaven forbid! Not Baptist. Saints, preserve me! Not anything but Lutheran. And unbeknown to me for years, a very conservative Lutheran!

It was only by dribs and drabs, bit by bit, that I eventually came to know there were other kinds of people, other sorts of Lutherans, other varieties of Christianity, other options. This emerging awareness came like a curtain slowly being pulled back to reveal windows, doors, and stage sets waiting for Act 3. One was not encouraged to be too curious. I was taught to respect my elders, obey the authorities, and not to ask too many questions. In high school, for example, the possibility of evolution on planet Earth was never entertained in any science class. Certain books could not be found in the library. Other people had to be doctrinally correct if we were to associate with them closely. Calvinists were not allowed participation in our Holy Communions. Seeing certain movies was off-limits. Dating girls of other religious traditions was verboten. I was being indoctrinated. Just like an adolescent Muslim boy gets to know the Koran and the hadith,[11] a Hindu girl the Vedas,[12] a Morman teenager *The Book*, and a Jewish boy his Torah, I was being confirmed (literally "made strong") in Lutheran schools. I was learning how "this" differs from "that." I was taught to respect the lines and boundaries, traveling down a one-lane, one-way highway.

Parochial school

I was enrolled as a first-grade student in St. John Lutheran Church Parochial School, York, Pennsylvania. It's interesting to note that the first school picture of me over by the blackboard in the striped shirt announces that I can write my name on the blackboard: "Andy."

11 The term *hadith* comes from the Arabic meaning "report," "account," or "narrative." *Hadiths* are second only to the Koran in developing Islamic jurisprudence and regarded as important tools for understanding the Koran and commentaries on it. See https://en.wikipedia.org/wiki/Hadith for more information.

12 The Vedas are a large body of texts originating in ancient India.

That's me on the left in the striped shirt.
I've written my name, "Andy" on the blackboard.

Inasmuch as my right hand holds an eraser, it appears as though I wrote my name with a piece of chalk in my left hand. I've always been left-handed when it comes to writing. That my single word is "Andy" says a lot about me, my education, and my life. Notice how I stare at the four letters of my name. Largely unaware until late in my life, nearly all of everything was about me. About Andy. It took me a long time to see that and eventually find ways to let go of such a sense of Andy. More about that later.

For our early formal education, Gordon, Art, and I went to St. John Lutheran Parochial School in York, Pennsylvania. We walked about a mile to and from school and always crossed the "inky-stinky" Codoros Creek as we trudged along sidewalks made of red-brick pavers. About school itself in the first to third and fourth grades, I remember nothing other than a certain Mr. Miller was my teacher, and I apparently made a fool of myself when seven years old in a school play—or maybe it was a dance performance. I've since made a fool of myself more memorably.

Learning grammar, collecting stuff, and making things

When Dad decided to take "a call" (as Lutherans then put it) to become pastor of Trinity Lutheran Church in Syracuse, New York, I became a student at Edward Smith Elementary School, again about a mile from home. Three memories stand out. First, I remember that in the sixth grade, my English teacher taught us the great distinction between the past and present perfect verb tenses. I was amazed at the difference in meaning between "I had built a snowman" and "I have built a snowman." Over the years I've used that example in English-grammar classes dozens of times. Second, when nine years old, I somehow managed to get my hands on large packets of cancelled stamps from countries around the world and was much interested in collecting stamps. A year later somebody took my picture with Miss Helen Angeloff, library assistant at the nearby branch library, and together we appeared in a local newspaper with this announcement:

> DISCUSS MUTUAL HOBBY—Stamp collecting is a major interest of both Andrew Harnack, 9, of 1040 Westcott St. and Miss Helen Angeloff, library assistant at Point Branch. Andrew frequently borrows books on stamps. Here he talks over some interesting stamps Miss Angeloff.[13]

Photograph published in *The Post-Standard*, Syracuse, New York (September22, 1947), 6.

Having spent thousands of hours in libraries, I'm especially appreciative that Miss Helen Angeloff made me feel welcome at an early age. I owe Miss Angeloff a big "thank-you" for blessing me with what has become a lifelong habit of collecting letters, notes,

[13] *The Post-Standard*, Syracuse, New York, September 22, 1947, 6.

scribblings on envelopes, unedited manuscripts, cards, doodlings, photos, and life records into boxes carried thither and yon from there to here.

Third, I remember enjoying the eighth-grade woodworking and electrical-shop classes in which we made coiled crystal radios by wrapping copper wires around and around oatmeal boxes. Very primitive stuff by today's standards but cutting edge for me back then. All of which may be why I still enjoy working in a workshop filled with tools, gadgets, and projects today.

More definitively Lutheran

And I become more Lutheran. At all our evening meals, after Mom brought in lots of delicious foods such as chicken dumplings, I listened to table prayers. Dad said prayers both before and after supper. They were from *Luther's Small Catechism* where it is recommended that fathers lead their families in a prayer like this one based on Psalm 145:

> The eyes of all look to You, [O Lord] and You give them their food at the proper time. You open Your hand and satisfy the desires of every living thing.
>
> Lord God, heavenly Father, bless us and these Your gifts which we receive from Your bountiful goodness, through Jesus Christ, our Lord. Amen.

Dad did it this way because he was soon to be my catechetical teacher and needed to set an example.

Most Lutheran kids went to Saturday catechetical classes for two years to learn what Luther wrote in his *Small Catechism*.[14]

[14] I still have that 212-page 1943 edition of *Luther's Small Catechism* published with this extended title: *A Short Explanation of Dr. Martin Luther's Small Catechism: A Handbook of Christian Doctrine* (Saint Louis, Missouri: Concordia Publishing House, 1943). Fifty years ago, like my father, I used it to teach catechumens in two parishes, one in upper New York and one in Louisiana. That 1943 edition, published by the Lu-

But after giving us catechetical instruction for two years, my father deemed the lot of us, twelve in all, not quite prepared for presentation to the congregation. As a consequence, memorizing and discussing Luther's *Catechism* continued for another twelve months. For twelve-year-old kids, the *Catechism* was quite a tome and not easily memorized.

At the end of our three years, standing in our white confirmation robes, we were marched out before the congregation to be publicly quizzed as to our knowledge and understanding of the *Catechism*. I remember this as one question I had to answer that my father as pastor presented to me:

> Pastor: "Andrew, what is the Eighth Commandment?"
>
> Andrew: "Thou shalt not bear false witness against thy neighbor."
>
> Pastor: "What does it mean?"
>
> Andrew: "We should fear and love God that we may not deceitfully belie, betray, slander, nor defame our neighbor, but defend him, speak well of him, and put the best construction on everything."

My response was correct! I had memorized all the *Catechism* and could spout it back word for word. Boy, oh boy, was I catechized—Lutheranized!

After the anxious but successful question-and-answer period was over, we catechumens were presented to the congregation, confirmed with the laying on of hands, blessed with a special Bible passage, and received as communicants into the congregation. All of us were so happy that we didn't have to go to catechetical classes any more.

---

theran Church Missouri-Synod (LC-MS), is full of fundamentalist, conservative, and institutional commentary. If required to teach catechumens today, I would use a good translation of Luther's original, perhaps like the one printed at the back of *Evangelical Lutheran Worship* (Augsburg Press, 2006); it's only seven pages long.

Delivering papers

Every school day Art, Gordon, and I slogged the ten blocks to and from Edward Smith Elementary School. Winters were difficult with snowballs flying everywhere, and sometimes we took alternative longer routes home to avoid getting smashed by the older boys.

As Art recently reminded me during our 2015 family reunion at Rock Island State Part in Tennessee, after school and especially on weekends, the three of us were paper boys like few others. In fact, my biggest childhood happiness—yes, indeed!—was delivering newspapers with my brothers. I don't remember exactly how it all got started, but I suspect my father was up to his usual frugalities: getting his three boys gainfully employed as soon as possible.

At any rate, in the late 1940s while I was in my sixth to eighth years in elementary school, the three of us delivered well over two hundred papers every day after school. Actually I think it was around three hundred. After picking up our wagonloads of the *Syracuse Herald-Journal*, our city's afternoon paper, we tromped throughout the many streets of our route, making sure that papers were delivered to front porches, through apartment buildings, personally put inside screen doors and under door mats. In the freezing winter weather of upper New York, we pulled sleds piled high with papers. Wearing winter parkas, heavy-wool socks, and ski boots, we sometimes found those evenings so cold that the boogers in our noses froze, and Mom had to thaw out our nearly frozen feet when we got home. During the balmy days of summer, we pedaled our Schwinn bikes with saddlebags heavy with papers slung over the back tires. That's the way paper used to be delivered, each to the customer's satisfaction. It paid off enormously, especially at Christmastime when the publishers gave the paperboys beautiful colored calendars to be given as "gifts" to our customers. Well, not exactly "gifts." They were actually little-disguised enticements for our customers to give us big tips as Christmas gifts. Although every week's income was good, our December bonanza was terrific. When we knocked on doors and gave our customers their calendars, they, in turn, gave us their gifts, usually a couple of bucks, sometimes five dollars, and once in a while a ten spot! The whole thing was so lucrative that each Christmas our piggy bank (well, my father's bank account!) was loaded up with $300–$500. I make the point that everything went into Dad's bank because none of us kids saw a penny of it. Too young to be financially savvy, Dad was our financial agent. We thought not a whit about it. It all seemed so normal, so right.

I was educated in the school of hard work and world economics. O, those were happy days! I had it made.

Boarding school

While in the eighth grade, I must have told my dad that I wanted to be a Lutheran pastor. For the oldest son of a Lutheran pastor to want to be like his daddy was not all that unusual. It's even possible that Dad made the decision for me. Whether the decision was his, mine, or jointly made, in 1951, as a fourteen-year old boy, I was sent off to Concordia Collegiate Institute in Bronxville, New York, to begin a twelve-year education for the Lutheran ministry. At any rate, my father thought it wasn't a bad idea and getting on that journey might do me some good. Whatever the reason, Mom and Dad drove me down to Bronxville where with thirty or so other young boys, we began our studies in foreign languages, classical music, world history, and mathematics. It was a real adventure for an innocent fourteen-year-old who knew nothing much about the facts of life, city life, and dormitory living.

My first two years in Bronxville were good ones. Classes were challenging. As a freshman I started to learn German and then Latin as a sophomore. Examinations were rigorous. To move up, for example, from German I to German II, you had to pass the New York State Regent's Exam. Needless to say, the pressure to pass was enormous. Flunking a Regents Exam meant going home.

Somehow I managed to climb the academic ladders in all my classes, even in high school and college. As for my prayer life, we all attended daily chapel for Matins (seldom doing Vespers because that was time for study and homework). Although we surely had table prayers at the common meals held in the refectory, I have no memory of them, perhaps because I always left the table early to work in the kitchen area as a dishwasher, operating an assembly-line machine that cleaned everyone's plates, glasses, and eating utensils, along with lots of pots and pans.

I rode the trains back and forth from school to home. Once when I had to spend the night in Grand Central Station, a very innocent me got picked up and taken to an apartment somewhere near the station. A man who told me he was an interior decorator showed me some black-and-white photographs of his recent visit to a brothel. It was all quite explicit. When I somehow expressed my desire to leave his place, he walked me back to the station. Such was my introduction to the sexier side of life. I now appreciate his not abusing me any more than showing me pictures. In spite of this loss of innocence, I continued to do well and stayed out of trouble.

During my freshman and sophomore years in high school, I was academically okay. On my own, far away from home, I managed. I only got into one fight with my roommate, one-eyed John Feeblecorn, who knocked me out. That was the first time I saw stars. A little later I watched a couple of guys box in the gym and decided it was not for me. Every school evening we were obliged to sit at our desks, four to a room, and do homework. If we had to go to the bathroom, actually the "locus" (Latin for "place"), we had to ask our "room deck," a senior, for permission. When it came to doing my laundry, Mom helped. Inasmuch as our dress code required a coat and tie and I had no iron for pressing, I sent all my shirts home in an aluminum case by mail. Mom then washed and pressed them, packed them into the case, and shipped them back to me. We mailed one another such cases about twice a month. And let me mention again the wonderful memory that goes along with it all: Mom always put a dollar bill into one of my newly ironed shirt pockets. Can you imagine my gratitude? I hope so.

During my freshman year at Concordia, I was introduced to "music appreciation" with an elderly lady playing 78-rpm vinyls of classical music and explaining the difference between concerti and symphonies. Ever since, I've loved such stuff. And I made a number of lifelong friends, especially Willy Wilkens and Jon Kessler; more about them later on.

I probably shouldn't mention this, but the memory is inescapably permanent. Among those in our small class, there was Donald Muchow, the Goody-Two Shoes who always sat in the front row. We made up a song about him; the lyrics go like this:

> This is the AK quartet;
> Muchow's the leader, you bet.
> He sits in the front of the class
> And kisses the teacher's fat ass.

That ditty and its melody have never left me. Years later I did some research to see whatever become of brownnoser Donald and was not too surprised to find out that not only was he born one day before me in 1937 but also that after graduating from seminary, he eventually become a Rear Admiral and Chief of Chaplains of the US Navy. Some might say that somehow those of us who sang his song had become quite prophetic. More truthfully—judgmental.

In addition to washing pots and pans, I worked in the school library and read my first novel, Herman Wouk's *The Caine Mutiny*, the narrative line of which I only faintly remember. I introduced myself to cigarettes, an introduction that evolved into a habit for almost two decades. Not knowing that cigarette smoke impaired one's breathing, I also ran around a track of sorts suspended as a balcony around and above the gymnasium. Downstairs in one of the toilet stalls, I masturbated for the first time. Nearly rocked myself off the porcelain. In my sophomore year, I almost got to kiss a redheaded Roman Catholic girl whom I had somehow met while walking around the neighborhood. When we got to her house, she simply smiled and walked inside.

Andy, Art, and Gordon getting ready to walk to St. John Lutheran Parochial School, York, PA

Andy 18 years old, barefoot but in working clothes

Andy, hitch-hiking from Indianapolis, IN to Ft. Wayne, IN

As Marty supervises, Andy and Dave turn out the glossies.

Oh no, another school!

I spent two years as a student in Bronxville and had to transfer out because Dad had accepted a call to be the pastor of St. Paul Lutheran Church in Indianapolis, Indiana. It was a big church, the downtown "mother" church. Huge. Moving to Indianapolis changed everything!

To continue my pre-ministerial education, I went to Concordia High School in Fort Wayne, Indiana, 120 miles away from home. It was all very different. Concordia was coeducational! Girls! Moreover, it was into high-school ROTC big time. Military! All male students had to sign up and participate in the school-wide ROTC program. Coming in as a high-school junior, I discovered to my horror that all my classmates were "officers" of some sort. Dressed up in their neatly pressed khakis and sporting smart caps, they decorated themselves with badges, insignias, pins, brass buttons, colorful chest ribbons, shoulder cords, and epaulets of rank, distinction, and honor. Me? I showed up in an ultra-plain khaki shirt and pants, black shoes polished, my lone brass belt buckle shining all by itself. Obviously inferior in rank and in the estimate of all my classmates, I soon detested everything about ROTC life, especially the business about M1 rifles and all the bang-bang that went along with them. To get away from guns and bullets, I bought myself a trumpet and joined the band, only to be assigned to toot-toot an undignified French horn. I trust you can imagine my unhappiness and developing disgust with authorities. One night in an act of defiance, I got a Mohawk haircut. The next day the Commandant summarily demanded that I come to his office so he could order me to get my whole head shaved! For the rest of the semester I had to wear a black wool cap from sunrise till sunset. Amazingly, I wore that "dunce cap" with pride!

Junior College

Not unexpectedly, my grades fell, especially my grades in Latin. But somehow I managed to graduate and move on, this time to the tiny (sixty students!) Concordia Junior College, just a block away from the high school. What all this had to do with being a ministerial student, I had no idea.

Every summer from my senior year in high school until I finished college, I worked on commercial construction sites in and around Indianapolis. Doing all sorts of sweaty jobs, I dug ditches for cement footings, waterproofed cinder blocks with tar, framed walls for cement pourings, hauled lumber, and helped out as a hod carrier for bricklayers. As a union apprentice carpenter, I was paid well, about $17 per hour. I bought an old '49 Chevy sedan, painted it green with a rigged-up vacuum cleaner, and drove myself to work. Coming home in the late afternoon, I was exhausted, dirty, and tanned. The great benefit of such work was that I got to know people outside the usual range of parsonage life. I found out how men cussed, told dirty jokes, and worked together as a team. I enjoyed it all.

After I graduated from high school, I stayed in the same dormitory but went to college in different buildings and classrooms. God blessed me as a college freshman with my first Greek professor, Eugene Nissen, one of the best teachers I've ever had. He came into my life at exactly the right time. After screwing things up at Concordia High School, I needed a great measure of academic discipline, intellectual excitement, and a sense of integrity that no uniform could provide.

As a freshman in college, I began to study Greek on a daily basis. Mr. Nissen set high standards of excellence that had to be met to receive passing grades. We studied Greek every day, and every day we were given a "90 percenter," that is, a quiz of Greek vocabulary, grammar, parsings, conjugations of verbs, declensions of nouns (regular and irregular), and translations of Greek texts that had to be accurate no less than 90 percent. And that included making the correct accent marks (acute, circumflex, enclitic, grave, proclitic, and recessive) where needed! If one of us scored less than 90 percent, the test had to be retaken as many times as necessary to reach the high 90 percent bar. Anything less was an F. No wonder we were required to spend two hours each weekday evening at our dormitory desks! Gradually such academic strictness gave me a new sense of life's purpose—to become a reader of the Bible in its original languages. At last I had a sense of what the future might bring. My disciplined study of Greek spilled over into other classes and subjects. I read Shakespeare and enjoyed Mr. Bente's humanities classes. Dr. Stach's Old Testament class was a real rip, especially when he acted out pagan dances to the heathen god Ba'al, his arms flapping about like a wild goose being goosed. He also had one habit that brought all sorts of titters to the class. In our second-floor classroom, when someone answered a question in a most inaccurate, pitiful, and wrongheaded way, old Stach would run to a side classroom window, open it dramatically, and honk a thick wad of spit out upon the lawn below. Then too he'd sometimes wrap his head with a thick rubber band and make it snap against the side of his forehead when he was showing us how to really think about something. He was weird. But we loved him. When he made a most delightfully funny observation, we were encouraged to stamp out feet on the floor, sometimes so vigorously that the poor teacher below on the first floor would send a student up to ask that we settle down. We loved it.

How I got back and forth from my home in Indianapolis to high school and junior college in Fort Wayne, Indiana, is an experience few youngsters can enjoy today. I hitchhiked. On Sunday afternoon, penurious Dad would drive me to the city limits of Indianapolis and drop me off on old State Highway 37 so that I could set up my luggage pieces with their "Please / Fort Wayne" signs taped on them and stick out my thumb for the 125 miles journey north to Fort Wayne. For trips home, I simply reversed directions and signs. As far as I can remember, Dad only drove up to Fort Wayne when I had to return for summer vacations with books and clothing. As a freshman or sophomore, I was not allowed to bring a car on campus.

My 1956 Concordia Junior College yearbook, the *Concordian*, tells me that I was surely one of that year's more quiet students. I belonged to no clubs and played no sports. I did join the choir one year and went on its tour to churches in Florida. To my delight, I was one of the yearbook's photographers. The school provided me with a terrific Speed Graphic, which I loaded up with four-by-six-inch negatives. That gem of a camera was just like the one I imagined journalist Clark Kent might occasionally have used in the Superman comics; it gave me such a sense of power. With it I took photos of everything: club meetings and officers, ball games, professors, staff, and so on. Late in the evenings and on weekends, I dropped down into a darkroom in the college's classroom basement, developed negs, and made prints in a wash of chemicals under the glow of a red safelight. In the yearbook there's a wee pix of me fiddling with an enlarger as two of my buddies watch on. I certainly was not a Clark Kent; I was simply a quiet student downstairs and away from the spotlight.

What happened next, however, took me into a really bright light, something like the light of creation's day one. Almost that miraculous. A big bang for me. After graduating from Concordia Junior College in 1957, I got to be among the first to attend the newly built Concordia Senior College, a genuinely unique school ready for its first class of students on the outskirts of Fort Wayne, Indiana.

Senior College

A little history. Prior to 1957, all Lutheran Church-Missouri Synod (LC-MS) pastors, my dad included, only went to high school and junior college before going on to seminary. They were properly introduced to German, Latin, and Greek, but when ready for ordination, they had no bachelor degrees, no master degrees. Yes, they were fairly well educated but not with any real academic credentials of substance. During the mid-fifties, however, the LC-MS, led by theological progressives, actively took steps to provide its seminary students with a stronger, more intellectually vibrant education. To make this happen, the Synod decided to bring all its pre-seminary graduates from each of its fourteen junior colleges across the nation

Concordia Senior College
Fort Wayne, Indianna, 1958

to one institution: Concordia Senior College, a one-of-a-kind pre-seminary school. In the junior-college graduating class of 1959, I was given the opportunity to get a first-class education.

When I transferred to Concordia Senior College, things became wonderful. The campus, classrooms, chapel, dormitories, and lawns were stunningly beautiful. With five hundred men daily singing Matins while classmate Joel Kuznik played the organ, things got to be a bit like heaven. Especially memorable was the singing of the magisterial "Te Deum," along with other canticles within morning prayer.

Designed by world-famous architect Eero Saarinen,[15] the campus itself was truly remarkable. In February 2014, fifty-five years after I graduated from that school, my first wife, Carol, sent me a magazine-sized package with this note:

> Andy, I picked up this magazine [*atomic ranch: midcentury marvels* (Winter 2013)] at the doctor's office. I wasn't interested in it, but it was the only magazine available. One article caught my interest, and I thought you also might like to read it.
>
> ~ Carol

I certainly did enjoy reading "Saarinen's Village: A Midwestern Midcentury Monastery."[16] It brought back so many memories. Although none of us at the time thought of it as a monastery, it without doubt was a "men's only" school of learning, different from anything I had ever experienced. The library, for example, was open 24/7. To check out a book, I simply took it off the shelf and placed

---

15 Eero Saarinen was a Finnish American architect and industrial designer famous for shaping his neofuturistic style according to the demands of the project: simple, sweeping, arching structural curves or machine-like rationalism. Among his several dozen famous designs are the Gateway Arch in St. Louis, Missouri; the chapel and Kresge Auditorium on the Massachusetts Institute of Technology campus; the Emma Hartman Noyes House at Vassar College; and the TWA Terminal in New York City.

16 Available at http://palni.contentdm.oclc.org/cdm/landingpage/collection/copcampus

a "shelf card" announcing my name and date in its place. When finished with the book, I put it back on the shelf. Everything was done on the honor system.

We ate our meals in common, and our classrooms were designed for discussion, conference-style. We studied all sorts of stuff never before placed before the eyes and investigation of LC-MS pre-seminary students: the history of scientific thought, classical and Hellenistic Greek, two years of Hebrew, and English literature, giving me my first reading of the romantic poets, Wordsworth becoming my favorite. We were even required to take gymnastics. I remember especially my learning to bounce on a trampoline, quietly farting as I danced up and down in the air. Saarinen topped the whole place off by making sure we had a nine-hole golf course in the back forty of the campus so that as pastors we'd know how to use a nine-iron, a wedge, and score a double eagle now and then.

Forty years later when I played a good bit of golf on a scruffy course near Sturbridge, Massachusetts, I made my first double eagle. So much a once-in-a-lifetime event that I asked my golfing companion Willie Wilkens, an old seminary friend, to record the event for posterity, selfies not possible yet. I even saved the tee and have it on my desk today.

At Concordia Senior College, I got a first-rate education. Not only did I continue my studies in Koine Greek, but I also enrolled in classical Greek courses and was introduced to Hebrew, a tough language for me. I got to translate two of Sophocles' tragedies: *Oedipus Rex* and *Antigone*. We studied the history of science and church history. I found out what evolutionary theory was all about. I majored in psychology, taking courses in abnormal, developmental, and cognitive psychology. Dr. Harold Haas, my primary instructor, was at the top of his game, and I enjoyed everything thrown at me.

With one exception. During a course on early developmental psychology, I was assigned to write and present a paper on "Thumb Sucking: Do's and Don'ts." When my turn to read the paper came around, toward the middle of my presentation, I mangled a lead-in to an important paragraph. I had written a section header titled "How to Avoid Thumb Sucking." For whatever reason—maybe a

Freudian slip!—out of my mouth came: "How to Avoid Some F***-ing." Oh my God! The uproar, foot-stomping, and table-slapping by my classmates were horrendous. And, of course, every time after that when I had to mention "sucking," I was terribly self-conscious about my earlier mispronunciation. Even when I correctly pronounced "sucking" whenever it had to be said, I could hear the snickers and giggles of my classmates. Hass dismissed the class early before the bell rang.

Above all, the most beautiful place was the chapel wherein all five hundred of us met daily for morning prayer as my classmate Joel Kuznik played the organ magnificently.

I learned to love liturgies and even took a course on the history of worship in the church. Nevertheless, my prayer life was fundamentally communal. Privately, I didn't pray a lot. Hardly at all.

Off to seminary

Concordia Theological Seminary
St. Louis, Missouri, 1960

I graduated from Saarinen's masterpiece in 1959. Because the Synod had added an extra year to the education of its pre-seminary students, that meant the real lapse of a seminary graduating class. To offset that unhappiness, the Synod asked a number of us Senior College graduates to fill the gap by going to seminary in St. Louis year around, reducing the usual four-year stint to three years. I signed up and soon began a thirty-six-month master's-level engagement with seminary studies. Once again, I was surprised and delighted at what happened. My seminary professors were cutting-edge theologians and experts in teaching Hebrew and Greek, some of the best in the country. All had first-rate degrees from schools like Harvard, Yale, and other distinguished institutions. For example, Frederick William Danker, who died in February 2012, was eulogized as

> a noted New Testament scholar and the pre-eminent Koine Greek lexicographer for two generations, working with F. Wilbur Gingrich as an editor of the *Greek-English Lexicon of the New Testament and Other Early Christian Literature*, starting in 1957 until the publication of the second edition in 1979, and as the only editor from 1979 until the publication of the 3rd edition, updating it with the results of modern scholarship, converting it to SGML to allow it to be easily published in electronic formats, and significantly improving the usability of the lexicon, as well as the typography.[17]

Dr. Edgar Krentz, under whom I took several wonderful classes, introduced me to modern biblical interpretation, especially the so-called historical critical method that has held pride of place for more than a century. Reading his 1975 publication of *The Historical-Critical Method* brought back refreshing seminary memories that still linger with me. My favorite passage of the book helps set up the overall point of the book:

> Historical Criticism produces only probable results. It relativizes everything. But faith needs certainty. Uneasy Christians ask whether those who make the historical confession that Jesus died under Pontius Pilate and rose again the third day can be content with mere probability. Defenders of historical criticism point out that the probability factor is actually a virtue. It removes the idolatry that confuses the temporal and the eternal and points out the

[17] "Frederick William Danker," available at https://en.wikipedia.org/wiki/Frederick_William_Danker.

> true nature of faith…It makes us hear the biblical proclamation as the first Christians did--without any security outside of the proclamation that confronts us with its demand for believing response-and this alone gives certainty to faith.[18]

In short, Krentz reminds us that if you need absolute certitude about what's in your Bible, you have no need of faith. Later in life when I was working as a pastor in Lafayette, Louisiana, I received a commendatory note from Professor Krentz that I treasure as a gift from a learned saint. More about all that in chapter 5.

Now a few words about my overall seminary education. In many respects, it was very good, good enough to set my thinking in new directions. Continuing my studies in Koine Greek and Hebrew, I studied under distinguished professors, notably Arthur Carl Piepkorn, Richard Caemerer, Edgar Krentz, Norman Habel, Arlis Ehlen, and John Damm. I also had to attend classes under less able instructors whose names I will not dignify with mention. These less-than-satisfactory teachers were most often of the more so-called orthodox persuasion, doctrinaire, and retro-scholastic with their minds set on teaching propositional theology. They liked everything set out in well-crafted sentences that both argued for and against decided points of view. Their classic text was Franz Pieper's *Christian Doctrine*, written with a full-scale endorsement of Biblical inerrancy and a sweeping condemnation of "Ich-theology," that is, anything that smacked of infused grace molding the spirituality of the inner self.[19] Any spirituality of pagan origin, whether Native American,

---

18 Edgar Krentz, *The Historical-Critical Method* (Minneapolis, MN: Augsburg Fortress, 1975), 76.

19 As a systematic theologian, Franz Pieper's magnum opus, *Christliche Dogmatik* (1917–24), provided the early twentieth-century world with a learned and extensive presentation of renewed seventeen-century orthodox (and markedly scholastic) Lutheran theology. Translated into English as *Christian Dogmatics* (1950–53), it continues to be the basic textbook of doctrinal theology in Lutheran Church–Missouri Synod. He was also the main author of the Missouri Synod's *A Brief Statement* (1932), an authoritative presentation of that church's doctrinal stance.

Hindu, Buddhist, or whatever, was dismissed outright. In fact, such realities were never mentioned.

Nearly everything was "Christ-for-us" theology with little or nothing said of "Christ in us." All was objective grace; nothing was developed in the area of subjective grace. Describing such Lutheran theology, Bengt R. Hoffman nicely spells it out:

> Christian certainty is said to be based on presumably inerrant statements in the Bible. These statements must be appropriated but this appropriation must not be linked to a spiritual-psychological process with man's soul. The transference of the gospel from word to man takes place on a purely dogmatic-rational level, as a reasoned acceptance of biblical formulations of truth. Luther's emphasis on "the external word" and "Christ for you" has become the sole theological message of the Reformation.[20]

Moving on to seminary in 1959 did not deepen or enlarge my prayer life. In fact, I found theological discussions about prayer dry, stale, and boring. We translated the Hebrew psalms with academic precision and continued to sing lustily in the chapel, always accompanied by accomplished organists and choirs. Singing and listening to Lutheran chorales was the backbone of my prayer life.

I learned very little about prayer other than what the books said were well-phrased collects, beautiful litanies, and pastoral prayers worthy of careful pronunciation. Nobody mentioned anything about Luther's love for and practice of mystical prayer. Not a word about John Tauler, the *Theologia Germanica*, and certainly complete and ignorant silence about the Desert Ammas and Abbas. Not a word about Eastern Orthodox spirituality, the Jesus Prayer, the Prayer of the Heart, and hesychasm. *Streng verboten*! Strictly forbidden! Except for classes in the exegesis of the Hebrew Scriptures and the New

---

[20] *Luther and the Mystics: A Re-examination of Luther's Spiritual Experience and his Relationship to the Mystics* (Minneapolis, MN: Augsburg Publishing House, 1976), 35.

Testament wherein I learned about higher and "form" criticism, nearly everything else was the teaching of sound doctrine and symbolics, that is, the branch of theology dealing with the study of the history and meaning of church creeds and confessions.

I certainly do not regret my seminary education. But now more than fifty years later, I'm so happy that many "Christ-in-us" contemplative saints have come to my rescue. While never denying that Christ died "for us" two thousand years ago, a truth I readily accept,[21] it's the "inner Christ" with whom I live, trust, and experience as an always and everywhere Presence in my life. The two of us, Andy and Jesus Christ, are a mass of tangled roots buried deep in the soil of my heart. I would not hesitate to describe this terrific *oneness* as N. Gordon Cosby does:

> Oneness was Jesus' thing. The world will never believe that anything divine has broken into our life until they are aware of this divine oneness in us. The oneness Jesus was pointing us to is not uniformity; it is not submissiveness. Conformity is not oneness. Oneness happens when each person is living from his or her own uniqueness and individuality.[22]

We're vine and branch, the sap of Holy Spirit flowing between us, uniting me to the every-where-ness of God's grace, love, light, truth, wisdom, humility, and cruciform glory. More about all of this later on.

All told, seminary was good for me. I appreciated studying "Techniques of Biblical Exegesis," "Homiletics and Persuasive Speech," "Theology of the Gospels," "Papacy and Empire," and "Readings in the Thought World of the New Testament." I

[21] Many today are reexamining our understandings of the "Christ's atonement." For a good overview of the options, see Ted Peters, "Models of Atonement," available at www.plts.edu/docs/ite_models_atonement.pdf.

[22] N. Gordon Cosby, *Seized by the Power of a Great Affection: Meditations on the Divine Encounter* (Washington, DC: Inward Outward, 2013), 24.

discovered who Karl Barth, Rudolf Bultmann, and Emil Brunner were. I learned what "demythologizing" meant. I felt comfortable with source, form, and redaction criticism of the Bible. In fact, all that I learned from my more progressive professors deepened my love for Scriptures and helped me delve more deeply and expansively into Biblical texts. One professor suggested that we all read Pierre Teilhard de Chardin's *The Divine Milieu*. I bought the book and quietly started to move away from my previous literal readings of God's Word into more profound contextual and heart-bending application of Torah and Gospel. I started reading the Bible from an evolutionary point of view. Then sixty years later on April 26 something wonderful happened, and I posted this note on Facebook:

> Last evening some kind person left a copy of Teilhard de Chardin's *The Divine Milieu Explained* by Louis M. Savary, along with a recent issue of *Christian Counseling Today*, at the garage door entrance of my home. While I have a slight hint as to that kind soul is, I'm really not sure. I want to say, "Thank you!" to whomever it might be. If it's YOU, please let me know! I first started reading Chardin in early 1960s, and now I can revisit Teilhard again, I want you to know that I'm already enjoying your book again. Please tell me who you are if you stopped by last evening and left me such a wonderful gift!

Learning American Sign Language and ministering to the deaf in Portland, Oregon

While at seminary, Larry Harris, one of my classmates, and I met Pastor George Kraus, another saint who changed the direction of my life. He too was a once-in-a-lifetime brother in the faith. Here's how the *Concordia Theological Quarterly* summed up his life after he died in 1989:

> During this forty-year ministry George Kraus served not only St. Matthew's Church for the Deaf in New York, but Prince of Peace Church for the Deaf in Minneapolis, Holy Cross Church for the Deaf in St. Louis, St. Peter's Church in Brooklyn, New York, and Redeemer Lutheran Church in Cape Elizabeth, Maine. After service to St. Matthew's Lutheran Church in New Britain, Connecticut, he came to Concordia Theological Seminary as associate professor in pastoral theology in 1982.
>
> In this seminary he initiated a program in the deaf ministry with which Dr. Kraus has been associated since his own seminary days. He was a major factor in involving the Lutheran Church-Missouri Synod in deaf ministry and was instrumental in the Mill Neck Manor Foundation. For his pioneer work in deaf ministry, he was recognized by the faculty of Concordia Seminary. Saint Louis, with the Doctor of Letters degree in 1982. At the seminary in Fort Wayne, he taught in the area of deaf ministry, Hispanic studies, Dogmatics, Pastoral Theology, and Homiletics. His course, "The Pastor's Devotional Life," was one of the most popular electives offered at the seminary.[23]

Because of Pastor Krauss's influence, in my final seminary year, I decided that I'd like to become a pastor to the deaf. As I attended deaf services at Holy Cross Church whose communicants were a healthy mix of black and white Christians, I witnessed how a pre-civil-rights community of love works with compassion for one another. And so I studied sign language and asked to be sent on my "vicarage" (a year of training before graduation) to a deaf congregation where, under the tutelage of another pastor for the deaf, I might learn how to minister to the hearing disabled. When the announcement came on "vicarage call day," my wife and I discovered we were going

---

[23] (Vol. 54; 3), 161-164.

to Hope Lutheran Church in Portland, Oregon, where under the direction of Pastor George Ring, I somehow learned to preach and teach in American Sign Language.

Larry Harris, Pastor George Krause, and me
Learning to "speak" the Good News in sign language

The experience was good and not so good. Pastor Ring was decidedly "low" church. Off went the clerical collar. Emotionally unstable, Pastor Ring needed me more than I needed him. Enough said. After a year in Oregon, Carol and I returned to the Midwest. While she worked as a nurse and gave birth to our first son, Kirk Anders, on February 27, 1962, I finished my seminary studies, bought another cheap black suit, a clerical black shirt, a rabat,[24] and another white collar—all in anticipation of becoming a pastor.

Toward more learning and another parish

In May 1962, I received my first "call" to ministry as a pastor. It came from the Eastern District of the LC-MS. I was instructed to go to Lima and East Avon, New York, and see if a new congregation might be established for a group of Lutherans living fifteen miles south of Rochester, New York. Carol, Kirk, and I got into our black Volkswagon Beetle and headed north.

While living as a pastor of The Church of the Epiphany in East Avon, New York, from 1962 to 1965, I enrolled myself at Colgate Rochester Divinity School, taking courses in patristics (the church fathers) and the history of the liturgy. While on that campus, like everyone in our nation, I was stunned to hear that President John F. Kennedy had been assassinated. Days later I found out that C. S. Lewis also died on November 22.

[24] A sleeveless, backless, vest-like garment extending to the waist, worn by a cleric beneath the clerical collar, especially in the Roman Catholic, Lutheran, and Anglican churches. Now going out of fashion.

In 1965, Carol and I, along with Kirk Anders, our firstborn, and his brother, Krister Martin, moved to Lafayette, Louisiana, where I became a town-and-gown pastor at Trinity Lutheran Church. Once there and eager to continue my education, I enrolled in an English literature master's program. That choice came about strangely. Earlier in 1964 while still in upper New York, I had gone out one afternoon to stroll around in the countryside. A little tired, I lay down on a gentle hillside of grass and fell asleep. When I awoke, it was raining, and I got thoroughly soaked a mile or so away from home. Drenched, I went home and to bed only to find that by the next day, something akin to pneumonia had damaged my lungs. Carol took me to a hospital in Rochester where for six weeks I spent a good deal of time in an oxygen tent and received fifty shots of penicillin. With little to do, I read lots and lots, one book determining the course of my life. I don't remember its title, but in page after page, it gave me the stories about England's greatest writers from Chaucer through T. S. Eliot. It was a whole new world to me, and I promised myself that I'd explore it if possible.

Getting to know English authors, some in depth

That possibility came to fruition in Lafayette where I found my parish office at Trinity just across the street from the University of Southwestern Louisiana. As a campus pastor ministering to students, it seemed good to me and "to the Holy Spirit" (as we say, justifying our decisions) to continue my study of English literature. In the summer of 1966, I enrolled in ENG 500, "20th Century Literature," a reading of James Joyce's *Dubliners* and *Ulysses* as my first graduate-level introduction to highfalutin and then-considered radical (if not quite pornographic) storytelling, along with a course in linguistics. I loved it. Eventually I read lots of poetry from the eighteenth through the twentieth centuries, earning As in every class. I wrote my master's thesis on "The Theology of Grace in T. S. Eliot's Later Poetry." In 1969, the university presented me a master's degree.

Off to Oklahoma and Oxford, England

Six years later in 1972, in addition to teaching full-time at St. John's College in Winfield, Kansas, I managed to get myself enrolled in another set of literature classes. Driving ninety miles each way from Winfield to Stillwater, Oklahoma, and often sleeping overnight on a couch in the Lutheran Student Center, I became a PhD candidate at Oklahoma State University. When I applied for program entrance, my seminary background, robust with Greek, Latin, German, and Hebrew, urged Dr. Shelley Berkley, my course advisor, to suggest that I concentrate on Old and Middle English and everything up to, but not beyond, 1660, roughly the blurry end of the English Renaissance. And so I began again. In the summer of 1973, I applied for and received an opportunity to study at Trinity College at Oxford University, England.

Trinity College
Oxford University, England

St. Andrew's Church
Bemerton, England

There I spent three months deep within Shakespeare's history plays while visiting every production of the Royal Shakespeare Theatre both in Avon and in London. I also visited the little church in Bemerton, near Salisbury in Wiltshire, made famous by George Herbert, whom I consider the best of all metaphysical poets. Several years later I authored three published essays on his poetry.[25]

[25] "George Herbert's 'Aaron': The Aesthetics of Shaped Typology," *English Language Notes* (September, 1976), 25-32; "Both Protestant and Catholic: George Herbert's 'To All Angels and Saints,'" *George Herbert Journal*, 11:1 (Fall, 1987), 23-39; and "Deconstruction and George Herbert," *Kentucky Philological Association Bulletin*, 10 (33-51.

Returning to the states, I continued learning all I could about Old and Middle English grammar, Chaucer, Spenser, Shakespeare, the metaphysical poets, and Milton, among dozens of other genres and writers. Three semesters of literary criticism gave me some eyes that could read with some discrimination. Again, all As. My dissertation thesis, "The Typological Divine: A Study in the Figural Expression of Renaissance Kingship," dedicated to Carol as "my *figura gratiae et rarissima lux*" (my gracious "figurer" and "most rare light") was approved; some even suggested that I get it published. I didn't. Getting things published came later.

The day when I received my PhD was one of the saddest in my life. It meant that school was over. No more classes. No more master teachers and professors. On that day, someone told me, "Andy, perk up! You should now be able to teach yourself." "Yeah, right," I murmured.

Learning, of course, didn't shut itself entirely down. In 1980, while teaching at Eastern Kentucky University in Richmond, Kentucky, I was awarded an opportunity to attend a National Endowment for the Humanities Summer Seminar, "Milton and the Fall into Reading," taught by no less than Stanley Fish at the Johns Hopkins University, Baltimore, Maryland. It was there that Derridean deconstructive theory entered my thinking. And I met my second wife, Paula Kopacz, a graduate of Columbia University, who had recently been teaching at Vassar. A highly intelligent woman. An amazing woman.

Since then things have not been so dramatic. Yes, I learned to teach online, publish some articles in juried academic journals, publish a book or two, and make lots of presentations at professional conferences. But all in all, things began to wind down, and I more or less considered myself educated.

Let me be blunt. I was both well-educated and at the same time quite (some would say "unbelievably") naïve. You have not heard the whole of the story. For the most part, let me now emphasize that as a student I never felt the need to challenge anyone or question much of anything for two reasons. First, my college and seminary teachers and professors were not overbearing or insufferably authoritarian.

They were, in fact, for the most part leading us progressively into new worlds of thought, imaginative engagement, and deep respect not only for the past but also for the best of emergent theology. To this day I can't remember anyone telling me I was seriously wrong in any of my thinking. Martin Luther and his gutsy defense of the Gospel was my spiritual hero. Understanding the *Book of Concord* in its historical setting allowed me to agree with Luther and at the same time honor Pope John XXIII and his efforts to renew the Church during the Second Vatican Council. If the conclusions of higher criticism made the Bible come alive, I could say so. Second, I assumed that everyone in the Lutheran Church–Missouri Synod was in general agreement that the spiritual life of the church was God-pleasing and acceptably orthodox. During the '50s, '60s, and early '70s, all was apparently okay. It was only later that I found out what ecclesial politics is all about.

I was still living in the first half of life, somewhat aware of changes about to occur in the second half but not anxious or worried or frustrated. I was simply a Lutheran pastor in what I thought was a moderately progressive national church: the LC-MS.

I was naïve.

Reflections on going to school

Never regret any kind of education. Whether it's learning how to weld steel, work as a chef, be a master gardener, become a kindergarten teacher, repair motorcycles, sell insurance, experience seminary life, spouse a wife or husband, become a monk, be an astronaut—whatever! All learning can be an opening. Even undesirable learning (such as becoming a drug addict) can ironically be a blessing. Think of King David learning how to seduce a woman or St. Paul learning how to participate in murdering Stephen; both of them and many more have fallen down (to use the old metaphor), only to be raised to wonderments and become spiritual miracles.

Always continue to be a student. When forty, learn how to jog; when fifty, try making pottery; when sixty, learn a new language (or relearn an old one) and read books; when you're seventy, take up a brand-new hobby like bird watching; and when eighty, follow your bliss: learn a bit about astronomy and look at the sky full of stars at night.

Always remember that life itself is schooling. Every day learn how to love. And don't get all puffed up about what you know.

But watch out! One's schooling can be an invitation to enormous ego enhancement, "look-at-me" intensification, and delirious preoccupation with knowing something about something. An academic gown is really a lot of tribal feathers! Believe me, there's nothing quite like getting a diploma for a PhD—and not realizing that it can also be an abbreviation for "Piled Higher and Drier," like a load of manure.

For Further Consideration

Applegate, Kathryn, and J. B. Stump, eds. *How I Changed My Mind about Evolution: Evangelicals Reflect on Faith and Science*. Downers Grove, IL: InterVarsity, 2016.

de Chardin, Pierre Teilhard. *The Divine Milieu: An Essay on the Interior Life*. New York: Harper & Brothers, 1960.

Savary, Louis M. *Teilhard de Chardin*: The Divine Milieu *Explained: A Spirituality for the 21st Century*. Mahwah, NJ: Paulist Press, 2007.

Chapter 3

HUSBAND AND FATHER

I have perfumed my bed
with myrrh, aloes, and cinnamon.
Come, let us take our fill
of love until the morning.
—Proverbs 7:17–18

The trouble with some women
is that they get all excited about nothing
—and then marry him.
—Cher

As husbands, I think one reason
we have some trouble with Paul's command
to love our wives "as Christ loved the church,"
is that we don't really and fully
know how Christ loves the church.
—Scott, *Journey to Surrender*

Chelsea is my sister's name.
—An inscription

on a small piece of paper
I found inside Kris's wallet after his death

Children are the hands by which we take hold heaven.
Henry Ward Beecher

The counsel of a Desert Father

Here's some good advice from Abba Poemen:

> A brother questioned Abba Poemen saying, "If I see my brother committing a sin, is it right to conceal it?" The old man said to him, "At the very moment when we hide our brother's fault, God hides our own and at the moment when we reveal our brother's fault, God reveals ours too."[26]

I'm providing the little conversation between Abba Poemen and a fellow monk because in writing this chapter, I may be tempted to intimate there's blame to be given for any number of sins, difficulties, and mistakes. May God deliver me from such temptations. If anyone is to be blamed within events about which I'm now going to describe, it's me.

All of which means that many pages in this chapter aren't easy to write because I've been married three times. Once to Carol, once to Paula, and now to June. For all that, much of my marrying life gives me a bothersome set of memories. Admittedly some are good, real good; others really not so good, disturbing to this day. More than several memories return as dreams, both as pleasant driftings and sometimes as nightmares. Like most young men brought up as I was, it was frankly inconceivable that I should ever divorce. Certainly not twice. And twice at my initiative. That was an absolute impossibility.

[26] *The Sayings of the Desert Fathers: The Alphabetical Collection*, trans. Benedicta Ward. (Kalamazoo, MI: Cistercian Publications, 1984), 175.

Nevertheless, I somehow managed the impossible. Often accompanied with lots of regret. You will, of course, forgive me if I leave out some of wished-to-be-forgotten details. Only the basics here.

Carol

The Wedding of Carol and Andy September 21, 1960

After a decade of dating, a long engagement, and a good bit of waiting, Carol Stellhorn and I married on September 21, 1960. It was a beautiful wedding as we came down the aisle in old St. Paul Lutheran Church near downtown Indianapolis.

The organist played Bach's "Jesu, Joy of Man's Desiring." I still like to listen to it as I'm doing now. The wedding reception at the parochial school was terrific. Lilian and Lester, Carol's parents, put so much effort into it. Afterward we drove off on an extended honeymoon, going cross-country all the way to Portland, Oregon, where Carol worked as a nurse and I spent the year on a "vicarage" assignment, training to be a pastor for the deaf. All went wonderfully well, and when we returned to St. Louis for my final year at Concordia Seminary, Carol was pregnant with Kirk Anders, later born on February 27, 1962.

For nearly all the twenty-two years we were married, all was blessed. Carol gave birth to three more wonderful children: Krister Martin, Lisa Marie, and Amy Katherine. I was happy, very much so. But as so often my experience, my academic ego, sensing advancement and something of a relatively distinguished career, got a violent hold on me, and I careened off into a series of plunges from which I have never quite recovered. Even to this day. While serving as a newly ordained pastor at the Church of the Epiphany in East Avon, New York, I took courses in patristic theology at Rochester

Divinity School. Nothing wrong with that. But I soon began biting into the tasty apple of self-preening academic knowledge. When the opportunity to serve as a campus pastor in Lafayette, Louisiana, came along, I seized it, knowing that my parish office would be across from the University of Southwestern Louisiana (home of the "Ragin' Cajuns"), now known as the University of Louisiana at Lafayette, where, as I guessed rightly, I could work on a master's degree. Again, nothing wrong. Reading and writing about James Joyce, the romantic poets, and T. S. Eliot gave me deep satisfaction. Fascinated with doing research, I wrote a master's thesis on Eliot. And by sponsoring a somewhat celebrated coffee spot in our parish hall where we often gathered several hundred for polylogs of all sorts (especially things political), I became known around town as something of a pastoral entrepreneur. All this self-serving acquisition of academic head-stuff slowly and surely proved itself a wedge between Carol and me. I was off in a direction neither one of us originally anticipated.

Again I became enamored with an academic life. Only this time I was not too smart. I took a position at St. John's Junior College in Winfield, Kansas. A stupid decision. As an exceptionally conservative school, I got myself into difficulties and out of a job because I would not sign the Missouri Synod's so-called *Brief Statement*,[27] a bit of fundamentalist nonsense that defied nearly all my theological convictions supported by academic research. Leaving the college because I was not conservative enough, I continued my doctoral studies at Oklahoma State University. Again, not a problem. Carol supported me 100 percent.

After getting my PhD at OSU in 1976 and moving to Kentucky to teach at EKU, I found myself firmly ensconced in academics. I loved it. Able to say what I thought (moderately progressive on the scale of things), I soon found myself serving as executive secretary and eventual president of the Kentucky Philological Society, the recipient of a NEH award at the Johns Hopkins University, a somewhat frequent publisher of articles in reviewed journals, a couple of books,

27 The text is available at https://www.creeds.net/lutheran/missouri.htm.

and an upcoming professor getting promotions on a regular basis. I was swimming freestyle in academics.

Not much of this helped talk and conversation in our marriage, and eventually I felt as though I were playing the eighty-eight keys of the matrimonial piano with missing fingers. A recipe for disaster. And it was not Carol's fault in the least. She was working full-time as an obstetrical nurse, bringing to life what some would claim to be 50 percent of the babies born in Madison County.

I had married a lovely, wonderful woman, a "saint," as many describe her. But being so utterly self-preoccupied, I didn't realize it. To give you some sense of how Carol treated me, let me simply say that when I asked for a divorce, she did her best to make me feel as comfortable as I could with that decision. She helped, not because she also wanted a divorce but because she wanted the best for me, even if that best was at her expense. On the day we signed the papers, she held my hand on the way to the courthouse. Yes, I seem to remember that Carol exhibited anger once, but she never let her justified frustration take hold of her in any mean-spirited way. Several years after my filing, together we took a long walk in the mountainous area south of Berea, Kentucky, and after a long conversation, she forgave me. And that forgiveness has lasted decades, so long and so real that today when we have opportunity, we go to Holy Communion together.

Paula

**Paula with Roshi in her lap,
Chelsea with two of her dolls,
and Andy with Scampy on his lap
The summer of 1995**

After receiving a grant from the National Endowment for the Humanities, I spent the summer of 1980 at the Johns Hopkins University studying the writings of John Milton. It was there I met Paula, a graduate of Columbia University, one-time professor at Vassar, and a distinguished American Renaissance scholar. I was profoundly impressed with her. We came to love each other. After several tries, she got a job at EKU, we taught classes together, team-taught in Kentucky's Governor's Scholars Program, did a number of weeklong summer Elderhostels, wrote articles for publication, and made joint presentations for fellow academics. She was and is a brilliant academician and scholar. I had a hard time keeping up with her.

Our greatest joy together was the gift of Chelsea, our adopted daughter. Our marriage was wonderful while it lasted, but far less so later on for reasons best left silent. I divorced Paula in the late '90s.

June

I lived by myself for a while until 2004 when I met June via match.com. Having dated numerous women over the course of two years, I found myself so lonely in February 2004 that I threw a three-hundred-mile-wide net out over the match.com landscape. What happened turned my life around and upside down. In the upper left-hand corner of a display featuring hundreds of women looking for suitable men, the picture of one attractive southern woman appeared. She called herself "jblueeyes."

Tired, but not too tired to press the "wink" button, I sent the lovely lady the simplest of messages: Wink! Wink! And I went to bed. The next morning I was surprised to find something of a return wink-wink. On Valentine's Day I took action and e-mailed the smiling lady. And thereupon things went uphill fast.

Luckily June kept a record of our correspondence from the time we met online on Valentine's Eve until we met in person two weeks later. Here is part of one of my early responses to one of June's match.com messages:

Sunday, February 22, 2004

Thanks so very much for responding—and so quickly. I'm not sure if in my previous email to you I've invited you to look at my homepage; but if not, here it is: www.english.edu.edu/Harnack.

Already I've started to write a somewhat longish letter that I'd like to send to you. However, in a few minutes I need to drive to Louisville to pick up a friend coming in from Puerto Rico. Realizing that this note doesn't contain a lot of information about me, I hope you'll allow us to continue our "talking" with each other later. I'll be sure to check my email either very late tonight or early tomorrow morning. In the meantime, I wish you a happy (but belated) Happy Valentine's Day . . . .

Grateful for your reply,
Andrew

After our initial sendings and replies, our e-mail correspondence flourished at a furious rate. Three or four a day. I told June that "politically I'm a mix of liberal and conservative, depending on the issue" and that "I'm quite comfortable with any religious tradition that encourages quiet reflection." Admitting that I couldn't dance, I confessed that I liked fine wine and good beer. As we batted e-mails back and forth, it soon became obvious that we shared much in common: faith in Christ, the deaths of sons, similar life-spans, and series of tragedies. Forthright about my previous marriages, I went into some detail about my recent divorce. However, as extensively as we wrote to one another, in nearly every communication, I found myself saying something like this:

June, both you and I must be cautious. It seems as though both of us have experienced enough emotional pain not to be otherwise. I'm not sure how I might

> convey to you that I'm neither a controlling person nor someone who feigns love; perhaps you can read that about myself in-between my lines and words. My older kids will certainly tell you that, as would my first wife. Older and wiser—yet still fully in love with being alive and being in God's presence—I would love to experience what marriage may yet—and in some ways, again—mean to me. I envy your long marriage to your husband. I frequently find myself watching with wonder older couples walking hand-in-hand, wish that I had a hand to hold. Perhaps I may, God willing.

As the days went by, more than anything I wanted June (as I had come to know her by name) to realize that Chelsea, with whom I was living on weekends and whose picture I had sent to June, was very special to me. And so I wrote:

> Now a word about Chelsea. My daughter is beautiful, inside and out. She's courteous (almost to a fault), obedient, studious, athletic, very sociable, hard working, and industrious. Next year she will be in the seventh grade at my university's Model Lab School. She never complains. In a few years she will be an exceptionally tall and attractive young woman. She wants to go to college. Well-mannered, gentle, and kind of everyone, she loves animals and her family. She will love you too.

By February 25, just eleven days after meeting, June was telling me lots about herself and her family. Within a fortnight I drove down to Barnesville, Georgia, to meet June. Lost in the final hour of driving, I finally knocked on her Holmes Street front door well after dusk. When she opened it, I asked for a hug and got a good squeeze. That night we went out for supper together at a little local Italian restaurant and got to know each other face-to-face. That was a Saturday night. On Sunday morning we attended worship together at her First Baptist Church, and I was given a real sense of how much people loved her. In many ways that settled it. I was going to woo this woman as best I could.

June and me
at the Greene Family Reunion
November 25, 2016

But first there was one obstacles: my kids' approval of June as a wife. My children, especially Amy, were leery of any woman interested in me. In fact, when I first told Amy with a phone call that I'd found someone named June, she summarily hung up on me. Amy had had enough of women in my life. Protective of her daddy, she wanted to interrogate firsthand any woman interested in me. With her approval necessary, Amy arranged for her sister, Lisa, June, and me to meet with her at her home in Nashville, Tennessee. That meeting took place and went well. June got my girls' approval, and plans for our marriage were made. Before we made our vows on June 26, 2004, I went to China, the trip of my life. And when I returned, everyone got together for a most beautiful wedding. The Rev. Robert Blythe, pastor of Chelsea's First Baptist Church in Richmond, Kentucky, and June's pastor, Garth Forster, officiated as Chelsea, Lisa, and Amy, along with June's daughters, Becky and Carole, June's son, Stan, and my brother, Arthur, stood by us as we became wife and husband. During the wedding I gifted June by reciting Wendell Berry's little poem of love, "The Wild Rose":

Sometimes hidden from me
in daily custom and in trust,
so that I live by you unaware
as by the beating of my heart,

Suddenly you flare in my sight,
a wild rose looming at the edge
of thicket, grace and light
where yesterday was only shade,

and once again I am blessed,
choosing again what I chose before.

It was a beautiful wedding.

I married into a very large family that annually gathers itself together for a family reunion held in honor of her first husband's mother, Annie Grace Greene. It's not unusual for forty or fifty to come and share a big feast at First Baptist Church in Barnesville, play games, and share the latest news. Everyone has been so kind to me, and I'm honored to be among them.

Although I'm still not good at it (ask June), I now have a deeper understanding of my life as a husband in marriage. After nearly two decades of daily prayer that began with the help of Buddhist friends who introduced me to silence, simple sitting, and a disciplined practice of seeing with awareness, my life began a slow turning. A turning and reorientation that finally caught the meaning of the Greek word *metanoia*, the Biblical word for repentance, which in all its fullness should be translated as "reorientation," "the widening of vision," and "the opening of the heart."

The paradox now is that while I've experienced two failed marriages and am happily married again for over fifteen years, I've undergone a transformation that keeps me not only appreciative of my past but also grateful for all I've come to know about myself and how I can live with another. Importantly I am able deeply to empathize with all who have undergone and experienced the tragedy of divorce. And more important, I have experienced not only God's grace and forgiveness of my terrible wrongs, but I've also come to know what the reconstruction of one's life looks like. Living within the forgiveness by my first wife, by her initiative, I'm reunited with Carol. Thank you, Carol; thank you, Lord. I'm still distant from Paula but would appreciate forgiveness. Help us, Lord. I'm approaching my sixteenth year with June and happily so. Praise to you, O Lord.

As I said, "Just the basics."

Thoughts about marriage and divorce

Most of us are at least vaguely aware of the consequences of our human miscalculations, driving our lives like cars with only one dim headlight working while we wend our way down a rutted country road. That's the way Tom Merton somewhere once described the wayward meanderings of our sin-prone lives. We only half know where we are as we convince ourselves we are not lost. Our lives—to some degree at times our whole selves—become distracted, off-center, road conditions being less than satisfactory. Sin, traditionally defined, lies at the heart of the matter. It's the cause of our restlessness. As a result, we experience a myriad of feelings rooted in alienation (a fancy word for being frayed), loneliness, shame, and meaninglessness. That was for me much of my midlife (please, Andy, no excuses here!) day and nighttime living. With guilt thrown in. Guilt, that shadow-side, the underbelly. Much of what I experienced came flooding in when my son, Krister, died in 1993, almost two years after Paula and I adopted Chelsea. I had never experienced the lowering of my heart, faith, and life to such an extreme after we found Kris dead in the wilderness of southern Kentucky. He had gone out to photograph the rising mists of a river. High on an embankment, he misgauged his footing and fell to his death. Within two years my marriage with Paula began to fall apart. I left her in great sadness. Details are not appropriate here. We divorced after living in the same house for five years.

Yet divorce need not separate us from someone we have loved. One may continue to love in residual ways, ways that urge compassion, friendship, and devotion to children. In many ways that describes my living after divorcing two wives whose lives are dear to me as I write. My first wife, Carol, and I often talk with one another. We are glad to see each other when the whole extended family gets together for reunions, birthdays, and holiday celebrations. Carol and

I have often received Holy Communion together even though we no longer wear what were once our wedding rings. And after the death of Chelsea (more about that in the next chapter), Paula recently shared brunch, heartfelt compassion, and hugs with Carol, June, and all my children. Both joys and tragedies urge us to hold on to each other.

So I would encourage anyone who has divorced a loved one to do whatever possible to let much of that love remain resident. As much as possible. Surely letters and phone calls keep even a loose knot from becoming completely untied. Just because a tree has been pruned does not mean it must die. After a season or two, even pruning can stimulate the growth of new leaves, perhaps a flower or two. All this requires the preservation and cultivation of good memories, perhaps the turning of pages in a photo album, maybe listening to an old shared song. Most importantly, we must hold one another in prayer, asking for forgiveness, reconciliation, and the best life can offer for one another. And if at all possible, now and then the sharing of coffee or a glass of wine during Christmastide.

And when in marriage, practice forgiveness. And try not to take arguments too seriously. A few days ago, June and I had a falling out with each other. After we'd forgiven each other, June said to me, "Andy, I hope you know I'm a hard-headed woman." I replied, "Yes, you are." To which she responded, "Well, at least we don't argue about that." We shared a smile.

If contemplating divorce, seek counseling.[28]

Fatherings

I'm the father of five children: Kirk, Krister, Lisa, Amy, and Chelsea. Two of my children, however, have died. Krister fell to his death in a wilderness climbing accident in 1993, and Chelsea was murdered on January 1, 2015.

---

28 For starters, I recommend, "The Best Marriage Advice from a Divorced Man," available at http://multisupermagazine.site/index.php/2018/04/28/the-best-marriage-advice-from-a-divorced-man/

Kirk, Michael, and Lora

Lisa, Timothy, and Katie

A Christmastide celebration with the Family, Jan, 2015

Amy, Kevin, Jackson, Mary Carol
and Hayden

Chelsea and Krister

See my big football!

Krister playing basketball
for his Model Lab School
Patriots

Chris and me hiking on the
Sheltowee Trace in
Kentucky

Krister Martin Harnack
Commander of the Supply Company
of the 103rd Forward Support
Battalion of the 35th Infantry Division

Holding Chelsea as a baby

Chelsea and me with
one of our favorite books,
Tolkien's *The Hobbit*

Chelsea hurdles to the
finish line as winner in the
100 meter sprint

Chelsea's Senior Year
High School Portrait

Chelsea and me
at an Eastern Kentucky University football game
with Mary, Carol and Kevin Kuhn

Kayaking with Chelsea on
the North Fork Kentucky River
Memorial Day, 2006

Boating together
On Jackson Lake, GA

The emotional and psychological pain of losing two children has been severe. When I'm alone, I often find myself quietly weeping. And when I find it necessary to share my continued grief with others, at times I grasp for words and need to pause while trembling to speak. Every day I walk past photographs of Kris and Chelsea and remember what it was like to be with them. I deeply feel their absence. I have no nearby graves to visit and for a long time wanted to create some kind of a memorial to them. Perhaps there will eventually be a medical clinic built on the property housing several dozen Haitian orphan girls at *Chez Moi*.[29] I would very much like that to happen. After Chelsea's death, I tilled a large swath of soil near the back fence surrounding my garden and planted several dozen beautiful, wild perennials in memory of Krister and Chelsea.

Although I mourn their deaths every day, I am nevertheless deeply grateful that both Kris and Chelsea are now in the heart of God.

During our Sunday liturgy, after everyone shares "the peace of the Lord," our little choir sings while the offerings are collected and brought to the altar by the ushers. The acolyte receives the gifts and lifts them to God. Then everyone rises, and the entire congregation often sings one of the loveliest of hymns, "Now the Silence." As mentioned in an earlier chapter, I sometimes quietly weep at the beauty of its imagery, poetry, and melody.[30] As a quietness hovers

---

29 More about *Chez Moi,* an orphanage for girls supported by Grace Missions, Inc., in chapter 11.

30 C. Michael Hawn reminds us that Jaroslav Vajda (1919–2008, one of the leading hymn writers in the twentieth century) was arguably the preeminent Lutheran hymn writer of his generation. His "Now the Silence" (1968) contains only fourteen lines with no punctuation. Just so, the incessant use of the word "Now" (sixteen times!) places the mystery of the Eucharist into the center of the singer's consciousness so that all who sing its simple melody enter a profound sensory experience, the essence of the embodiment of the Incarnation. "The Lord's Supper" is thus no longer relegated to the past as a memorial event, but is the reality of "Now" as we see "the vessel brimmed for pouring" and participate in "the joyful celebration." Communion reveals itself as a manifestation of "the Son's epiphany" through which we receive "the Father's blessing."

About the music to which the poem is set, Hawn aptly notes that, composed by Lutheran Carl Schalk (b. 1929), it wonderfully complements the beauty of the over the congregation, our pastor, raising her or his hands, re-presents Jesus' Passover blessing of bread and wine as the Holy Spirit descends upon us in holy communion. Within these words, this music, and this Silence, God brings Kris and Chelsea to me as once again I enter the eternal Now with Christ.

During the past two decades, I have received continued help in coping with my sorrow. In our Centering Prayer group, we've recently been reading Martin Laird's *A Sunlit Absence: Silence, Awareness, and Contemplation*. As someone who practices centering prayer as I do, Laird lovingly encourages me to see that whatever difficulties I, and others like me, experience in meditation—boredom, lethargy, arrogance, depression, grief, anxiety—not as obstacles to be overcome but as opportunities to practice surrender.[31]

And during the past year, I've also come across wonderful words written hundreds of years ago by Meister Eckhart, my beloved medieval Christian mystic, whose short sermons I treasure, reading one almost daily, and about whom I will say more in the final chapter of this little book. Here's what Meister Eckhart says about the presence of pain in one's life:

> However great [one's] suffering may be, if it comes through God, then God suffers first from it. Indeed, by the truth that is God, there never was so tiny a pang of sorrow that befell a man, not the least little discomfort or inconvenience, but if he placed it in God, then it would pain God incomparably more than that man, and incommode God more than man himself. But if God endures this for the sake of such benefit as He intends for you thereby, and if you will endure that which God endures and which comes to

hymn's text. As Vajda himself once noted, "Carl Schalk's collaboration with me on this hymn and others prompts an expression of appreciation to him and to all musicians, without whom…hymn texts, no matter how good, would die." Hawn's more extended background story for this hymn, "History of Hymns: 'Now the Silence,'" is available at https://www.umcdiscipleship.org/resources/history-of-hymns-now-the-silence.

31 Much more about centering prayer and contemplative practice in Chapter 9.

> you through Him, then it inevitably becomes godlike, so that shame is like honour, bitterness like sweetness and the blackest darkness like the brightest light. It takes all its savour from God and becomes godlike: for whatever comes to such a man conforms to God, because he seeks nothing else and has no taste for anything else. Accordingly, he gets hold of God in all bitterness just as in the greatest sweetness.[32]

And near the end of *The Book of Divine Comfort*, Eckhart adds this conviction:

> Whatever someone good suffers for God's sake, he suffers in God, and God is with Him in his suffering. If my suffering is in God and god suffers with me, how then can my suffering be painful when suffering loses its pain, and my pain is in God and my pain is God? In truth, as God is truth and wherever I find truth I find my god, the truth—so likewise, neither more nor less, whenever I find pure suffering in God and for God, there I find God, my suffering.[33]

What this means is that God and I suffer together. God loves me so much that he allows himself to suffer with me, and I am so united to God that my suffering is his suffering. We grieve together.

If you are grieving over the loss of someone you love, I urge you to read William Paul Young's *The Shack* or watch the movie. My friend Jayne Mouchet gave me her used copy when she sensed I needed help; it was an enormous blessing, greatly helping me understand, appreciate, and welcome the love of the Most Holy Trinity into my life in times of sorrow, darkness, and weeping.

---

32 Meister Eckhart, "The Talks of Instruction," *Meister Eckhart: Sermons & Treatises*, vol. III, trans. and ed. M. O'C. Walshe (Rockport, MA: Element, 1987), 27–28.

33 Ibid., 96.

My family and I also rejoice together. When Amy, Lisa, Kirk—and all in our families, all in my big extended family—love and forgive and celebrate birthdays, Christmases, vacations, and reunions together, we do all united with God. All our sufferings and joys are one in God. Nothing separates us from the love of God in Christ: not tears, not laughter, not frustrations, not distance, not nearness, not unhappiness, not anxiety, not hope, not sickness, not grief, not giddiness, not mirth, not dejection, not hope, not death, not resurrections. As moms and dads and brothers and sisters and children and grandchildren and generations to come, we are one.

I'm also so happy that Kirk, Lisa, and Amy are alive and well. They've made me a grandfather now some nine times. And a great-grandfather of seven (with more to come, I hope).

Yes, I am blessed. Although Kirk, Lisa, and Amy now live some distance from my home in Georgia, I get to see, talk with, and hold Kirk, Lisa, and Amy almost as often as I need or wish to be with them. And more often than many granddads, I get to hug and hold most of my grandchildren and great-grandchildren at least once.

Chapter 4

PASTOR AND PROFESSOR

The biblical fact is that
there are no successful churches.
There are, instead, communities of sinners.
In these communities of sinners,
one of the sinners is called pastor.
—Eugene Peterson

The great thing in the world is not so much where we stand,
as in what direction we are moving.
—Oliver Wendell Holmes

So what does a good teacher do? Create tension
—but just the right amount.
—Donald Norman

A first parish

Upon graduating from seminary, Carol and I were sent by the Lutheran Church–Missouri Synod (LC-MS) to East Avon, New York, to work as what today is known as a "church planter." Sporting a crew cut and collar, I was ordained as a Lutheran pastor on Sunday, July 15, 1962, in Pinnacle Lutheran Church, Rochester, New York. My father preached the sermon. For nearly three years, a small group of committed Lutherans met in an upstairs room in the back of a volunteer fire-department station. Everything was makeshift. Frequently on Saturday nights, the room was occupied by locals who loved to drink and leave without a lot of cleanup. On Sundays I'd arrive early, arrange the chairs, and set up a folding table for the Eucharist. Unaccustomed to weekly preaching and quite unsure of myself, I often found it necessary to vomit in the men's toilet to settle my tummy and relieve my anxieties. I imagine that I looked awful a time or two. When it came time to do Vacation Bible School, we pitched a huge tent and became something of Lutheran circus. Eventually, however, we gathered ourselves together—about ten families—and with the Eastern District's underwriting, we bought three acres south of the Highway 20 between East Avon and Lima, New York.

The building we planted was and still is beautiful. Happenstance allowed us to find a stained-glass worker who earlier in his life had worked on the chapel at West Point. Several craftsmen in the congregation designed and built the pulpit. The cone-shaped lights that hang in the sanctuary were made of copper, and to give them a lovely patina, the entire church council (it was all men) took them outside so that we could pee all over them. The uric acid did its job; my goodness, that green patina! We were so ecumenical in everything. Students from a nearby Roman Catholic minor seminary came and helped us paint and lay tile. When we dedicated the building, my father came and preached. And the biggest wonder of all is that somehow I managed to stay out of trouble during my first pastorate. Carol gave birth to our second son, Krister, on April 21, 1963, and I was able to go unnoticed as a liberal and quite liturgical Lutheran in the Missouri Synod.

The Installation

of

The Rev. H. Andrew Harnack

as Lutheran Pastor

for the Avon-East Avon-Lima-Livonia area

Pinnacle Lutheran Church

Pinnacle Rd. & Stone Rd.

Rochester, New York

The Fourth Sunday after Trinity

SUNDAY, JULY 15, 1962 - 3:00 P. M.

Ordination Bulletin

Sanctuary
The Lutheran Church of the Epiphany
East Avon, New York

At my parish desk
Trinity Lutheran Church
Lafayette, Louisiana

Trinity Litheran Church
Lafayette, Louisiana

A second parish, a coffee house, and more schooling

But as good as it was, I wanted somehow to be with young people, be near a university, be more politically active. And so I let it be known that I was looking for a town-gown or campus ministry. Although I'm still not sure if my dad had something to do with it, nonetheless I did get another "call," an invitation to serve at Trinity Lutheran Church in Lafayette, Louisiana. Carol, Kirk, Krister, and I moved there in the summer of 1966.

For many years I lived a fairly restricted intellectual life, empty of any acquaintance with American, British, world, or secular literature of any kind. My education was exceptionally parochial, conservatively Lutheran. Unexpectedly, my interest in non-theological literature had its origins in a hospital stay. While pastoring at the Church of the Epiphany in East Avon, New York, I had gone out walking one summer afternoon. Finding myself tired, I lay down on a grassy knoll. I fell asleep only to be awakened by thunder in a rainstorm, soaked to the bones. By the time I got home, I had what appeared to be a bad cold with lots of coughing. It turned out to be a lung infection that landed me in a Rochester hospital for several weeks. While there, I managed somehow to take along a pile of books, one containing biographies of famous English writers like Wordsworth, Coleridge, and Byron. I found their lives amazingly interesting and the possibility of reading their poetry a genuinely hoped-for realization. When Carol, Kirk, Kris, and I later moved to Lafayette, the chance to read such unfamiliar literature became a reality inasmuch as Trinity Lutheran Church was located directly across the street from the university. It was only a two-minute walk from my parish office to the Department of English, British poetry, and literature.

My first graduate class took me to James Joyce, his short stories in *Dubliners*, and, of course, *Ulysses*. It was a new kind of Greek to me, and I loved it. Eventually I earned a master's degree, Dr. Mary Dickerson steering me through my thesis on T. S. Eliot.

I gained a bit of notoriety by opening a parish coffee house. The late 1960s and early 1970s were times of civil unrest and serious disagreements within the LC-MS. Convinced that the church must work for justice, oppose unjust wars, and stand up for the marginalized, I asked my congregation on August 4, 1966, to create a coffee house on Sunday evenings so that university students and faculty might gather for entertainment and conversations. We called it "The Arena," imagining it to be something—on very small scale!—like the Roman Colosseum where martyrs died in witness to the Gospel. We bought large coffee urns to make Louisiana-style steamed espresso coffee served in demitasse cups.

Taking turns, thirty dedicated parishioners worked each Sunday evening serving students hot teas and coffees at very nominal charge. We invited poets, musicians, storytellers, local choirs, and quartets to read, play, sing, and encouraged discussions about local, state, and national events. After opening our doors on October 26, 1966, hundreds of students arrived each Sunday evening to hear presentations on topics like the legality of state miscegenation laws, goings-on at the Second Vatican Council, and civil rights happenings.

Each week in the *Daily Advertiser*'s theatre section, my friend Dave Miller previewed upcoming events. From my archive of saved clippings, here is a typical announcement, the exact date of which I've lost:

> Tonight at the Arena Coffee House, a polylog, a choir, and film will be featured. The polylog (everybody invited) will be led by Dr. Patricia Rickels, and will be on the National AAUP proposal for academic freedom for students. It begins about 8:00 p.m.
>
> At 9, the Jesuit seminarians from St. Charles in Grand Coteau will sing liturgical folk music. Then, at 10, the film, "The Parable," will be shown. This is the movie that was shown at the New York World's Fair in the Protestant Pavilion. Those who have seen it spare nothing in their praises.[34]

---

[34] *Parable* is a 1964 American short Christian film written and directed by Rolf Forsberg, made for the Lutheran Council and became popular when first screened at the

On April, 1967, *The Forum*, the university's student newspaper, published this note of appreciation:

THANKS TO THE ARENA

> In the fall semester of the 1966–67 term, the U.S.L. campus was greeted with something which has become extremely popular around the country—a coffee house.
>
> The coffee house was conceived to offer an opportunity to students, faculty members, and anyone else who might be interested to participate in dialogue and free discussion in a healthy atmosphere. It also a place for talented students to perform in a number of different fields.
>
> The coffee house was met with excited approval by a large number of people. Participation was excellent and students attended in large, enthusiastic numbers. The coffee house has been consistently serving a crowd of anywhere between 250 and 400 people per night. It has obviously alleviated a heretofore conspicuous void in campus activity.
>
> The Forum would like to take this opportunity to express its thanks to Pastor Andrew Harnack and the congregation of Trinity Lutheran Church for making the coffee house possible.
>
> —Roger Asher

1964 New York World's Fair in 1964, and again in 1965 at the Protestant Pavilion. The film depicts Christ as a clown and the world as a circus and is considered both a revolutionary Christian film and one which proved to be influential. For more information, visit https://en.wikipedia.org/wiki/Parable_(film). In 2012, the film was selected for preservation in the US National Film Registry by the Library of Congress as being "culturally, historically, or aesthetically significant."

Subversive and un-American

In the spring of 1967, a small bag of poop hit the fan. Inasmuch as everyone was engaged in the national discussion about the war in Vietnam, I asked the faculty in the Department of Political Science to form a five-member panel, each panelist articulating a view on the spectrum of opinions and arguments for and against the war: far right, right of center, center, left of center, and far left. I asked these panelists to place the five options in a hat, take turns drawing out a position, and then articulate that viewpoint regardless of personal opinion. They agreed to do so.

In scheduling events for that discussion on an early Sunday night in March 1967, I also asked my friend Art Emery, a Quaker and committed pacifist, to spell out the overall position of the Quakers (known also as the Religious Society of Friends) about the Vietnam War. A few hours before he was to arrive, Art phoned to say that he could not make it, but his wife would be glad to come on his behalf. That sounded fine. After she arrived, I introduced her, and she took her place on a stool under a stage light. It was then that she explained how the Quakers were attempting to help the wounded and needy on both sides of the conflict, South and North, as reported in *Quakers in the World*.[35] Because Quakers in the United States were sending monies to both sides fighting in the war, President Lyndon Johnson had frozen the assets of the American Friends Service Committee

---

35 In 1966, as US involvement in the war continued to escalate, the AFSC sponsored David and Mary Stickney to run a medical clinic in Quang Ngai Province, which by then was flooded with over one hundred thousand refugees. The clinic specialized in making prosthetic limbs, eventually dealing with as many as sixty-five cases a month. Throughout the war, the Stickneys refused to accept any military protection for the clinic.

In the autumn of 1966, aware that the need for humanitarian aid was even greater in North Vietnam than in the South, the AFSC applied for permission to send $6k of aid to North Vietnam. The US government refused on grounds that the North Vietnamese would not allow independent observers to ensure the aid reached civilians only. The AFSC knew that to proceed would put them in violation of the 1917 Trading with the Enemy Act and backed down. In response, a new, more radical group called "A Quaker Action Group (AQAG)" formed and took charge of the operation for North Vietnam.

Money began to be funneled through the Canadian Friends Service Committee. The US Treasury department asked the Royal Bank of Canada to stop checks being

(AFSC) so that no monies got to North Vietnam. Unable to transfer monies via banks in the United States, many Quakers decided to carry cash gathered in the United States to the Canadian border where funds were handed over to Canadian Quakers who, in turn, sent financial aid to humanitarian workers in North Vietnam. In this way, the Quakers, Art's wife explained, were able to show love to our enemies as Jesus urged us to do.

I remember well what happened next. Under the spotlight in the semidark coffee house, Art's wife pulled out a long pin from her hair, took off her black French beret, turned it upside down, and asked all who wanted to contribute to Canadian Friends Service Committee to place contributions into her hat. She then promised to make sure such money would eventually get to aid workers in North Vietnam.

REPORTER SAYS 2 'PARROT RED LINE'

Zippert, Emery Probed At Meet

Quite frankly, because I was busy elsewhere, I didn't pay much attention either to her talk or to her request. But one person in the audience did. Because Dave Miller, my friend and reporter for the local newspaper, was out of town and could not attend that night's coffee-house program, a substitute from the paper had come to report on goings-on. Unknown to any of us, he was a member of the John Birch Society. On Monday morning a week later, he made sure the front page of the *Daily Advertiser* ran this screaming two-inch, blocked letter headline: "REPORTER SAYS 2 'PARROT RED

---

paid to CFSC. When that request was refused, they wrote to US banks asking them not to honor the checks.

An ad hoc Quaker underground then came into effect. The personal bank accounts of Canadian Friends were used to channel money to the CFSC. American Friends drove over the border carrying bundles of cash, while others walked over the Peace Bridge from Buffalo, New York, to Niagara, Ontario, carrying medical supplies. ("Peace Witness and Relief Efforts during the Vietnam War," available at http://www.quakersintheworld.org/quakers-in-action/315.)

LINE.'" In the article itself, he put Art on full display, calling him a traitor, guilty of treason.

By association, I was publicly accused to being a communist[36] and eventually found out that my name had been listed by the House Un-American Activities Committee[37] as an enemy of the state for sponsoring the likes of Art's wife, a speaker in the coffee house.

Many in Lafayette came to my rescue by writing letters of support to the newspaper and to my parish. I received, for example, the following letter from a well-known and highly respected Roman Catholic priest who ministered to students and faculty at the Southwestern Catholic Center:

> March 10, 1967
> Congregation of Trinity Lutheran Church
> c/o Pastor H. Andrew Harnack
> 1402 Johnston Street
> Lafayette, Louisiana 70501
>
> Dear Friends in Christ:
>
> We have long wanted to commend you for the Christ-like spirit of concern and generosity your growing community has manifested in the City of

---

36 That was not the first time I have been called a communist. Forty-eight years later a Barnesvillian Tea Party enthusiast, Robert Heiney, labeled me a friend of "slobbering Visogoths in the Orwellian named Department of Homeland Security." In early November 2011, I had published a tongue-in-cheek article in the local paper suggesting that Barack Obama, with Tea Party help, might make a good president of the United States. Heiney didn't appreciate my humor.

37 The House Un-American Activities Committee (HUAC) was an investigative committee of the US House of Representatives. It was originally created in 1938 to uncover citizens with Nazi ties within the United States. However, it has become better known for its role in investigating alleged disloyalty and subversive activities on the part of private citizens, public employees, and those organizations suspected of having ties to Communism. In 1969, the House changed the committee's name to "House Committee on Internal Security." When the House abolished the committee in 1975, its functions were transferred to the House Judiciary Committee.

Lafayette, particularly in reference to the community and others in the University ambit. Recent events give added point to my personal gratitude and that of your Christian brothers collaborating in the apostolate of our day. Criticism is a normal concomitant in any positive effort to serve in a public area; although sensitive to it, we cannot allow it to determine our goals and condition our efforts.

Certainly Christ spoke through the smokescreen of confusion and discord in an occupied country where Roman, natives and assorted visiting pagans found His message not too congenial. Your leadership among our Christian communities is encouraging to all of us who seek to let Christ be known and loved by all who manage to approach Him and reach Him in us. We thank Pastor Harnack and all of you for the witness you give so generously and wholesomely.

Let us remain united in prayer and public witness to the present love of our Lord.

Yours in Christ,
Monsignor Alexander O. Sigur and Staff

In spite of such support, as you might imagine, Trinity's parishioners were more than a little upset at the publicity our congregation had earned. Before the service on the following Sunday, I called for a congregational meeting to discuss the matter. I was apprehensive. Perhaps we'd have to shut down the coffee house.

What happened next was a surprise. To the best of my memory, one of our parishioners, Captain Bill Stricker, the University's Commandant of the ROTC in the Department of Military Science, came to the service in full uniform. Bill and I were close friends; a fervent supporter of our coffee-house ministry, he always showed up early to set up tables, put on his apron, and make coffee. As I watched him take a seat at the back of the sanctuary, I thought his arrival in full uniform unusual. Bill usually came in civvies.

After Holy Communion, I called the meeting to order, telling everyone why we were meeting (as if they needed to know!). It was then that Captain Stricker raised his hand and asked for permission to address the congregation. I asked him to come forward. Standing before us all, Bill began by telling us that he is always proud to wear the uniform of an army officer; "today," he said, "being no exception." Then Bill told us why he wears his uniform. "It's because I want to protect the rights of American citizens to say whatever they wish in a place like our Arena Coffee House. I am willing," he said, "to lay down my life so that we can invite Quakers to speak to us about their convictions. I may disagree, but I want everyone to have the right to speak without harassment." Bill went on to praise the ministry of the coffee house and urged everyone in the congregation to continue their support. He closed with these words: "I will be here tonight to brew coffee for our students. I ask you to join me and help clean up after they leave. Thank you for giving me this opportunity to speak." And with that he walked back to his seat.

Within seconds someone raised a hand and motioned that we adjourn the meeting. Another seconded that option. All said, "Aye." No one said, "Nay." The motion passed. All stood, and I said a prayer. As we left the sanctuary, everyone once again shared the peace of Christ. And we all went home.

Of all the accolades and appreciations I received, none meant more to me than one from Dr. Edgar Krentz, one of my New Testament professors at Concordia Seminary in St. Louis. On November 13, 1967, he sent me this note:

> Dear Andrew:
>
> After reading the article on your coffee-house in the November 1967 *Advance*, I thought I should just drop you a short note to say it made exciting reading. I'm sure that you are finding it a means of getting through to many people who otherwise would never give you the time of day.

> Congratulations on the creative use of imagination and church facilities.
>
> Yours in Christ,
> Edgar Krentz (signature)

To be your student, Dr. Krentz, was a blessing I will never forget. I thank you for your scholarship, note, and friendship. May God bless you.

We continued to keep the coffee house open for the rest of the year but eventually found ourselves exhausted. Luckily for us, the Presbyterian Church down the street came to our rescue and offered to take things over so that we could catch our breath and go about a parish ministry in more usual fashion. Thank you, dear Calvinist friends!

Ministry in Lafayette proved to be wonderful. The congregation and I got along swimmingly. I was able to study English literature, hold hands with my neighbors, grow spiritually, and most of all enjoy the hours when I went to my parish study early in the morning and poured myself into the Scriptures, preparing sermons for the next Sunday. As a Lutheran pastor, I usually preached on the lectionary reading assigned for a particular Sunday.

Teaching and tenure troubles

As much as I enjoyed pastoring in both New York and Louisiana, I soon wanted very much to teach English literature to Lutheran college students so that they might grow in the ability to read well, enjoy the wisdom of great poetry and epics, and discover for themselves something in addition to the teachings of conservative Christianity. Earning a master's degree at USL was enough to qualify me for a teaching position at St. John's College in Winfield, Kansas, where I taught British literature, the history of art, and writing courses until it became impossible to continue. After teaching there for five exciting years, I was up for tenure—if only I would sign a certain document. Sadly, both the college and I declared myself ineligible for such a signature. So I had to leave, saying with Dorothy, "Toto, I've a feeling we're not in Kansas anymore."

The reason for my leaving Kansas began years before I arrived as events within the Missouri-Synod inevitably proved themselves disastrous for my personal life. For a number of years, but especially between 1970 and 1976, ultraconservative and fundamentalist Lutherans in the Synod infiltrated and took over numerous administrative positions in seminaries, schools, and district offices. They wanted to clean house and get rid of liberals and broad-minded progressives. Administrative censors started sitting in on classroom discussions. Suffice it to say that I got caught up in the turmoil tearing the Synod apart with its newly instituted demands. All professors teaching in Synod colleges and seminaries were summarily required to sign the so-called *Brief Statement.*[38] I opposed the theology of that document declaring it un-Lutheran, fundamentalist in orientation, intellectually unsupportable, reactionary, and unworthy of acceptance as an article of faith. Other Christians in other traditions (noticeably those in the Southern Baptist Convention) were experiencing similar "house cleanings."[39] I attended gatherings of protest and

---

38 Originally written in German by Franz Pieper (1852), this document was adopted in 1932 as an authoritative presentation of the Missouri-Synod's doctrinal stance and later recast as *A Statement of Scriptural and Confessional Principles* in 1972. Essentially a product of the nineteenth century, it does not reflect the consensus of sound and general well-accepted biblical scholarship since the mid-1950s. For the full text of *A Statement of Scriptural and Confessional Principles*, see "Doctrinal Position [of the Lutheran Church-Missouri Synod]," available at http://www.lcms.org/doctrine/scripturalprinciples.

39 For the past thirty years, many have witnessed with dismay an intense struggle within the Southern Baptist Convention (SBC). Fundamentalist in theological orientation, a conservative "revival" overwhelmed progressive seminaries, churches, and schools. Its initiators called it a "Conservative Resurgence" as James C. Hefley describes it enthusiastically in *The Conservative Resurgence in the Southern Baptist Convention* (Hannibal, MO: Hannibal Books, 1991). Its detractors labeled it a "Fundamentalist Takeover." Russell H. Dilday, president of the Southwestern Baptist Theological Seminary from 1978 to 1994, described the resurgence as having fragmented Southern Baptist fellowship and as being "far more serious than a controversy." Dilday described it as being "a self-destructive, contentious, one-sided feud that at times took on combative characteristics." Since 1979, Southern Baptists had become polarized into two major groups: moderates and conservatives. Reflecting the conservative majority votes of delegates at the 1979 annual meeting of the SBC,

eventually got myself ousted by refusing to sign the *Brief Statement.* As theologically conservative as I was in the 1970s, signing it meant that I would teach what I did not believe. At my ordination I vowed to teach in the spirit and witness of the historic *Book of Concord.*[40] I, along with hundreds of other professors and pastors, was unable to put my signature to another theological document, especially one that required teaching and preaching Scripture as inerrant, that is, historically reliable in all details. My understanding and reading of Scripture was and is that I love the Bible but not to make it an idol it was never designed to be. If I had penned my name to the *Brief*

---

the new national organization officers replaced all leaders of Southern Baptist agencies with presumably more conservative people (often dubbed "fundamentalist" by dissenters). To review opposing viewpoints expressed during this controversy, consult Rob James and Gary Leazer, *The Fundamentalist Takeover in the Southern Baptist Convention: A Brief History* (Timisoara, Romania: Impact Media, 1999); Fisher Humphreys, *The Way We Were: How Southern Baptist Theology Has Changed and What It Means to All* (Macon, GA: Smyth & Helwys, 2002); and James C. Hefley, *The Truth in Crisis: The Conservative Resurgence in the Southern Baptist Convention*, vol. 6 (Garland, TX: Hannibal Books, 2005).

40 The *Book of Concord* was compiled by a group of theologians led by Jakob Andreae and Martin Chemnitz at the behest of their rulers, who desired an end to the religious controversies in their territories that arose among Lutherans after the death of Martin Luther in 1546. Following the preface written by Andreae and Chemnitz (1578–80), the Three Ecumenical Creeds (Apostles', Nicene, and Athanasian) were placed at the beginning to declare that Lutheran teaching and doctrine fully agree with that of the ancient Christian church.

Also included are statements of faith from the earliest years of the Lutheran Reformation (1529–77): *The Augsburg Confession* and *The Apology of the Augsburg Confession*, both by Philipp Melanchthon, the catechisms of Martin Luther, his *Smalcald Articles*, and Melanchthon's *Formula of Concord.*

The Augsburg Confession, delivered to Emperor Charles V at Augsburg during the great Diet in the year 1530, has singular importance as the unanimous consensus and exposition of Christian faith articulated by Lutherans. *The Apology*, *the Smalcald Articles*, the *Treatise*, and the *Formula of Concord* explain, defend, or serve as addenda to *The Augsburg Confession*. At their ordinations, Lutheran pastors vow to serve the church in accordance with the teachings of the *Book of Concord.* To this day *The Augsburg Confession* remains the basic definition of what it means to be Lutheran.

Statement, I would have been required to teach the creation stories as science.[41] Good God, deliver me from that!

[41] Here's what the *Brief Statement* requires one to teach and preach about creation:

> We teach that God has created heaven and earth, and that in the manner and in the space of time recorded in the Holy Scriptures, especially Gen. 1 and 2, namely, by His almighty creative word, and in six days. We reject every doctrine which denies or limits the work of creation as taught in Scripture. In our days it is denied or limited by those who assert, ostensibly in deference to science, that the world came into existence through a process of evolution; that is, that it has, in immense periods of time, developed more or less of itself. Since no man was present when it pleased God to create the world, we must look for a reliable account of creation to God's own record, found in God's own book, the Bible. We accept God's own record with full confidence and confess with Luther's Catechism: "I believe that God has made me and all creatures."

In addition to such fundamentalist thinking, the *Statement* also requires one to believe that the Roman Catholic pope is the Anti-Christ:

> As to the Antichrist we teach that the prophecies of the Holy Scriptures concerning the Antichrist, 2 Thess. 2:3–12; 1 John 2:18, have been fulfilled in the Pope of Rome and his dominion. All the features of the Antichrist as drawn in these prophecies, including the most abominable and horrible ones, for example, that the Antichrist "as God sitteth in the temple of God," 2 Thess. 2:4; that he anathematizes the very heart of the Gospel of Christ, that is, the doctrine of the forgiveness of sins by grace alone, for Christ's sake alone, through faith alone, without any merit or worthiness in man (Rom. 3:20–28; Gal. 2:16); that he recognizes only those as members of the Christian Church who bow to his authority; and that, like a deluge, he had inundated the whole Church with his antichristian doctrines till God revealed him through the Reformation—these very features are the outstanding characteristics of the Papacy. (Cf. *Smalcald Articles*, Triglot, p. 515, Paragraphs 39–41; p. 401, Paragraph 45; M. pp. 336, 258.) Hence, we subscribe to the statement of our Confessions that the Pope is "the very Antichrist." (*Smalcald Articles*, Triglot, p. 475, Paragraph 10; M., p. 308.)

God preserve us from such nonsense.

God did deliver me. Dr. Michael Stelmachowicz, the president of the college, called me into his office. Understanding my inability to sign the *Statement* as a matter of conscience, he offered to provide me with a scholarship underwriting tuition for an upcoming sabbatical. As a member of Aid Association for Lutheran's Board of Directions, Dr. Stelmachowicz managed my reception of $10,000 for further graduate study. I owe him decades of gratitude.

While teaching British literature at St. John's, along with courses in composition, I knew deep down that the more enlightened and progressive movement in the Synod was fast coming to an end. For that reason, I had already taken deliberate steps to enroll myself in a doctoral program at Oklahoma State University's Department of English. For nearly a year, I was driving to and from Stillwater, Oklahoma, during the summer and on week nights for classes on John Milton, Edmond Spenser, and other Renaissance authors. Again a whole new world opened up.

Seminex

It was at this time that the great Concordia Seminary "Walk-Out" took place on the morning of February 19, 1974. Forty-five of fifty faculty members at the Seminary marched themselves off the campus into self-exile to form Seminex, a "Seminary in Exile."

Rather than being summarily dismissed and thrown off the seminary campus, they declared themselves protestors, departing the campus in dramatic fashion. Singing "The Church's One Foundation," they processed to the main quadrangle, where students planted white cemetery crosses bearing names of the exile faculty, and then they marched to the gothic entryway known as the Walter Arch. They boarded it up with wooden frames bearing the single word "EXILED."[42] I marched with them in spirit and hope into what I knew would eventually become my Babylonian Exile.

---

[42] Wikipedia continues the story:

> Television crews clustered round as the procession exited the campus, and, in a nearby park on DeMun Avenue, Tietjen preached on the text from Hebrews 13:13–14 which declares that "there is no permanent city for us here on earth; we are looking for the city which is to come." The event attracted a great deal of media attention, although the seminary's Board of Control subsequently accused the students of disingenuous posturing, noting that several had returned to the seminary cafeteria for lunch immediately after their departure into "exile." It is not clear how the news media came to be present.
>
> The next day, classes officially began at Concordia Seminary in Exile (Seminex), which was first located at facilities provided by Eden Seminary and Saint Louis University. Since Seminex was not yet an accredited school, an arrangement was made with the Lutheran School of Theology at Chicago (LSTC) whereby the first class of Seminex graduates would officially receive their diplomas from LSTC. The first graduation was held in the neo-gothic quadrangle of Washington University in St. Louis. John Tietjen, who in October 1974 was finally removed as president of Concordia Seminary, was elected president of Seminex in February 1975.
>
> Within a year and a half of its inception, Seminex had acquired its own facilities, making its home in midtown St. Louis (now generally known as the Grand Center area): first at 607 North Grand Boulevard and then, following water damage to that building, at 539 North Grand. No longer acknowledging the legitimacy of Concordia Seminary and its new administration led by Martin Scharlemann, Seminex faculty and students referred to that institution simply as "801," after its address at 801 DeMun Avenue. However, facing legal action from Concordia, the exiled seminary eventually changed its official name from "Concordia Seminary in Exile" to "Christ Seminary-Seminex" in October 1977. https://en.wikipedia.org/wiki/Seminex.

The purge of progressive scholars from the Synod was extensive, a profoundly sad affair, family splitting, and unnecessary. For a good review of the debacle, I recommend Frederick W. Danker, *No Room in the Brotherhood: The Preus-Otten Purge of Missouri* (St. Louis, MO: Clayton Publishing, 1977). Also consider watching *Seminex: Memories of a Church Divided, A Documentary* by Tim Frakes; available for purchase at http://www.frakesproductions.com/2015/seminex-memories-of-a-church-divided-a-documentary-by-tim-frakes/.

More schooling and a PhD

Unable to stay on at St. John College, Carol, the children, and I moved to Stillwater, Oklahoma; we set up a home in federal housing; and did the best we could to feed, house, and nurture our children. Carol worked nights, and I studied feverishly, around the clock. It was not easy. Carol had to work long hours as a nurse. I had to teach classes, take classes, and write a dissertation. Somehow after two years of intense labor, I sat for my qualifying exams, passed them, published a small book, got an article published, and began searching for employment.

That was extremely difficult. Jimmy Carter was president, interest rates were in the upper teens, and few were hiring. I sent out over eight hundred letters with my résumé. For a brief moment, I thought I had a job at Fort Hays State University. Invited for an interview, I met all the faculty in the Department of English and thought all was going well. One of my colleagues even told me privately that I was a shoo-in. Indeed, all went well until I sat down privately at the end of the day with the departmental chair. As we chatted, he pulled out a recent copy of the *New York Times*. There on the front page was a photo of a gay-pride parade. One of his faculty was caught marching behind a street-wide banner, clearly showing his support for the fired-up demonstration. The chairperson put the paper down and asked if I would include myself in such a demonstration. "Well, I don't think so," I said. Then came the next question. "Would you ever consider being a faculty advisor to a gay group on campus?" That question gave me some pause. I answered by saying that while I'm as straight as a telephone pole, nevertheless I did believe that gays had certain employment and housing rights that needed to be protected. After a few minutes of closing chitchat, we shook hands and I left. When I got back to Stillwater, Oklahoma, I fully expected a contract in the mail. I knew, of course, that if an envelope arrived bulging with documents to be signed, then I had the job. A thin envelope would indicate otherwise. Six days later the thin envelope arrived in my mailbox.

Eastern Kentucky University

So I had to start all over. In a last-ditch effort, a friend and I flew to Philadelphia to put ourselves on display at the annual Conference on College Composition and Communication. Posting a résumé on one of the bulletin boards in the conference lobby, I expected nothing. Then it happened. On the last night of the conference while I sat dejectedly on my bed, Dr. Kelly Thompson, chair of the Department of English at Eastern Kentucky University in Richmond, Kentucky, rang me up and asked if he might see me the next morning. You bet he could!

Dr. Thompson wanted to hire me because I could teach composition and the Bible as literature. That was right down my alley. I got the job and was hired for an annual salary of $13,000, enough to buy bread, some gasoline, and make a house payment. I was overjoyed and began a teaching career at EKU that lasted thirty-six years. During that time, I taught undergraduate courses in Renaissance literature, surveys of world literature, honors rhetoric, developmental writing, freshman composition, the Bible as literature—and for two semesters: New Testament Greek (my own father taking the course!). At the graduate level, I taught the history of rhetoric and directed several students in the writing of their theses. Eventually I become the director of the writing program. For six years I supervised the administration of EKU's writing requirement, the mandatory writing of a thesis-driven essay that every junior-level student had to compose under strict observation, an essay evaluated by a team of faculty readers from all university departments. I published articles in professional journals and a series of books with Greenhaven and St. Martin's presses, frequently taught off-campus classes for a little extra money, and began online teaching, becoming the first online instructor in the Commonwealth of Kentucky. I served on numerous committees and was highly involved in community service, the Human Rights Commission of Madison County as one opportunity. I loved it, looking forward each day to being on campus so that I could teach, help students, and nourish faculty professionally. I lead a busy life as both student and teacher, retiring in 2004.[43]

But not without a bit of notoriety. In my second-semester freshman writing classes, ENG 102, I found it difficult to teach researched writing using the MLA style of documentation when all the students were writing on dozens of topics. Who knew—especially with the advent of the Internet and the ease with which students might copy and paste information—when any one student was plagiarizing? I didn't. Consequently, I decided to design a course in which all students in any single class were to do research and write on one topic. Yes, they could share sources; but more importantly, I could keep track of their documentation with relative ease. So I contracted with Greenhaven Press and published three textbooks in their Opposing Viewpoints series: one on the rights of animals

43 Somehow I managed to publish six books, nearly a dozen articles in professional journals, four in electronic publications. Having been awarded a National Endowment for the Humanities scholarship, I spent the summer of 1980 at the John Hopkins University studying John Milton's prose works, especially his *Areopagitica*. As to presentations at professional meetings, from 1975 to 2002, I gave sixty of them. During six summers, Paula Kopacz and I taught weeklong Elderhostel programs on Henry David Thoreau, Homer's *Odyssey*, Herman Melville's *Moby Dick*, and the poetry of Emily Dickinson. We also team-taught in two Governor Scholar Programs. In 1983 and 1993, I was given two sabbaticals, both resulting in publications. From 1988 to 1989, I was elected president of the Kentucky Philological Society, having served from many years as its executive secretary. Throughout my academic career, I maintained memberships in a variety of professional organizations: National Council of Teachers of English, the Modern Language Association, and the George Herbert Society, to mention a few. I served on numerous committees and boards while teaching at EKU: the Distance Education Committee, the Computer Communications Ethics Committee, the University Information and Technology Committee, the University Writing Requirement Advisory Committee, the Sabbatical Review Committee, among others. In addition, I led many faculty workshops, conferences, and seminars, notably the Mina P. Shaughnessay Conferences for Teachers of Writing. Over a span of almost thirty years within one college and two universities, I taught over thirty-five undergraduate and graduate courses in everything from classical mythology, editing and stylistics, Renaissance literature, Koine Greek, honors composition, basic writing, Internet rhetoric, short stories and films of Woody Allen, and contemporary literary theory. Twice I took students to Kings College, London, for a course titled "Tolkien and His Circle." I was awarded an "Excellence in Teaching Award" by the College of Arts and Humanities in 1985 and inducted into the Eastern Kentucky University's Society of Foundation Professors in 1998.

and another on the topic of adoption. Each contained thirty essays and extended bibliographies for and against a controversial topic. This meant that from day one my students, having not yet entered the library, already had over thirty essays available for citation and bibliographies containing lists of material for further investigation. And to help them along, I published an accompanying manual, *Writing Research Papers: A Student Guide for Use with OPPOSING VIEWPOINTS*, detailing the step-by-step process for producing a first-class research essay. With everyone working together on one topic, the class discussions were lively and argumentative, with just the right kind of instruction that I enjoyed providing.

But, of course, things got around, so much so that in the official history of Eastern Kentucky University, I later found this paragraph penned by William E. Ellis, a distinguished historian:

> Eastern could not escape what one expert called "the cacophony of teaching," in which subject matter became the extension of a professor's political, social, or intellectual mind-set. Eastern had its own version of chattering classes, sometimes "blathering" might have been more correct, as the professoriate often went off on tangents. The Eastern "left" mostly copied trends in larger universities, being more reactive than proactive. A few professors pushed ideological hobbyhorses. For example, one zealot required some of his English survey classes to indulge his dedication to animal rights, which *The Progress* gleefully lampooned in a cartoon showing the professor shoving a chicken down the throat of a student.[44]

I was that "blathering" professor. Would that Ellis had taken my freshman course on good documentation and accurate reporting. If

[44] William E. Ellis, *A History of Eastern Kentucky University* (Lexington, KY: University Press of Kentucky, 2005), 178.

that paragraph had come to my desk, I'd have written a few notes in the margins of his paper:

1. Who is the "one expert"? Citation, please.
2. Please note that ENG 102 is not a survey class; it's a course on how to do research on a topic and support a thesis—either pro or con!—on a topic of interest.
3. The cartoon does not show me shoving a chicken down a student's throat. It's a rat! Hereafter, please provide accurate descriptive information.

In fairness, however, it must also be said that historian Ellis is generally more reliable in much of his other reportage.[45]

Foundation Professor

Dr. Joanne Glasser, President of Eastern Kentucky University, presents me with a plaque in 1998 certifying that I had benn inducted into The Society of Foundation Professors

In 1987, the Eastern Kentucky University Foundation established a program to recognize "creative, self-motivated exemplars of the ideal college professor." All full-time tenured faculty were and are eligible for the two-year professorship, which comes with a substantial extra salary stipend. Basing its decisions for selection on

[45] Last year I read Ellis's *A Man of Books*, and *A Man of the People: E.Y. Mullins and The Crisis of Moderate Southern Baptist Leadership* (Macon, GA: Mercer UP, 2000) and found it remarkably instructive.

the University's criteria for promotion, tenure, and merit, a committee of previously awarded faculty choses one or two for induction into the Society of Foundation Professors. In 1998, near the end of my teaching career, I was delighted to be inducted into the Society of Foundation Professors.[46]

Teaching at Eastern Kentucky University proved to be God's response to my dissatisfaction with years spent in the prison garb of a pastor in the conservative Missouri-Syond Lutheran Church. I grew spiritually at EKU. By giving me opportunities to meet dedicated teachers, able administrators, respected scholars, and intelligent students on a daily basis, God blessed me richly. Yes, I had to spend some time outside the institutional church, but a remarkable series of events made it possible for me to return to a much more charitable expression of Lutheranism. Today I am a happy communicant in the Evangelical Lutheran Church in America, once again living in the Good News, news that assures me that I am deeply embedded in the heart of God.

---

46 For more information about The Society of Foundation Professors, visit http://foundationprofessors.eku.edu.

Chapter 5

BOXED-IN

Betwixt the stirrup and the ground,
Mercy I asked, mercy I found.
—William Camden

Get a prayer-book in your hand,
And stand betwixt two churchmen.
—Shakespeare, *Richard III*, Act 3, Scene 7

People demand freedom of speech to make up for
the freedom of thought which they avoid.
—Soren Kierkegaard

If I had a message to my contemporaries, it is surely this:
Be anything you like, be madmen, drunks, and bastards of every shape,
but at all costs avoid one thing:
success...If you are too obsessed with success, you will forget to live.
If you have learned only how to be a success,
your life has probably been wasted.
—Thomas Merton, *Love and Living*

For now we see indirectly, as in a mirror,
but then face to face.
Now I know in part,
but then I will know fully,
as I am fully known.
—Saint Paul, Corinthians 13:12

A better box

Well into my early forties, I lived what I imagined as a profoundly thoughtful life. The sad truth, however, is that I was largely unaware of my walled-in, firmly bordered life. I did not realize the extent to which I was in fact living within a complex set of dualities, a life of well-defined boundaries. Living in a box, I thought my box was better, if not the best of all boxes. It's what I later labeled as my "comparative mode of thinking." Actually I was quite proud of it all. My box was better than your box. It just was.

That was because I grew up and learned to think with a thoroughly dualistic approach to almost everything. My thinking was structured in binaries, my awareness keyed to boundaries that required me always to be for something and always against its opposite. I was for *this* and not for *that*. I was a Lutheran and not a Baptist. I was white, not black. I was reasonably smart, not stupid. I was oriented toward language, not mathematics. I was somehow basically anti-authoritarian, not a conformist. I was an optimist, not a pessimist. I liked to read Shakespeare, not junk novels. I preferred good music to most of the stuff on the radio. I was not an athlete, but a spectator of sports. Politically I was a Democrat and not a Republican. The labels I put on my life were nearly always for something and opposed to something else. I loved bumper stickers advertising my convictions. I could argue for the right side of nearly any topic. Good Aristotelian logic was my forte. I was good at debating.

Better is always binary

I was taught at an early age to think in binary fashion, in sets of twos. In my early teens, I was taught that only Lutherans live in Biblical light; Roman Catholics muck around in too much tradition. I'm saved; most people aren't. The Bible's six-day creation story doesn't allow for evolution. A few years later, I learned Biblical Greek in college. Knowing some Greek, I was surely going to be a better pastor than the Pentecostal preacher who doesn't know Koine Greek. Getting an education made me superior to those who had only a high-school diploma or only one master's degree. Fifteen years later I was convinced that getting two master's degrees and a PhD (along with some postdoctoral work) separated me from other academics who really were not all that well educated.[47] I knew how to vote intelligently; others didn't. Good liturgy outdid awful free-style worship. My baptism was better than yours. And so on. Of course, I didn't parade all this around on a placard, but within I knew it to be true. I was right most of the time. O yes, I'd pretend to lean and bend now and then, but mostly for the sake of appearance. Deep down, I knew I lived and thought on the right side of damn near everything.

Most of us are aware that our lives are organized in binary fashion. It comes naturally. With the flick of a switch, we turn on

---

[47] I earned by BA from Concordia Senior College in 1957; a BD from Concordia Theological Seminary, St. Louis, Missouri, in 1962; an MA from the University of Southwestern Louisiana, Lafayette, Louisiana, in 1969; a MMin from Concordia Seminary, St. Louis, Missouri, in 1971. I attended Oxford University (Trinity College), England, in the summer of 1973 and was awarded a PhD from Oklahoma State University in 1976; as a postdoctoral student, I studied at the Johns Hopkins University in 1980.

and light our house lights. We know that in a basketball game, one team either wins or loses. We can usually choose to take showers in either hot or cold water. In other words, as a friend of mine once said, "Something in relation to something else can be left or right, up or down, or in or out." Of course, not all binaries are dangerous. Many like Richard Rohr recognize that lots of dualistic or binary thinking have been beneficial to our culture. "In fact, it is necessary in many if not most situations." Rohr is quite willing, as all must, to own up to his own tendencies toward such ways of thinking. That said, it is also necessary to say with Rohr that dualistic thinking is "completely inadequate for the major questions and dilemmas of life."[48]

Historian Frances Stoner says that "we construct borders, literally and figuratively, to fortify our sense of who we are."[49] That's true. During my early years as a university professor, I was more than once asked to participate in Oxford-style public debates by the Department of Philosophy. I enjoyed taking one side of an argument, smashing my opponent's logic, and declaring myself the winner. Here, for example, is how I entered the fray in one EKU Oxford-style debate on whether or not animals have *rights* before a packed auditorium of seven hundred students:

> Hello, everybody! Before I begin, I want to thank Michael for representing so well his very bad argument that only human beings have rights, and in anticipating what Eilene will say about rocks having rights, I want to say in advance that her arguments are just as lousy. That said, I know you're wondering how in the world I'm going to argue that all sentient beings—human and non-human—possess rights. Let me begin.[50]

48 Richard Rohr, *The Naked Now: Learning to See as the Mystics See* (New York: Crossroad, 2013), 32, 40.

49 Qtd. "Wit & Wisdom," *The Week*, December 22/29, 2017, 17.

50 Personal manuscript.

Students were not my only audience. From 1975 to 2002, I made nearly fifty presentations at meetings of organizations such as the Modern Language Association, the Kentucky Philological Association, the Conference on College Composition and Communication, the International Milton Symposium, and a Conference on Christianity and Literature, among many others. Always wanting to be better than others, I chose whatever would give me an edge when it came to having an upper hand. It's for that reason that I chose to get a doctorate in English Renaissance literature, the somewhat archaic hard stuff that only a few might master. Or so I thought. When it came time for me to advertise myself in a job listing with the Modern Language Association, the ad in 1976 read like this:

> Searching for an opportunity to teach Greek, Old and/or Middle English, Renaissance Literature, Literary Criticism, and Professional Writing. Well published in academic journals.

Truth to be told, I wasn't all that *well published.* Eventually, however, I was able to publish in juried professional periodicals like the *George Herbert Journal*, books with Greenhaven and St. Martin's Press, and with Gene Kleppinger an early 1996 online trend-setting essay, "Beyond the MLA Handbook: Documenting Electronic Sources on the Internet"[51] At EKU I was the first person to teach online. Eventually my earliest self-promotions got me a decent job, quick promotions, and something of a reputation for excellence. I was what many others were not—up and up.

But it came at an enormous cost. Thinking in profoundly binary fashion, I developed an ego that was terribly difficult to undo, stubbornly defensive, saturated with self-praise, and deplorably resistant to change. The change toward the diminishment of my ego took place over many years, and there is still great demand for its continuing disappearance. But somehow—I'm not sure I know

[51] Available at http://kairos.technorhetoric.net/1.2/inbox/mla_archive.html.

the process as well as one might hope—my damn ego has slowly dissolved so that others tell me that today I'm a somewhat different Andy. Simply getting older, of course, has done a lot to change me. White haired, I appreciate my physical waning because, as you might expect, I'm more mellow, less convinced about lots of stuff, and much more appreciative of differences, opposite points of views, antitheses, paradoxes, the so-called heterodox, even the cacodoxical[52] (I still love to show off with big words, don't I?).

Boxing in God

The awful thing about our living in a binary thought world is that we also put God in a box so that he looks and acts just like us. Binarians make God a projection of their own thinking. God becomes a mirror image of their mental activity and lives. Because I was a binary thinker, my God had to be a binary God. Think about it. If people read the Bible literally, surely God must have written it to be taken literally. If they think that violence is the answer to violence, God surely agrees with them. If they think that the edicts of their government are always to be obeyed, God

52 Cacodoxical simply means "heretical" or "of a perverse opinion." While one can locate its meaning and etymology online, the word is no longer listed in any recently published paper dictionary. You will, however, find it in the twenty-pound, 3,210-page unabridged second edition of *Webster's New International Dictionary of the English Language* (Springfield, MA: Merriam-Webster, 1945). In 1951, my father was given that massive dictionary as a gift from the Ladies Aid Society of Trinity Lutheran Church, Syracuse, New York. It's a treasure in my library.

must have set up rulers and governments to be obeyed without question. If they are uncomfortable with the LGBTQ community, without doubt God is equally if not more uncomfortable with gays and lesbians. In all these instances, binarians are able to cite proof passages from the Bible. Read your Bible like we do, they say, and you'll see the same God as we do. Of course, they can't imagine they are in fact shoving God into a binary box!

I was once quite binarian and boxed-in. I read my Bible as my conservative church taught me to read it, and I expected others to read it just like me.

All this is not to say that I didn't suspect something was haywire. The box in which I once lived wasn't taped so tightly shut that I couldn't see some light slipping in from a crack or two. As a youngster I was told that the Bible was inerrant. Everything in it was historically true. Even upon entering college, I thought the Bible was word for word "the inerrant Word of God" as so many of my conservative classmates and teachers (and my father) required me to believe. Upon entering seminary four years later, I was not so sure. Able to read the Old Testament in Hebrew and the New Testament in Greek, I knew the text of the Bible fairly well. In my annotated edition of the Hebrew and Greek texts, the notes at the bottom of each page showed me what manuscripts supported (or didn't support) individual words, phrases, sentences, and stories. I knew, for example, that the early seventeenth-century translators of the King James Version (KJV) based their work on a set of Greek manuscripts collectively known as the Textus Receptus. For that reason, a good bit of 1611 KJV translation was not only idiosyncratic but also less than a good reliable witness to the original texts. Take, for example, the KJV's inclusion of the story about the woman taken in adultery in John 7:53–8:11. Today we know that "the evidence for the non-Johannine origin of the pericope of the adultress is overwhelming."[53] While the story has the earmarks of historical veracity, it is "obviously a piece of oral tradition which circulated

[53] For a detailed discussion, see Bruce M. Metzger, *A Textual Commentary on the Greek New Testament* (Stuttgart, Germany: United Bible Societies, 1975), 219–22.

in certain parts of the western church." That doesn't make it any less worthy of study and possibly a preacher's text. This is but one glaring instance of a translation's faulty reliance on poor documental evidence. There are others, some serious. The manuscript collection (the so-called Byzantine text) for many early English translators was often, unbeknownst to them, disfigured and corrupt. We've come a long way since the early seventeenth century in publishing better Bibles.

Encountering God in my box

Trying to figure out how to trust a particular biblical translation, however, proved not nearly so great a problem as trying to figure out what sort of a God is in the Bible, in my box. I found myself asking lots of questions. Is the Bible simply a box for God? Have we somehow managed to package God by composing stories that make him what we want him to be? Were some of the Biblical writers like the egregious Jerry Falwell who infamously opined that 9/11 was God's judgment on America for its tolerance of homosexuality? Did some Biblical writers describe God as angry because they also were angry?

In a seminary class on the Old Testament, I was shocked to read in the Hebrew text that God demanded that the Israelites commit genocide, murdering and "utterly destroying" thousands of innocent people in Deuteronomy 7:

> When the Lord your God brings you into the land that you are about to enter and occupy, and he clears away many nations before you—the Hittites, the Girgashites, the Amorites, the Canaanites, the Perizzites, the Hivites, and the Jebusites, seven nations mightier and more numerous than you—and when the Lord your God gives them over to you and you defeat them, then you must utterly destroy them. Make no covenant with them and show them no mercy. Do not intermarry with them, giving your

> daughters to their sons or taking their daughters for your sons, for that would turn away your children from following me, to serve other gods. Then the anger of the Lord would be kindled against you, and he would destroy you quickly. But this is how you must deal with them: break down their altars, smash their pillars, hew down their sacred poles, and burn their idols with fire. For you are a people holy to the Lord your God; the Lord your God has chosen you out of all the peoples on earth to be his people, his treasured possession. (1–6)

And thirteen chapters later, God does it again:

> When you draw near to a town to fight against it, offer it terms of peace. If it accepts your terms of peace and surrenders to you, then all the people in it shall serve you at forced labor. If it does not submit to you peacefully, but makes war against you, then you shall besiege it; and when the Lord your God gives it into your hand, you shall put all its males to the sword. You may, however, take as your booty the women, the children, livestock, and everything else in the town, all its spoil. You may enjoy the spoil of your enemies, which the Lord your God has given you. Thus you shall treat all the towns that are very far from you, which are not towns of the nations here. But as for the towns of these peoples that the Lord your God is giving you as an inheritance, you must not let anything that breathes remain alive. You shall annihilate them—the Hittites and the Amorites, the Canaanites and the Perizzites, the Hivites and the Jebusites—just as the Lord your God has commanded, so that they may not teach you to do all the abhorrent things that they do for their gods, and you thus sin against the Lord your God. (10–18)

A biblical 9/11

Many of you reading this page remember what happened on Tuesday, September 11, 2001. I remember that day well and will never forget what happened. I was teaching at EKU when I heard screams from nearby classrooms. Rushing into the hallway, students told me to go watch a tv right away. I ran to the teacher's lounge where a CBS news reporter was telling our nation that that U.S. was under attack! Four passenger jets had been highjacked and two jets had just destroyed New York City's Twin Towers, one had hit the Pentagon, and a fourth had crashed into a field in Shankesville, Pennsylvania. Later that week I found out that a total of 2,996 people were killed (including the 19 hijackers) and more than 6,000 others injured. I also remembered reading about something very similar happening in a well-known Old Testament story. When the Israelites built a golden calf to worship instead of God (as reported in Exodus 32), their leader, Moses, told the sons of Levi, "Go back and forth from gate to gate, throughout the camp, and each of you kill your brother, your friend, and your neighbor." After the sons of Levi killed three thousand random people, Moses told them, ""Today you have ordained yourselves for the service of the Lord, each one at the cost of his son and of his brother, that God may bestow a blessing upon you this day." Thus, the Levites, one of the most important religious orders, was established by an act of terror, and those who killed nearly three thousand fellow human beings were blessed by the Lord. It was a biblical foreshadowing of 9/11.

Such a violent God!

The following genocidal commands are not isolated instances of God's approval of violence. For all the cuteness of Sunday-school leaflets showing smiling animals sheltered in Noah's boat, how does one justify the extermination of all human beings except the lucky eight in the ark? We may surely ask, "Were so many millions justly exterminated?" And why were the firstborn among the Egyptians killed? Surely these children were loved by their parents. And why were the Amalekites annihilated by Saul with God's approval? They surely didn't deserve their deaths.

And what are we to make of verses like these:

- Whoever strikes father or mother shall be put death. (Exod. 21:15)
- Whoever kidnaps a person, whether that person has been sold or is still held in possession, shall be put to death. (Exod. 21:16)
- Whoever does any work on the sabbath day shall be put to death. (Exod. 31:15b)
- If a man commits adultery with the wife of his neighbor, both the adulterer and the adultress shall be put to death. (Lev. 20:10)
- If a man lies with a male as with a woman, both of them have committed an abomination; they shall be put to death. (Lev. 20:13a)
- If a man has sexual relations with an animal, he shall be put to death; and you shall kill the animal. If a woman approaches any animal and has sexual relations with it, you shall kill the woman and the animal; they shall be put to death, their blood is upon them. (Lev. 20:15–16)
- A man or a woman who is a medium or a wizard shall be stoned to death; their blood is upon them. (Lev. 20:27)
- One who blasphemes the name of the Lord shall be put to death; the whole congregation shall stone the blasphemer. Aliens as well as citizen, when they blaspheme the Name, shall be put to death. (Lev. 24:16)
- Anyone who kills a human being shall be put to death. (Lev. 24:17)

Many Christians don't know that such verses are in their Bibles. Like Nicholas Kristof, I was not surprised by the account of a Dutch team that disguised a Bible as the Koran and read some of its more violent passages to people on the street. The reaction, when people thought it was the Koran, was along the lines of: "That's why Muslims are so violent!" When they were told everything was actually in the Bible, there was some embarrassment.[54]

I also knew, of course, that some Christians in my conservative tradition are convinced that such divine thinking and behavior are justified.[55] But I also knew that many scholars had concluded that the biblical death commands and accounts of extermination are exaggerated, fictional, or metaphorical at best.[56] After all, promoting God as a punitive lawgiver is one sure way that tribal leaders can make sure things go their way. Strict commands with harsh punishments, especially when endorsed by a clan's Deity, will do much to keep communal law and order. And inasmuch as the Hebrew Bible is obviously the national epic of the Jewish people, the epic's episodes, told and shaped by the king's storytellers, understandably promote the notion that "might makes right." Moreover, those who write

---

54 *The Holy Quran Experiment*. Video report available on https://www.youtube.com/watch?v=zEnWw_lH4tQ.

55 See, for example, "Why Did God Condone Such Terrible Violence in the Old Testament?" Available at http://www.gotquestions.org/Old-Testament-violence.html.

56 In the archaeological community, the Battle of Jericho is very thoroughly studied, and the consensus of modern scholars is that the story of battle and the associated extermination are a "pious fiction" and did not happen as described in the book of Joshua. Even the story itself contains internal problems. For example, the book of Joshua describes the extermination of the Canaanite tribes, yet at a later time, Judges 1:1–2:5 suggests that the extermination was not complete. For a good review of the evidence, see Hans Van Wees, "Genocide in the Ancient World," in *The Oxford Handbook of Genocide Studies*, ed. Donald Bloxham and A. Dirk Moses (Oxford University Press, 2010), 239–58.

Perhaps the best overview of the Bible's portrait of God as an angry, vindictive, brutal, and vengeful judge is Eric A. Seibert's *Disturbing Divine Behavior: Troubling Old Testament Images of God* (Minneapolis, MN: Fortress P, 2009). Seibert urges us to realize that there are six hundred passages of explicit violence in the Hebrew Bible, one thousand verses where God's own violent actions of punishment are described, one hundred passages where Yahweh expressly commands others to kill people, and several stories where God irrationally kills or tries to kill for no apparent reason (e.g., Exod. 4:24–26). Seibert faces these challenges head-on by confronting the problem of "virtuous" violence and urging people to engage in an ethically responsible reading of these troublesome texts. He offers a variety of reading strategies designed to critique textually sanctioned violence, while still finding ways to use even the most difficult texts constructively, thus providing a desperately needed approach to the violence of Scripture that can help us live more peaceably in a world plagued by religious violence.

down the history of the victorious almost always promote the idea that surely God is on the side of the winners. Everything, including genocide and all sorts of punishments, gets God's approval.

When trying to make sense of the Bible's divine mandates for exterminating humans, I found lots of explanations larded with twisted hermeneutical logic. And as for declaring such stories unhistorical, it seems to me that most violent Biblical stories might well have real historical foundations. But here was the problem: finding them horrific and unforgettable, I never discovered such stories spiritually transformative. In short, I wish they weren't in the Bible. I did not want to have this oft-times Hebrew violent deity as my God. If God is both full of grace and at the same time as violent as he is often described in the Hebrew Scriptures, I found him woefully schizophrenic, a divine Jekyll and Hyde, simultaneously psychopathic and unbalanced. Whatever was I to do with such a double-minded God?

Re-seeing God

As I studied the Bible and Christian history, especially with the help of scholars and others outside my tradition, I soon discovered that not only does the Bible give voices to many competing memories, visions, convictions, opinions, testimonies, judgments, declarations, and facts but also that Christians are not at all in agreement on many teachings, doctrines, and moral values. The Bible does not come to us self-explanatory from a bookshelf in Barnes and Noble. It comes to us as a library of books, manuscript by manuscript over many centuries, from a host of writers and traditions. For example, in the Hebrew Scriptures, the two creation accounts in the opening chapters of Genesis are not in agreement with each other. The first is a six-day creation story; the second a one-day account. Each is quite different from the other.[57] In the New Testament, while the Synoptic Gospels

[57] Many Bibles call attention to the marked differences between the two accounts. See, for example, *The New Interpreter's Study Bible: New Revised Standard Version with Apocrypha* (Nashville: Abington, 2003), 5–10. Concerning these two accounts, my

present the Last Supper as a Passover meal, the Gospel of John makes no explicit mention that the Last Supper was a Passover meal and presents the official Jewish Passover feast as beginning in the evening a few hours after the death of Jesus. Then too we have many versions of what people call "the Bible," many of which contains different books, translation peculiarities, and doctrinal emphases. Few are aware, for example, that the original King James Version (KJV, 1611) contained the Apocrypha.[58] That's because no modern version of the KJV includes the once highly treasured printings of I and II Maccabees, Tobit, and Judith. While the KJV (known also as the Authorized Version) remains among the most widely sold, modern critical New Testament translations differ substantially from it in a number of passages, primarily because modern translations rely on source manuscripts not then accessible to early seventeenth-century Biblical scholarship. Thus, in the Old Testament of the KJV, there are many differences from modern translations that are based not only on manuscript differences but on different understandings of ancient Hebrew vocabulary or grammar. For example, in modern translations it is clear that Job 28:1–11 is referring throughout to

---

understanding is that neither is based on good science or historical fact. Although they do not agree in presenting a sequence of events and are authored by different representatives of two distinctive communities (the first priestly, the second agrarian), an unknown but brilliant editor placed them side by side as an introduction, not to observable history, but to the main character of the Bible: God! The first creation story introduces us to our transcendent, all-powerful, majestic God. The second story introduces to an immanent and companionable God who is unembarrassed to keep befriending humankind until man is happy, not just with his gardens and animals but with another human being, the gift of a wife. The God of the first story is heavenly, transcendent, far above us; his story name is Yahweh, and he simply says words and thing are done. The God of the second story is down-to-earth; his story name is Elohim, and he makes us out of dirt, converses with us personally, and even walks with us when we head off in the wrong direction. Together these two stories about God prefigure what we experience in Jesus, the truly Human One ("Son of Man") who compassionately walks with us, always and everywhere introducing us to all that is divine. The compassionate Creator of the two creation stories meets us fully in Jesus.

58 Even fewer are aware that in the original 1611 [KJV] Bible an appreciable proportion of the relatively few references placed here and there in the margins of the canonical books [i.e., Matthew, Luke, etc.] directed the reader's attention to passages in the Apocrypha. To become more acquainted about the Apocrypha, see Bruce M. Metzger, *An Introduction to the Apocrypha* (New York: Oxford University Press, 1957).

mining operations, which is not at all apparent from the text of the Authorized Version.

One might well be able to write a whole library of books that uncover and present the numerous difficulties that truly close readings of the Bible make apparent. This is not to say that the Bible is a composite of falsehoods; it is truly a wonderful testimony to our various understandings of God, especially to our hearing the voice of Jesus as the Word of God. But that said, we must also confess that the Bible is open to many interpretations, many competing for our attention.

As I began to appreciate how variously the Bible can be read, I found myself often living between various and often opposing interpretations. What I had inherited as the *right* way to read and understand again and again stood challenged by others. Slowly but surely the cardboard walls of my received house of faith were perforated with holes that turned into windows and then into doors of possible escape. I frequently ventured out into new and previously unknown worlds. I learned to read the Bible like a Quaker, like a Baptist, like a liberal, like a Methodist, like a seeker. My binary thinking became multiple thinking, and I learned to hold a variety of competing thoughts in creative tension, not knowing exactly what to think. I was betwixt and between. I was more than binary; I was multiple and many.

So eventually I had to ask whatever was I to do with myself. I found myself pushing the box apart. The top of my box was opening up, and its bottom was falling apart. My box was comng apart. I began to rethink and reimagine what I thought about people who were not in my box, who are not Lutherans. Not Christians. And what about Taoists? Buddhists? Hindus? Jews? Muslims? What about atheists and agnostics? What about people who are different? Gays and lesbians? The transgendered? What about Democrats? Neo-Nazis? Libertarians? Green Party-ers? People in the Coffee Party? What about the uneducated? Evolutionists? Fundamentalists? The very wealthy? Liberals? Crooks? Rioters? Immigrants? Rednecks? Pious Protestants? And you? Me?

And what was I to do with my God? Was he really so obviously Lutheran? At times I even began to ask myself, "Would God recognize himself as a Christian?" Would Jesus be a Lutheran? Or had I made the Holy Trinity Lutherans? Had I managed to stuff the Holy Spirit into a crate, pulled down the flaps over him, and taped my boxed-in God shut? I ask you: Have most, if not all of us, done something like that?

Yes, what about me? Boxed-in Andy? Must I always be in one box? Always on one side of an argument? One side of two or many ways of thinking, the right side? The best side? And, if so, must God usually, if not always, also be in my better box? If so, who put him there? Me? Why would I do that?

When asking such questions, I often found no clear answers. My inability to make sense out of things frequently overwhelmed me. I felt intellectually naked, raw, unvarnished, sometimes even uncivilized. Without guidance, grace, and prayer. What some have called "the Dark Night." I stopped going to church. The sun had set.

For Further Consideration

Evans, Rachel Held. *Inspired: Slaying Giants, Walking on Water, and Loving the Bible Again.* Nashville, TN: Nelson Books, 2018.

Fleischer, Matthew Curtis. *The Old Testament Case for Nonviolence.* Oklamona City, OK: Epic Octavius the Triumphant, 2017.

Hayward, David. *Questions Are the Answer: nakedpastor and the search for understanding.* London: Darton, Longman, and Todd, 2015.

Seibert, Eric A. *Disturbing Divine Behavior: Troubling Old Testament Images of God.* Minneapolis, MN: Fortress P, 2009.

Chapter 6

COMING TO KNOW MYSELF, MY TRUE SELF

God will not look you over for medals,
degrees, or diplomas—but for scars.
—Elbert Hubbard,

I poke and prod
prod and poke
inside and out
my blemishes and wounds
scarred recovery and discovery
of what is yet untouched.
The markers of pain are the
milestones of my journey to wholeness
it is in my breaking I am made.
—Talitha Fraser

An Empty sort of mind can see what's in front of it.
An Overstuffed mind is unable to.
While the Clear mind listens to a bird singing,
the Stuffed-Full-of-Knowledge-and-Cleverness mind wonders what kind of bird is singing.
The more Stuffed Up it is, the less it can hear
through its own ears and see through its own eyes.
—Benjamin Hoff, *The Tao of Pooh*

The mind that is the prisoner of conventional ideas, and the will that is the captive of its own desire, cannot accept the seeds of an unfamiliar truth and a supernatural desire...I must learn therefore to let go of the familiar and the usual and consent to what is new and unknown to me. I must learn to "leave myself" in order to find myself by yielding to the love of God.
—Thomas Merton, *New Seeds of Contemplation*

You are never too old to dream a new dream.
—C. S. Lewis

I had an opportunity to teach the history of art in the early 1970s at St. John's College in Winfield, Kansas. Having never taught anything about art before, I threw myself into learning what I didn't know. I chose H. W. Janson's *History of Art: A Survey of the Major Visual Arts from the Dawn of History to the Present Day* as our textbook. It was huge: 9" × 14," 616 pages, weighed almost six pounds, and contained nearly 900 pictures. It was so big that it took two semesters for my students and me to work through it.

We studied many famous works of art and architecture: the Parthenon, Nike of Samothrace, the interior of St. Vitale in Ravenna, Islamic architecture, the Bayeux Tapestry, Gothic art (especially altar pieces such Matthias Grunewald's *The Crucifixion*), the works of Cranach and Durer, and of course, lots of baroque, neoclassical, impressionistic, and twentieth-century masterpieces. Years later, several of my students sent me appreciative postcards and letters saying they appreciated our classwork as they were traveling aboard in Italy, Greece, and Germany.

Ambroise Vollard
by Pablo Picasso

Like many others, I have been deeply impressed with one modern artist: Picasso. To this day I still see myself standing before his *Guernica*, the *Les Demoiselles d'Avignon*, and especially his portrait of Ambroise Vollard. Picasso once asked this provocative question: "Who sees the human face correctly: the photographer, the mirror, or the painter?" To no one's surprise, Picasso thought it was the painter. Often, when painting a person, Picasso painted with more than one face. Vollard's face, in fact, resembles a field of broken glass.[59] Vollard is seen in Picasso's painting as a many "faceted" person, a multidimensional man. Although I am no Vollard, that's how I began to see myself in the early 1970s. Yes, I can tell the chronological story of my life and have someone take a photograph of me, but there was and is lots in me uncaught by a time line or a camera.

My persona

Each of us has a persona,[60] the public mask, facade, or personality we promote in everyday life. According to Carl Jung, the persona is the social face the individual presented to the world—"a kind of mask, designed on the one hand to make a definite impression upon others, and on the other to conceal the true nature of the

[59] For an excellent analysis of Pablo Picasso's painting of Ambroise Vollard, visit "Portrait of Ambroise Vollard by Picasso" (1910), available at http://cubismsite.com/cubist-paintings/ambroise-vollard/.

[60] The word "persona" comes from the ancient Greek theater tradition. It's the word designating the large mask that a Greek actor used to portray the character he was personifying. The primary function of the mask was not to hide the actor but to give information about the character. The *persona* is the mask or role that a person plays in society. While it gives information to an audience, it can certainly be used to hide the ego.

individual."[61] Right now mine is that of a retired professor who used to be a Lutheran pastor.

Robert A. Johnson refers to the persona as our "psychological clothing":

> The persona refers to that aspect of the ego that we present to the world for its approval. It is like a mask, and we can hide behind it. As a social role the concept of the persona is useful in allowing an individual to move in and out of relationships without being too vulnerable. A persona can be the oil to ease potential social friction. A persona provides for some predictability of relationship. For example, the personas of doctor and patient or of student and teacher can be useful in knowing what to do, when, and where. Other examples of the persona are: mother, father, husband, wife, lawyer, judge, policeman, baker. A persona becomes a problem only when a person becomes too attached to it and cannot put it aside. For example, when someone who is a judge is a "judge" all the time at work and at home. Or perhaps, a teacher who is in her role all the time. When a person cannot move flexibly between roles then the persona not only hides the person from others but also from himself. It is difficult for such a person to have appropriate self-knowledge.[62]

What you see on the next page is my persona. Actually it's a selfie that I took of myself several years ago. It's on the back cover of the first and second editions of this book. I usually carry about ten business-size cards of it in my wallet and give them away to people

---

61 C. G. June, *Two Essays on Analytical Psychology* (London: Pantheon Books, 1953), 190.

62 Robert A. Johnson, *Owning Your Own Shadow*, Part 1, available at http://www.spiritsite.com/writing/robjoh/part4.shtml.

whenever I imagine that someone would like to get to know me. It makes me look pretty good doesn't it?

But there's more to me than what you see. In fact, there is a largely hidden me, the darker aspects of me personality that late in my life I discovered and confronted, a "me" that now needs to be acknowledged.

Andy's persona

My false and phony self

Let me introduce you to something within me, something I've found difficult to look at, get a hold of, to grasp. It's what many call my "false self."[63] I found about the reality of the false self in the mid-1960s when pastoring at The Church of the Epiphany in East Avon, New York. That's when I first started reading Thomas Merton.[64] For the past fifty years, I've never stopped reading Merton. In fact, I owe so much to him that I have a photograph of him looking down on me near my bed so that every night as I go to sleep, I can say, "Hi, Tom! Thanks for helping me understand who I am." In his *New Seeds of Contemplation*, Merton describes the false self this way:

> Every one of us is shadowed by an illusory person: a false self. This is the man [or woman] that I want

[63] False and true self are concepts introduced into psychoanalysis in 1960 by D. W. Winnicott. In the last half century, we have seen Winnicott's ideas extended and applied in a variety of contexts, both in psychoanalysis and beyond. Contemplatives such as Thomas Merton, Thomas Keating, Basil Pennington, and Richard Rohr have enriched Winnicott's initial observations with Christian content and understandings.

[64] Thomas Merton (1915–68) is arguably the most influential American Roman Catholic author of the twentieth century. His autobiography, *The Seven Story Mountain*, has sold over one million copies and has been translated into over fifteen languages. He wrote over sixty other books and hundreds of poems and articles on topics ranging from monastic spirituality to civil rights, nonviolence, and the nuclear-arms race. For more biographical and bibliographical information, visit The Thomas Merton Center at Bellarmine University, available at http://merton.org.

> myself to be but who cannot exist, because God does not know anything about him [or her]. And to be unknown of God is altogether too much privacy.[65]

Richard Rohr fully agrees. Commenting on Merton's insight, Rohr describes the false self as simply a fragile "creation of the mind, a social construct":

> It doesn't exist except in the world of perception—which is where we live most of our lives—instead of in God's Eternal Now. When you die, what dies is your false self because it never really existed to begin with. It simply lives in your thoughts and projections. *It's what you want yourself to be and what you want others to think you are.* [my italics] It's very tied up with status symbols and reputation.
>
> Whenever you are offended, it's usually because your self-image has not been worshiped or it has been momentarily exposed. The false self will quickly react with a vengeance to any offenses against it because all it has is its own fragile assumptions about itself.[66]

As narcissists we spend a lot of time creating and defending our false selves even though all our false selves are illusions. Our false selves are imaginative figments of our egotistical thinking. It's who we think we are. To get away from self-created illusions about ourselves to real life, authentic life, a True Self, we must be rescued from such pretending, bragging, and ego to genuine authenticity. As Merton

65 I no longer have the clothbound 1962 edition of *New Seeds of Contemplation*. This quotation and the ones that follow are from a later edition (New York: New Directions, 1972), 34.

66 "The Illusion of the Autonomous Self," *Daily Meditation*, August 3, 2016, available at https://cac.org/illusion-autonomous-self-2016-08-03/

says, "The free son of God must be saved from the conformist slave of fantasy, passion and convention."[67]

My shadow-self

Yes, there is indeed lots more because all of us are many faceted. Helen Keller, who was both blind and deaf, tells us of yet another truth about herself—and ourselves:

> We are all complex. I wish I were made of just one self—consistent, wise and loving—a self I should never wish to get rid of at any time or place, which would move graciously through my autobiography "trailing clouds of glory"...It is no use trying to reconcile the multitude of egos that compose me. I cannot fathom them myself. I ask myself questions that I cannot answer. I find my heart aching when I expected to find it rejoicing; tears flow from my eyes when my lips were formed to smile. I preach love, brotherhood and peace, but I am conscious of antagonisms, and lo! I find myself brandishing a sword and making ready for battle.[68]

Underneath one's persona, there are realities that we avoid knowing intimately. They are part of our darker sides. They are part of the dark truth we all need to know about ourselves. It took me many years of introspection before I began seeing Andy's complexity—not only my persona and false self, but also my bogus or smaller self, my shadow self. I eventually came to know a dark truth about myself, something about my flickering shadow self.

---

67 Merton, *New Seeds of Contemplation*, 38.

68 Helen Keller, *Midstream: My Later Life*, cited in *Inward Outward: Seeking the Depths*, available at http://inwardoutward.org/quote-source/midstream-my-later-life/.

Here's how Daniel H. Johnston, a clinical psychologist teaching at Mercer University School of Medicine, describes each person's shadow:

> One's shadow is composed of the dark and unknown realities of personality. It is created when we make "unchosen" choices. It's an interior decision about which you are largely unaware. For example, if, as a child you choose to be tough, then you are not tender and vice versa. In a choice to be an athlete you may give up the options to be a musician or an artist. You learn to either keep your feelings in or to let them out.
>
> Choices are made and direction is given to personality development. The shadow can be viewed as the unlived life resulting from a certain pattern of life choices. Thomas Moore in *The Care of the Soul* tells us that, "The person we choose to be… automatically creates a dark double—the person we choose not to be."[69]

My shadow is my dark (in the sense of hidden, not necessarily bad) double. It's my cave underneath my hill. For better or for worse, it developed within me within a history that I may not like to recognize. To see and be aware of it, I needed to become a spelunker. Crawling in my life's cave, I have been surprised to see stuff that's scary. It just came with the territory, becoming Andy. Importantly, of course, we need to realize, as Johnston reminds us, that sometimes life choices are not freely made; they are often made for us:

> We are taught as children to grow up one way and not another and have little choice. Boys may be taught not to cry and girls not to be assertive. Some elements

[69] "The Shadow: Our Darker Side," available at, http://www.lessons4living.com/shadow.htm.

> of the shadow can indeed be potentially harmful and do not need to be acted out. Uncontrolled anger, impulsive sexuality, lying, and stealing are shadow potentials that are best kept in the shadow and the socialization process sees that they are. The shadow contains not only the positive of potential life choices "not made" but the negative potential of unbridled acting out. Most often the shadow comes to be seen as entirely negative and its recognition is resisted. If a person strongly denies the shadow then he may be overly focused on the persona. He may only know himself as persona and this is all that is shown to society.[70]

How to work effectively with the shadow self in one's interior life is a vital consideration on the journey to spiritual maturation.

Going inwardly down with Carl Jung

In the late 1950s, Dr. Harold Haas, my psychology professor at Concordia Senior College, introduced me to Jung. At that time, however, I had only the faintest idea as to Jung's importance in anyone's understanding of inner growth, especially his teachings about the stages of life that have direct relevance to Christian maturity and prayer. As I grew older and looked over the decades of my life, eventually I learned to see what had happened deep within me from day one. To help me understand and describe my "inside where God is," the gift of Carl Jung and his writings kept coming into my life as I become more introspective.

Understanding Jung is admittedly not always easy, and I know this is not the place to lay out a detailed presentation of Jung's teachings. That said, for me to share my life's story with you, we need to be basically familiar with Jung's archetypes. An archetype

70 Ibid.

may simply be defined as a tendency to experience things in a certain way; an archetype is an "organizing principle" much like a black hole in space, that is, it's a well-defined creative emptiness that wants to be filled. Archetypes are spaces for ciphers that need encryption.

Already in the fourth century, St. Augustine speaks of archetypes as ideas given to us by God that are not yet formed. They are divinely given patterns or images that God has lovingly implanted in us. Entering the world of thought, imagination, longing, and desire, we discover images and intimations of God that are already deeply rooted within us. Such archetypes are part of our proto-conscious life.

All of us have many archetypal patterns and wellsprings. Our lives need filling with certain basic shapes. Everyone, Jung says, possesses four main archetypal potentialities needing realization: the shadow, the anima, the animus, and the self.[71] The self represents our need to maintain inner stability and balance by reconciling whatever opposites in life we encounter. The self as a creative center shapes each person into a hoped-for and well-balanced being. The self is thus on a journey, and what we observe about its development is expressed in many wonderful, often unforgettable, and sometimes terrifying images, symbols, stories, and dreams. When it develops well, the self becomes integrated, whole, and well defined.

During my formative years as a Lutheran, no one emphasized the importance, the plausibility, or the power of inner spiritual experience. As a Lutheran, I was simply taught to believe my pastor (in my case, my father) and certain doctrines or teachings. I was especially taught to believe the Bible. Whether it's preacher or the Bible, as Richard Rohr once said, "They're both the same game, I'm sorry to say":

---

71 The literature on Jungian archetypes is extensive. For starters, I recommend *The Essential Jung.* Selected and Introduced by Anthy Storr (Princeton, NJ: Princeton, University Press, 1983); C. G. Jung, *Memories, Dreams, Reflections* (New York: Vintage, 1989); and Deirdre Bair, *Jung: A Biography* (Boston: Little, Brown, and Company, 2003).

> It's all about trusting something that is outside of yourself. When this is encouraged, there is little deep conviction or passion, but only hard-headed and often arrogant "belief"—which then feels like a game of pretend both to the believer and to those who observe such people. We give people answers that are extrinsic to the soul and to anything one knows from the inside out. "Holiness" largely becomes a matter of intellect and will, instead of an inner trust and any inner dialogue of love. It makes you think that the one with the most willpower wins, and the one who understands things the best is the beloved of God—the opposite of most Biblical heroes. It keeps us gazing at our own "performance" instead of searching for the Divine in us and in all things.[72]

Jung, whom I read in college as a psych major, eventually helped me realize that I needed to bring externalized religion back to its internal foundations. He taught me to see, as Rohr observes, how institutional religion keeps emphasizing

> the split and unbridgeable distance between the Creator and Creation, between God and the human, between inner and outer, between the One and the many. In spite of the ecological unity of all creation, Christianity too often began by emphasizing a problem ("original sin") instead of beginning with the wonderful unity between creation and Creator (original blessing), which we called "Christ" or the Primal Anointing of all things.[73]

How true!

---

72 "Beginning with Blessing," Richard Rohr's *Daily Meditation*, October 6, 2015.

73 Ibid.

Decidings

I've come to realize that whoever I am, I've never made a real *big decision* to become or be so-and-so or such-and-such. If changes occurred inside of me, they were done in slow motion. It has been a very gradual process with scores of minor, mostly hidden, settlements and adjustments, a few rough adjustments, many fine tunings. St. Paul has let me know how it takes place:

> What I'm getting at, friends, is that you should simply keep on doing what you've done from the beginning. When I was living among you, you lived in responsive obedience. Now that I'm separated from you, keep it up. Better yet, redouble your efforts. Be energetic in your life of salvation, reverent and sensitive before God. That energy is God's energy, an energy deep within you, God himself willing and working at what will give him the most pleasure. (Phil. 2:12, *The Message*)

All this had been increasingly apparent to me in the past twenty or thirty years, especially since my daughter Chelsea came into my life in 1992. As I have said elsewhere, it was my taking Chelsea to a black Baptist church that introduced me to a theology wherein making decisions is so critically important. Having attended her church for ten years and going often to a white Baptist church with my wife June for another fifteen years, I know that Baptists plead for decisions at the end of every service; it's the altar call, the climax of worship, the sermonic peroration, often emotional. Baptist preachers preach for a decision. As I sit in the Baptist pews, having often attended the Lutheran Eucharist just an hour before, I find myself knowing full well that my own decision for Christ was clearly a gift and process that grew slowly, incrementally, often hidden from my conscious awareness. It was not a one-time event. It's a process that has been going on for years, ever since infancy. Deep within me an insistent voice reminds me that in Christ God has made a decision about all human beings and about me that gives me the privilege of a long-nuanced response, developed since birth over decades and years, a response to an invitation that in the end asks the question Jesus gave to Peter: "Do you love me?" Jesus asks, "Peter, do you have my kind of love for people?" That's a question that requires a real answer. One's whole life is a series of decisions, often hidden, answering that question.

A flickering light

For the first half of my life (even though I was an ordained pastor) I was not aware that God was somehow and mysteriously underneath or deep down in my basement caves, shaping my archetypal Self, my own deep well filled with living water, images, and Spirit. Throughout t the first decades of my life, I was taught that at birth I entered the world with what some Christians still call "original sin."[74] I had inherited sinfulness from my first parents, Adam and Eve. Yes, I knew that somehow my baptism as an infant brought me into God's family, but I had no "native goodness." Only in the second half of my life did I realize that as a fetus in my mother's womb I possessed "original goodness," to use Eknath Easwaran's phrase, that is, a spark of divinity hidden inside every one of us.[75] And ever since, God has been fanning that flaming spark by rearranging airflows, turning valves, re-wiring circuitries, leveling pathways, throwing out trash, replacing nervous fuses, and getting me ready for a time when

74 Historically Lutherans have taught teach that, since Adam and Eve fell into sin (Genesis 3), all people are "brought forth in iniquity" and conceived in sin (Psalm 51:5). This sin is a hereditary sickness that prevents us from fearing, loving, and trusting in God above all things, because "every intention of the thoughts of [humankind's] heart [is] only evil continually" (Genesis 6:5). This inborn sickness causes us to commit all kinds of evil deeds and merits only God's eternal wrath.

75 Lutherans everywhere are no longer insisting that everyone's fetal identity is best described as inheriting "original sin." See, for example, "Original Sin or Original Blessing," a sermon preached by Pastor Monte Stevens of North Riverdale Lutheran Church, Dayton, Ohio; available at https://www.nrlchurch.org/sermons-for-life/sermons-2012/original-sin-or-original-blessing/.

I wouldn't need to live in any basement. My life was changing from the inside out. I was experiencing what one of my friends calls "dark grace."

Counterbalancing conversations

My interior life grew in balancing counterbalances. Early on I became suspicious of literalistic readings of the Bible when I listened to fundamentalist teachers of biology. What I found in one classroom was different from what I found in another. In college I was told the conservative view of creation. My biology professor, who should have known better, told me half truths about the story of creation in Genesis. I knew early on that there was not simply one creation story, but two, each told by a different narrator; placed side by side, they contained contrasts, contradictions that could only be stitched together by some editor working with a plausible metanarrative conviction.[76] The reading of Scripture in seminary was, of course, an eye-opener. Yes, we had fundamentalists on the faculty. But more important, we had professors like Frederick W. Danker, who brought the best of biblical scholarship to our attention. By the time I got

---

76 See "The Two Biblical Stories of Creation" at http://bibleresources.bible.com/passagesearchresults.php?passage1=Genesis+2&version1=9 for a good side-by-side display of the two stories. After you see the differences and the quite apparent inconsistencies, let each story introduce you, each in its own way, to the main character in the Bible—God. Who God is requires two stories! The first story tells us that God is transcendent, an utterly Other Being who from a great distance creates the world in orderly fashion. The second story tells us that he is not only transcendent, but he is also wonderfully immanent, companionable, among us here and now. Moreover, walks and talks with us. He will do whatever is necessary to help us. When he finds Adam lonely and unsatisfied with animals as potential friends, he will try another form of creation and so made Eve, a woman whom Adam recognizes as part of himself. Together, the two stories introduce us, not to science but to God who is both beyond us and with us, previewing the God we come to know as Jesus Christ.

Realizing that it takes two different creation stories to introduce us to the fullness of God who is both transcendent and immanent, an unknown but wise Hebrew editor stitched these two stories together so that we are presented with God in all his glory and caring intimacy. Getting to know who God is as a person is what the opening chapters of Genesis are all about. It isn't science.

through seminary, the art of higher textual criticism made good sense to me. In fact, I learned to appreciate the demythologizing of Rudolf Bultmann,[77] the "religionless" Christianity of Bonhoeffer,[78] and the ethical relativism of Joseph Fletcher.[79] I also deeply appreciated the sacramental theology of Dr. Arthur Carl Piepkorn whose writings on and about the Lutheran Confessions I deeply appreciated. I left seminary with a self for the most part leaning left and right, sometimes balanced, stable, open to change, and engagingly welcome to all people, ideas, and viewpoints.

Inside the inner me

Yes, over the years I have been vaguely aware that something hidden within me was happening. Something was going on somewhere in the middle, corners, and eventually at the bottom

---

77 *Jesus Christ and Mythology* (New York: Scribner, 1958) serves as an excellent introduction to Bultmann's theology. It consists of two groups of lectures Bultmann gave at Yale and Vanderbilt in 1951, and I read them in seminary before the lectures were advertised as appropriate for students unacquainted with his work. I had read a good deal about Bultmann's thought in other books, but this was the first of his actual works I read, and it certainly got me wondering.

78 Lutheran pastor and theologian Dietrich Bonhoeffer was executed by the Nazis on April 9, 1945. During his months in prison prior to his execution, Bonhoeffer wrote several letters to his friend Eberhard Bethge in which he shared his developing conviction that we Christians must learn to live a "religious Christianity." To understand what Bonhoeffer was advocating, I recommend two opportunities: first, spend some time in Kurt Struckmeyer's blog "Invitation," available at followingjesus.org; and second, read Ralf Wustenberg, *A Theology of Life: Dieterich Bonhoeffer's Religionless Christianity* (Grand Rapids, MI, Eerdmans, 1998). For those wishing to know more about Bonhoffer, two resources are invaluable: Eberhard Bethge, *Dietrich Bonhoeffer: A Biography* (Minneapolis: Fortress Press, 2000) and Charles Marsh, *Strange Glory: A Life of Dietrich Bonhoeffer* (New York Knopf, 2014).

79 Igniting a firestorm of controversy upon its publication in 1966, Joseph Fletcher's *Situation Ethics* was hailed by many as a much-needed reformation of morality—and as an invitation to anarchy by others. Proposing an ethic of loving concern, Fletcher suggests that certain acts—such as lying, premarital sex, adultery, or even murder—might be morally right, depending on the circumstances. Hotly debated on television, in magazines and newspapers, in churches, and in the classroom, Fletcher's provocative thesis remains a powerful force in contemporary discussions of morality.

of my life. As strange as it sounds, I was experiencing stuff about which I was by and large unaware. I was undergoing the experience of discovering several Andys.

How does one describe what has been going on in his or her life? Obviously our memories keep some sort of record, for the most part retrievable. But get this! In addition to remembered stuff, there are also real interior events that remain largely unremembered. Such stuff, Carl Jung contends (correctly, I believe), has been stored in each person's "collective unconscious," where it is stored, hidden away, and buried at the bottom of everyone's life but available for inspection. Down in the seat of our souls, in the cave of our hearts, packed away in the cellar of our human house, there is, Jung asserts, a level of unconscious reality we share with other members of the human species, it's "the form of the world into which [a person] is born that is already inborn in him, as a virtual image."[80] Saul McLeod explains:

> The human mind has innate characteristics "imprinted" on it as a result of evolution. These universal predispositions stem from our ancestral past. Fear of the dark, or of snakes and spiders might be examples and it is interesting that this idea has recently been revived in the theory of prepared conditioning. However more important than isolated tendencies are those aspects of the collective unconscious that have developed into separate sub-systems of the personality. Jung called these ancestral memories and images archetypes.[81]

80 *Collected Works*, vol. 12 (1953), 188.

81 "Simply Psychology," retrieved October 13, 2014, at http://www.simplypsychology.org/carl-jung.html.

The Enneagram

As I explored the underside of my interior life, about twenty years ago I received a larger and valuable understanding of who I am when a friend introduced me to the Enneagram, a gift from countless spiritual guides. For many it's proven to be a powerful resource for personal and collective transformation. Stemming from the Greek words *ennea* (nine) and *grammos* (a written symbol), the nine-pointed Enneagram symbol represents nine distinct strategies for relating to the self, others and the world. Each of the nine Enneagram types has a different pattern of thinking, feeling and acting that arises from a deeper inner motivation or worldview. The Enneagram fosters greater understanding through a universal language that transcends gender, religion, nationality and culture. While we are all unique, we share common experiences.

It didn't take me long to find out that I'm basically a Type 2, that is, I relate to myself, others, and the world as a helper. Getting to know myself as such a 2 was enlightening, truthful, embarrassing, disturbing, and challenging. At their worst, immature and naïve 2s (as often I am) frequently fail to see themselves as aggressive and/or selfish in their behaviors. Unhealthy 2s can be domineering and coercive, and 2s at times feel entitled to get anything they want from others: the repayment of old debts, money, sexual favors. Able to excuse and rationalize what they do since, they can feel abused and victimized by others and become bitterly resentful and angry. Somatization of their aggressions sometimes results in chronic health problems as they vindicate themselves by "falling apart" and burdening others.

What can be described as "average helpers" want to be close (and closer) to others, often becoming overly friendly, emotionally demonstrative, and seemingly full of good intentions. We 2s like to flatter folks and will even go out of our way to help, serve, and befriend others. At times we will even create needs within others so they can be of assistance. When I'm quiet and listen to myself, that's who I am sometimes. Thankfully, however, it's possible to be a mature Type 2. Realizing that as a child, 2s may come to realize that they might not have received as much parental love as they had hoped for, wanted, or needed. Mature 2s come to rely on Divine Love as the gift they continue to need. Moreover, mature 2s insightfully realize that they need to take care of themselves without exhausting their energies in loving others. They must, as Scripture says, "love your neighbor as yourself." Mature 2s understand that helping others requires good energy, a heart that beats well, and a brain that solves problems. For 2s to become deeply unselfish, humble, and altruistic, they will do well to give unconditional love both to self and to others. Caring and concerned about their own needs, they can then become genuinely thoughtful, warm-hearted, forgiving, sincere, empathetic, and compassionate. For me, this means that I need to quietly immerse myself contemplatively in God's love regularly every morning, afternoon, evening, and night.

Determining one's personality type through the Enneagram gives us insights into who we are fundamentally, what our weaknesses are, and what we might do to improve ourselves and the lives of others. With these awarenesses we can step outside of our limited perspective. Ideally, our personality is an effective way to express ourselves, but challenges arise when our point of view becomes rigid and we get stuck in automatic habits. By discovering these unconscious patterns, we can lead more fulfilling lives, enjoy healthier relationships, and connect to our true essence.

My memories have often proved themselves to be blessings and gifts from God. For example, God designed me with spiritual DNA so that from conception I have possessed a longing for the Divine.

A deep, inconsolable longing, yearning, the feeling of needing something or Someone when we don't even know what or Who it is. In *The Weight of Glory*, Lewis tells us that

> [It's] a secret we cannot hide and cannot tell, though we desire to do both. We cannot tell it because it is a desire for something that has never actually appeared in our experience. We cannot hide it because our experience is constantly suggesting it, and we betray ourselves like lovers at the mention of a name.[82]

In his *Confessions* St. Augustine thanked God for this unconscious imprint with this prayer: "You have made us for yourself, and our hearts are restless, until they can find rest in you." Echoing Augustine, Richard Rohr tells us that "our unique little bit of heaven is installed by the Manufacturer within the product, at the beginning!" God has placed a "chip" in us so that we have a "homing" device, sometimes called the deeper "I" that steers us into His presence. Some say it's called the image or impress of God to which Genesis alludes: "Humankind was created as God's reflection: in the divine image God created them; female and male, God made them" (1:27). From the beginning everybody is marked, stamped, and ticketed for a Godward journey. It's in us on day one; we just don't know it on the day we were born. After our natal day, we come to sense its presence.

Like you, the evolution of my deepest interior life is best described as occurring somewhere subterranean, in-the-cellar, hidden, quietly, barely noticeable. During the past fifty years, I have been slowly becoming aware of another and more secretively quiet Andy. By way of explanation, let me share with you an excerpt from a journal entry I wrote on December 20, 2011:

---

82 *The Weight of Glory and Other Addresses* (New York: HarperCollins, 1980), 30.

> Lynn Hall, the author of novels for juvenile and young adult readers, says that we do not change as we grow older, we just become more clearly ourselves. I think that's true, and her observation reminds me of something that Dr. David S. Berkeley, my dissertation adviser, once said about John Milton: "he simply flowered and become more and more of what he truly was." In some important ways I too have been becoming more and more of what I have always been. By that I mean that my inner core, my spiritual innards, so to speak, have for years been organizing themselves into something of a stem that has eventually flowered (some would say "weeded") into something with defined leaves and petals, or perhaps, depending on your point of view, a clearly defined roadside chickweed or sunflower. To my mind, St. Paul says it nicely: "Even though on the outside it often looks like things are falling apart on us, on the inside where God is making new life, not a day goes by without his unfolding grace." (2 Cor. 4:16)

Not a day goes by!

Emptyful

For the first half of my life, most of my memories and dreams came and went while I was a pastor in a conservative Lutheran church denomination. I prayed that things would be all right. God, however, did not answer my prayers as I had hoped he would. God gave me the best of all replies—he completely undid me and filled me with the mystery of his Presence.

With two divorces registered in the court records, the loss of "pasturing" as a pastor, the deaths of Kris and Chelsea, along with gut realizations of moral failure, I bottomed out and came to the limits of my own energies. I was in need of rescue, help, and a profound reorientation. Ironically, in a place of powerlessness, I was in a valley exactly where I needed to be. Having ruined my marriages, I was near the undoing of fatherly relationships with my children. Aware of both my public and private self-images, I realized that my way of life wasn't working. I sensed that there might and possibly must be another way, but I didn't know where to find it. Some, like Saint John of the Cross, have called my experience the "dark night of the soul." That designation implies nothing sinister; it simply tells us that our eventual liberation takes place in hidden ways, "beneath our knowledge and understanding."[83] The truth is that I did not find liberation. It came to me. I was at the point and place where what I had known as religion was slowly (very slowly) morphing into a new spirituality, a new freedom in Christ.

Finding my True Self

Eventually I came to know another Self (with a capital S). Hebrew Scriptures tell us in Genesis that we are created in God's image. This archetypal Self is deeply connected with God's image. Each of us is to grow up in that image. This Self is what St. Paul calls the "mystery of Christ within us." As our True Self, the ever-and-everywhere-present Christ unfolds within us from the moment we begin to live. Here is how St. Paul describes the way we become aware of the Christ within:

---

[83] Fifty years ago Lutherans were not encouraged to read anything by Saint John of the Cross. He was too "Catholic." In the mid-twentieth century, I was given the impression that when John talked about the "dark night of the soul," he was describing a time of suffering and tribulation, almost entirely unpleasant. Today we realize that "the dark night of the soul," in John's original sense, is "in no way sinister or negative." As Gerald G. May in *The Dark Night of the Soul: A Psychiatrist Explains the Connection between Darkness and Spiritual Growth* (New York: HarperOne, 2004) repeatedly reminds us, "The only characteristic of the experience of the dark night that is certain is its obscurity. One simply does not comprehend clearly what is happening" (68). Most often one's "dark night" is an experience of hidden transformation when God works with an individual for liberation, often involving a blurring of one's beliefs so that one "feels *a part* of all things instead of *apart from* them" (88–89). Today Lutherans are encouraged to appreciate God's hidden work during "the dark night of the soul," and annually on December 14, they celebrate the witness of John of the Cross as a "renewer of the church."

> What actually took place is this: I tried keeping rules and working my head off to please God, and it didn't work. So I quit being a "law man" so that I could be God's man. Christ's life showed me how, and enabled me to do it. I identified myself completely with him. Indeed, I have been crucified with Christ. My ego is no longer central. It is no longer important that I appear righteous before you or have your good opinion, and I am no longer driven to impress God. Christ lives in me. The life you see me living is not "mine," but it is lived by faith in the Son of God, who loved me and gave himself for me. I am not going to go back on that.
>
> Is it not clear to you that to go back to that old rule-keeping, peer-pleasing religion would be an abandonment of everything personal and free in my relationship with God? I refuse to do that, to repudiate God's grace. If a living relationship with God could come by rule-keeping, then Christ died unnecessarily. (Gal. 2:19–21, *The Message*)

The True Self, especially as understood by Christian contemplatives, is God's gift to each person upon conception, our "original goodness," as we name it now.[84] It is our spiritual DNA, the image of God within, our innermost being or soul, the "polestar" of our personal universe, the interior gyroscope that wants each of us to spin with God. The True Self is our Center: the "cave of our heart." Thomas Merton says it's *le point vierge*, the "virgin point":

> At the center of our being is a point of nothingness which is untouched by sin and by illusion, a point of pure truth, a point or spark which belongs entirely to God, which is never at our disposal, from which

---

84 See, for example, Eknath Easwaran's *Original Goodness: A Commentary on the Beatitudes*, 2nd Edition (Nilgiri Press, 1996) and Clint Adams, "The Original Goodness"; available at https://www.revivesf.com/revival-blog/2018/10/16/the-original-goodness.

> God disposes of our lives, which is inaccessible to the fantasies of our own mind or the brutalities of our own will. This little point of nothingness and of absolute poverty is the pure glory of God in us. It is so to speak his name written in us...like a pure diamond, blazing with the invisible light of heaven. It is in everybody, and if we could see it we would see these billions of points of light coming together in the face and blaze of a sun that would make all the darkness and cruelty of life vanish completely.[85]

The Cosmic Christ Within

Slowly I became conscious of my True Inner Self, the Universal Christ. Yes, I was in a box, but even "inside" I knew there was a Presence, an emerging awareness of an archetypal Self whom I would come to know intimately as Christ. As St. Paul likes to say it:

> My ego is no longer central. It is no longer important that I appear righteous before you or have your good opinion, and I am no longer driven to impress God. Christ lives in me. The life you see me living is not

[85] Thomas Merton, *Conjectures of a Guilty Bystander* (New York: Image, 1966), 155.

> "mine," but it is lived by faith in the Son of God, who loved me and gave himself for me. (Gal. 2:20)

So God undid me. At times I was deeply depressed. Empty. It was a slow falling, but falling it was. I went down like water flows down. Sometimes I went down in drops, and at other times it was like the north Georgia's Chattahoochee River flowing south in the spring—swift, splashing over rocks. Falling. I saw descent and humility in a new light. I saw new people in unfamiliar corners, people I wanted to meet. I started holding hands with strangers and singing "We Shall Overcome." I fell down to where it was all right to say, "I'm not sure," "I was wrong," and "That's something I never thought of before." I fell down and found myself among people mistreated, on the margins, and in the gutters. I fell down and started to say, "Can I help you?" I fell and found myself sitting with Buddhists, reading the Taoist teachers, and rethinking who I was with my Jewish brothers and sisters. I fell down and found myself in Haiti, back in the mountains, listening to people singing as they walked to work along a dirt road. I was going down in humility, service, solidarity, risk, and grace, learning to be different on behalf of outcasts and outsiders. God was reintroducing mystery to me: I was finding God through descent.[86]

I end this chapter with a little story.

> A university professor went to visit a famous Zen master. While the master quietly served tea, the professor talked about Zen. The master poured the visitor's cup to the brim and then kept pouring. The professor watched the overflowing cup until he could no longer restrain himself. "It's full! No more will go in!" the professor blurted. "This is you," the master replied. "How can I show you, Zen, unless you first empty your cup?"

---

86 Those of you who have read Brian D. McLaren's *We Make the Road by Walking* (New York: Jericho, 2014) will surely recognize that my description of going downward owes much to his chapter 46: "Spirit of Service." Reading it was for me a refreshing discovery of all that has taken place in my life.

How could God show me Christ unless somehow my cup became empty? My cup was and is more like a bucket. A huge bucket that needed to be turned over, whacked, cracked, smashed, and remade. The cup of my life was not only filled with unpleasant nastiness, but at times, many times, it was also stained and hardly worth keeping. At least it seemed to me as I got to look at myself honestly—unflinchingly. I did not like what I saw. I did not like myself. I certainly didn't love myself. I experienced emptiness.

But once the cup was empty, it was no longer simply empty. It stood and stands ready to receive. I wanted and still want filling. And so here I ask my first two wives, Carol and Paula, to forgive me and fill my cup and life with mercy and forgiveness. I don't want to be full of myself. I want to be immersed in God's love, which may come to me through forgiveness. Especially from Carol and Paula and from my children. I abandoned them when they needed a father and the model of a good husband. I left them on their own, and each in his or her own way has suffered because of my prideful egotism, my inability to love, and my need for self-gratification. Kirk, Lisa, and Amy, I ask you to forgive me.

What I've described in this chapter some say is a time when one is in "liminal space."[87] I was in-between the time when I began to think critically, beginning to move out of a bourgeois mind-set, and learning to step out of my comfort zone. Side streets and detours began to interest me. I especially liked dirt roads, especially when the car I was driving had only one headlight. More than once I drove off the road and into a ditch, sometimes a deep embankment. I experienced running out of gas and spiritual hitchhiking. Frequently decentered, I had to walk slowly, feeling my way through the woods, always looking up to find the moon, hoping it was full enough to shed some light on where I was. Learning the art of letting go of known securities, I began to tolerate ambiguity and paradox. Time

---

87 The word "liminal" comes from the Latin word *limens*, which means, "threshold." You enter such space when you have left the tried and true but have not yet been able to replace it with anything else. It's when you are between your old comfort zone and any possible new answer.

and again I experienced the weakening of my ego. Now and then it actually died. I often felt empty.

Ralph Waldo Emerson once said, "When it is dark enough, you can see the stars." The lights of our culture—TV, movies, social media, billboards, the glitter of downtown, and the neighborhood malls—make it difficult for us to get into really dark places, into our inner selves so that we can see the North Star, any star. For me physically, it sometimes meant going out in a canoe at 2:00 a.m. on woodland-circled Leadmine Lake in Massachusetts. When the lights of the houses along the shore and in the woods around the lake went out, I could even see the Milky Way. Just as we need to get away from lights to see the stars, so we need to get away from the highway lights of our culture, personal lives, any number of religious traditions, and past experiences to explore the darkness within. How we go there may require a map, a guidebook, someone to lead the way, someone to turn off the lights, someone to hold our hand as we travel by moonlight. We must not be afraid of what it may take to explore who we are inside. We may take even take a flashlight if that will help.

We are not to be unduly afraid of such life-changing experiences. Yes, things can be dark. But, as Richard Rohr reminds us:

> There is a gravitas in the second half of life, but it is now held up by a much deeper lightness, or "okayness." Our mature years are characterized by a kind of bright sadness and a sober happiness, if that makes any sense. There is still darkness in the second half of life—in fact maybe even more. But there is now a changed capacity to hold it creatively and with less anxiety. It is what John of the Cross called "luminous darkness," and it explains the simultaneous coexistence of deep suffering and intense joy that we see in the saints, which is almost impossible for most of us to imagine.
>
> Life is much more spacious now, the boundaries of the container having been enlarged by the constant addition of new experiences and relationships. You

are like an expandable suitcase, and you became so almost without your noticing. Now you are just here, and here holds more than enough. Such "hereness," however, has its own heft, authority, and influence.

One's growing sense of infinity and spaciousness is no longer found just "out there" but most especially "in here." The inner and the outer have become one. You can trust your inner experience now, because even God has allowed it, used it, received it, and refined it. As St. Augustine dramatically put it in his *Confessions*:

> You were within, but I was without. You were with me, but I was not with you. So you called, you shouted, you broke through my deafness, you flared, blazed, and banished my blindness, you lavished your fragrance, and I gasped.[88]

For Further Reading

Balswick, Jack O., Pamela Ebstyne King, and Kevin S. Reimer. *The Reciprocating Self: Human Development in Theological Perspective* (Downers Grove, IL: InterVarsity Press, 2016).

Chestnut, Beatrice. *The Complete Enneagram: 27 Paths to Greater Self-Knowledge* (Berkeley, CA: She Writes Press, 2013).

Cron, Ian Morgan, and Suzanne Stabile. *The Road Back to You: An Enneagram Journey to Self-Discovery* (Downers Grove, IL: InterVarsity Press, 2016).

Easwaran, Eknath. *Original Goodness: On the Beatitudes of the Sermon on the Mount* (Tomales, CA: Nilgiri Press, 1996).

88 "Luminous Darkness," *Daily Meditation*, October 24, 2014, available at, http://st-johnsquamish.ca/richard-rohr-a-bright-sadness/.

Heuertz, Christopher. *The Sacred Enneagram: Finding Your Unique Path to Spiritual Growth* (San Francisco: HarperCollins, 2017).

Jung, C. G., *The Undiscovered Self with Symbols and the Interpretation of Dreams* (Princeton: Princeton University Press,1990).

Palmer, Helen. *The Enneagram in Love and Work: Understanding Your Intimate & Business Relationships* (San Francisco, CA: HarperCollins, 1995.

Riso, Don Richard, and Russ Hudson. *The Wisdom of the Enneagram: The Complete Guide to Psychological and Spiritual Growth for the Nine Personality Types* (New York: Bantam Books, 1999).

Rohr, Richard, and Andreas Ebert; trans. Peter Heinegg. *The Enneagram: A Christian Perspective* (New York: Crossroad Publishing, 2014.

Rohr, Richard. *The Universal Christ: How a Forgotten Reality Can Change Everything We See, Hope For, and Believe* (New York: Convergent, 2019).

Sheppard, Lynette. *The Everyday Enneagram: A Personality Map for Enhancing Your Work, Love, and Life . . . Every Day* (Petaluma, CA: Nine Points Press, 2000).

Chapter 7

ONE'D & THREE'D

Mysticism involves
significant life-transforming events
and changes in consciousness.
A mystical experience may seem
as insignificant as the Butterfly Effect
—Carl McColman

The shell must break apart
if what is inside is to come out,
for if you want the kernel,
you must break the shell.
—Meister Eckhart

The power which I cannot explain or know or name I call God. God is not God's name. God is my name for the mystery that looms within and arches beyond the limits of my being. When I pray to God, God's answer comes to me from within, not beyond. God's answer is yes, not to the specifics of my prayer but in response to my hunger for meaning and peace.
—F. Forrester Church

Three folds of the cloth, yet only one napkin is there,
Three joints in the finger, but still only one finger fair,
Three leaves of the shamrock, yet no more than one shamrock to wear,
Frost, snowflakes and ice, all in water their origin share,
Three Persons in God: to one God alone we make our prayer.
—A Celtic Prayer

Lord, who hast formed me out of mud,
And hast redeemed me through thy blood,
And sanctified me to do good;
Purge all my sins done heretofore:
For I confess my heavy score,
And I will strive to sin no more.
Enrich my heart, mouth, hands in me,
With faith, with hope, with charity;
That I may run, rise, rest with thee.
--George Herbert, "Trinity Sunday"

One'd

In my mid-thirties I was living betwixt, between, and within lots and lots of dualities (me/others, my God/your God, straight/gay, and so on). Comfortable and adept in binary thinking. I was convinced that my thoughts, decisions, and actions were generally better than what others thought, how they argued, what they did. Then something happened to me in my mid-thirties that I never anticipated or expected. I was given a wee peek into what it means to see, live, and experience life without judgments, without bad and good, without good and better, without *this* and *that*. I saw a world without borders, fences, rooms, and walls. I was taken into a Vastness. I was given an out-of-the-box experience.

What I hope to tell you about in these next pages will be difficult to describe. I've started, hesitated, stopped, and given up doing these pages many times. Often what I want to say seems beyond words. But I will try nonetheless.

It happened to me while I was walking on the spacious green lawn in front of the library on the Oklahoma State University campus. It happened in the middle of the afternoon on July 22, 1976. Earlier in the afternoon, I had been in the top floor of the OSU library working in my graduate carrel on a chapter of my dissertation, the one I eventually titled "Royal Typology in Shakespeare's *Cybeline*." As I came down the stairs to the main lobby, I passed the front desk, went through the massive library doors, and continued down the wide steps onto the great lawn. It was a beautiful day. I expected nothing. I began my mile-long walk north to home on Arrowhead Drive. The sky was big and blue. There were no clouds. I wore no hat, carried no books. Sunshine everywhere. I was aware of the warmth of the sun, the wideness of the sky, and the field of green over which I made my way.

The lawn in front of the Library at Oklahoma State University

Then it happened. Without expectation, I had no head. My head disappeared. Everything above my shoulders evaporated like the imprint of a bird disappearing in the sky. I was nowhere and everywhere. Where my head used to be was a vast emptiness. A great fullness. Not the simplest whisper of a breeze wafting through what once was my noggin. I was simply, completely, and quietly unheaded. I experienced the absence of me and everything and at the same time the Allness of Everything. It was the No-thing of me and All of Everywhere.

I'm not sure how long the All and Nothing lasted. Perhaps minutes, maybe a nanosecond. Maybe five minutes. Time and space as I usually knew such dimensions disappeared. Vastness was the only reality. I entered a No-whereness and Now-hereness that I had never experienced before.

Or after. Today, some forty years later, the memory remains intense, albeit diffuse. I have tried to understand (in the literal sense—

to stand under again) what happened, but to no avail. Experiencing that Presence of an Absence, as I now tend to put it, changed me profoundly. Never in my life had I ever imagined such a happening. No one ever intimated to me the possibility of such a Nothing/Allness. Not a word about it in college, seminary, or graduate work. Well, not quite. While reading the so-called metaphysical poets—Donne and Herbert, the best known—I had come across Thomas Traherne and poems like his "Poverty" wherein he writes:

> For I forgot my ease and health,
> Nor did I think of hands or eyes,
> Nor soul nor body prize;
> I neither thought the sun,
> Nor moon, nor stars, nor people, mine,
> Though they did around about me shine;
> And therefore was I quite undone.[89]

But at the time such thoughts seemed strange and out of my range of experience. I had, of course, come across St. Paul mentioning that someone (presumably himself) had been taken up into a "third heaven" (2 Cor. 12:2), but until my "lawn experience" I had no way of knowing experientially what he meant by those words. Now I have some felt sense as to what happened to him.

Comparing myself to Paul, I suppose I could say that I had been taken up into heaven, but that expression doesn't capture what I experienced. It would be better to say that I had been un-Andy'd, de-Andy'd. My sense of self disappeared. I was noheaded.[90] I entered what the Greeks call *kenosis* (emptiness).[91] Simultaneously No-thing-

---

89 Thomas Traherne, "Poverty," in *Seventeenth-Century Prose and Poetry*, eds. Alexander M. Witherspoon and Frank J. Warnke (New York: Harcourt), 1026.

90 For a superb discussion, see Douglas Edison Harding, *Having No Head: Zen and the Recovery of the Obvious* (London: The Shollond Trust, 2012) and www.headlessway.org.

91 The Greek noun is *kenosis* (emptiness); St. Paul uses its verbal form kenoō (to empty, to make void) as he quotes an early Christian hymn in Philippians 2:5–8, urging us to be like Christ:

> Let the same mind be in you that was in Christ Jesus,

ness and Allness happened to me. Something or someone eliminated me (well, eliminated everything but awareness), took me into the All, enveloped me in No-thing-ness, and allowed me to experience what I found out others have described as "cosmic or unitive consciousness," a term I find too abstract to convey much of anything except an experience about which descriptions are nearly useless. After all, to describe No-thing-ness and Every-thing-ness is quite impossible.

Headless on that lawn, time did not exist, and within the suchness of that timelessness, I was unaware of any beginning, middle, or ending. Seconds, minutes, distance, depth, upness, downness, and all boundaries were simply absent. There was not a taint or hint of time or space. Later I read and noted in one of my journal entries that somewhere Meister Eckhart says, "Time is what keeps the light from reaching us." Light had reached me; on the lawn I was all Now. I had been given the privilege of entering the nonbinary world, the nondual world to which the word "God" points.

Not so unusual

Ralph Waldo Emerson's "transparent eye-ball" experience, illustrated by Christopher Pearce Cranch, ca. 1836-38

who, though he was in the form of God,
did not regard equality with God
as something to be exploited,
but emptied himself,
taking the form of a slave,
being born in human likeness.
And being found in human form,
he humbled himself
and became obedient to the point of death—
even death on a cross.

As unusual as I thought it was, what happened to me is not all that unusual. Gregory of Nyssa, Evagrius Ponticus, Meister Eckhart, Teresa of Avila, John Tauler, Henry Suso, Emerson, Rumi, Thomas Merton, among thousands of other recipients have penned poems and paragraphs making allusions and creating metaphors to help themselves and others sense what happens.[92] Emerson, for example, described it as a moment when he became a "transparent eye-ball":

> Standing on bare ground—my head bathed by the blithe air, and uplifted into infinite spaces—all mean egotism vanishes. I become a transparent eye-ball; I am nothing; I see all; the currents of the Universal Being circulate through me; I am part or particle of God.[93]

Five hundred years earlier, the Dominican Meister Eckhart (c. 1260–c. 1328) told us this truth about Reality, life with and in God: "The eye through which I see God is the same eye through which God sees me; my eye and God's eye are one eye, one seeing, one knowing, one love." [94] Mystical experiences, as Ken Vincent reminds us, can happen at any time: "St. Teresa had a mystical experience while cooking eggs for her convent—she reportedly burned the eggs!"[95] And you need not be a Baptist, Lutheran, Roman Catholic, or Presbyterian to be caught, netted, or enmeshed in a mystical experience. People

92 Steven Fanning in *Mystics of the Christian Tradition* (New York: Routledge, 2001) lists hundreds who in Christ have not only talked about God but who have also entered and experienced what the word God points toward. His time line of mystics from the second to the twentieth centuries (257–58) lists over eighty mystics from Clement of Alexandria to Thomas Merton. Many more are included in the book's chapters.

93 Ralph Waldo Emerson, "Nature," *Essays and Lectures* (New York: The Library of America, 1983), 10.

94 For yet another wonderful retelling of oneness with everything, read the remembrance of what happened to Freerick Frank when he was but five years old in an excerpt from "The Awakening Eye," available at http://lifespanleaern.org/ipnb2019.

95 *The Golden Thread: God's Promise of Universal Salvation.* (Lincoln, NE: Universe, 2005), 46.

have experienced the inexplicable Divine Presence intimately in every century, everywhere, in all religious traditions, and in all walks of life.

As I later learned from dear friends, I was and am not alone in the Nothingness and Allness of Everything. I was simply, along with many others— Christians, Buddhists, Hindi, whatever—made One, that is, radically united with the All, the mystery of God. Julian of Norwich in the fourteenth century described our common experience when she called the happening a "one-ing." St. Teresa also experienced it—and said it so well: "My soul has been carried away, and usually my head as well, without my being able to prevent it."

I realize, of course, that many think that what I and others have experienced may be so "out of it" as to be considered "unchristian." So to those who lean toward that assessment, I wish to say a word or two; after all, "You too may well be caught up in the Allness! the Nowness! the Everywhereness! Yes, you too!" And it's good to know that even the theologically conservative may be "one'd."

For my theologically conservative friends

In early November 2014, June and I, along with our friend Ellen, drove to Arden, North Carolina, where at Lutheridge we spent four days with the Scottish contemplative John Philip Newell and Georgia's own and wonderful theologian Barbara Brown Taylor.[96] The weekend confirmed all that I had experienced decades ago on the grassy lawn of OSU.

96 John Philip Newell is a poet, peacemaker, and scholar. In 2011, he received the Contemplative Voices Award from the Shalem Institute in Washington, DC. John Philip divides his time between Edinburgh with his family where he does most of his writing and the United States where he teaches and preaches across the nation. Formerly Warden of Iona Abbey in the Western Isles of Scotland, he is now Companion Theologian for the American Spirituality Center of Casa del Sol at Ghost Ranch in the high desert of New Mexico where he and his wife spend their summers. As the cofounder of Heartbeat: A Journey Towards Earth's Wellbeing, he is an ordained Church of Scotland minister with a passion for peace among the great wisdom traditions of humanity. With a PhD from the University of Edinburgh, he is internationally acclaimed for his work in the field of Celtic spirituality. He has authored sixteen books, including *Listening for the Heartbeat of God, Praying with the*

As confirming as that November weekend proved itself to be, something equally wonderful happened. During some free time, I found an e-book on "one-ing" that I now recommend to all my Baptist friends, many of whom have entered my life when I married June. Marshall Davis, a pastor in mainline and evangelical congregations for forty years, recently published *Experiencing God Directly: The Way of Christian Nonduality.*[97] What I like about Davis's book is its straightforward truthfulness, things made plain in simple terms. Here's an excerpt from chapter 2: "UnBorn Again":

> Evangelical Christians are not born again. That is my assessment from ministering among evangelicals for most of my life. I know evangelicals well. I would consider myself one. I earned two graduate degrees from the Southern Baptist Theological Seminary in Louisville, Kentucky. I have served as senior pastor of Southern Baptist churches and American Baptist churches (a more moderate, but still evangelical denomination.) I have known evangelicals—clergy

Earth, A New Harmony: the Spirit, the Earth, & the Human Soul, and *The Rebirthing of God: Christianity's Struggle for New Beginnings.*

Taylor, writer, teacher, and preacher, is the Butman Professor of Religion at Piedmont College in rural northeast Georgia. An Episcopal priest since 1984, she is the author of twelve books, including the *New York Times* best seller *An Altar in the World.* Her first memoir, *Leaving Church,* met with widespread critical acclaim. Barbara was recently featured on the cover of *Time* magazine with a story about her new book *Learning to Walk in the Dark,* and she has been named to the *Time* 100—*Time* magazine's list of the one hundred most influential people in the world for 2014. Barbara and her husband, Ed, live on a working farm in the foothills of the Appalachians with wild turkeys, red foxes, two old Quarter horses, and too many chickens.

97 *Experiencing God Directly,* along with others by Davis such as *Living Presence: A Guide to Everyday Awareness of God,* and his translation of Brother Lawrence's *The Practice of the Presence of God* are currently available only in Kindle editions.

> and laity—for a long time. My opinion is that very few are "born again" in the way that Jesus describes it.
>
> I am not suggesting that evangelicals are not "saved," in the way in which they understand salvation—in terms of life in heaven after death. Evangelicals certainly believe in Jesus Christ as Lord and Savior, and they trust in Christ for eternal life. If that is what it means to be born again, then evangelicals are born again. That is what evangelicals mean by the term "born again," but that is not what Jesus meant when he used that phrase.

Having said that, Davis next retells the story of Nicodemus meeting Jesus when in the dead of night Jesus clarifies what it's like to be "born again" (or better translated, as Davis prefers, "born from above"). Baptist Davis then makes this astute observation:

> Jesus is saying that being born again is a spiritual reality, not a physical one. He describes it as like the wind blowing through the Palestinian countryside. "The wind blows where it wishes, and you hear the sound of it, but cannot tell where it comes from and where it goes. So is everyone who is born of the Spirit." Jesus describes being spiritually reborn in terms of unknowing. We don't know where the wind comes from and where it is going. (It is helpful to know that both the Greek and Hebrew words for wind can also be translated "spirit.") One who is born again doesn't know if he is coming or going. He is just blowing in the wind.
>
> This is a description of nondual awareness. Nonduality is best described in terms of what it is not. In classic Christian spirituality this is known as the *via negativa*, the way of negation. It is also known as negative theology or apophatic theology (from the Greek word meaning "to deny"). Being born again

> is "not this" and "not that." If you try to describe it, you are missing it. Nothing one can say about it is true without immediately saying the opposite. Even balancing a statement with its opposite misses the mark, because it makes the truth dualistic, and God is nondual. The Lord is One.

If that's not a good-enough tease for you to read *Experiencing God Directly*, then listen to this recommendation by Paul R. Smith, another Baptist pastor:

> As a Baptist pastor like Davis, I was delighted to see how he found the Kingdom of God as nondual awareness in his experience and then right there in the Bible itself. While I came to this through the integral philosophy of Ken Wilber, it has been life changing for both of us. Davis does a superb job of opening up Jesus' teaching with the new eyes of one who is experiencing the joy of God's presence—nondual reality. If you wish to seriously follow Jesus, his teaching and model, this book will open it all up in quite remarkable ways.
>
> A few years ago I printed out all the verses in the canonical Gospels and the Gospel of Thomas that referenced the Kingdom of God. Then I substituted "nondual consciousness" for the words "Kingdom of God." There was no turning back. I discovered what Davis did: This was what Jesus focused his entire teaching on. And Davis puts it more succinctly in seventy pages than anyone else I have found. He makes it easily available to all. Run, do not walk, your fingers to www.amazon.com and get a copy. And then share it with your Christian friends and

> those who have left Christianity because they wanted more. Here is the "more" they are looking for.[98]

I recommend Davis and mention the many transformative experiences of other Christians neither to verify my own nor to place myself into some privileged circle of friends. To the contrary, it's my suspicion that nearly everyone at one time or another has fallen into some kind of cosmic consciousness or at least maintains a faint memory of such as experience. Perhaps like C. S. Lewis, they need simply to remember what was almost forgotten:

> The first is itself the memory of memory. As I stood beside a flowering currant bush on a summer day there suddenly arose in me without warning, as if from a depth not of years but of centuries, the memory of that earlier morning at the Old House when my brother had brought his toy garden into the nursery. It is difficult to find words strong enough for the sensation which came over me; Milton's "enormous bliss" of Eden (giving the full, ancient meaning to enormous) comes somewhere near it. It was a sensation, of course, of desire; but of desire for what? Not, certainly, for a biscuit tin filled with moss, nor even (though that came into it) for my own past—and before I knew what I desired, the desire itself was gone, the whole glimpse withdrawn, the world turned commonplace again, or only stirred by a longing for the longing which had just ceased. It had taken only a moment of time; and in a certain sense everything else that had ever happened to me was insignificant in comparison.[99]

---

98 https://www.amazon.com/Experiencing-God-Directly-Christian-Nonduality/dp/1521325022#customerReviews.

99 C. S. Lewis, *Surprised by Joy* (New York: Harcourt Brace Jovanovich, 1955), 16.

So "Good-bye" to some theological templates

I'm getting ready now to tell you about a change in my life. Like many, perhaps including you, I was "schooled," to use Diana Butler Bass's apt phrase, "in vertical theology." Forty years ago, I slowly came to realize that "Western Culture, especially Western Christianity [had] imprinted a certain theological template upon [my] spiritual imagination."[100] If you were to have asked me what I thought about God forty years ago, my answer would have echoed the her words:

> God exists far off from the world and does humankind a favor when choosing to draw close. [My] sermons declared that God's holiness was foreign to us and sin separated us from God. Yes, humanity was made in God's image, but we had so messed things up in the Garden of Eden that any trace of God in us was obscured, if not destroyed. Whether conservative or liberal, most American churches teach some form of the idea that God exists in holy isolation, untouched by the messiness of creation, and that we, God's children, are morally and spiritually filthy, bereft of all goodness, utterly unworthy to stand before the Divine Presence. In its crudest form, the role of

---

100 *Grounded: Finding God in the World—A Spiritual Revolution* (New York: HarperOne, 2015). Arguing that what in America appears to be a religious decline actually signals a major transformation in how people understand and experience God. The distant God of conventional religion has given way to a more intimate sense of the sacred that is with us in the world. This shift, from a vertical understanding of God to a God found on the horizons of nature and human community, is at the heart of a spiritual revolution that surrounds us—and that is challenging not only religious institutions but political and social ones as well. Exploring this cultural turn, Bass unpacks how people are finding new spiritual ground by discovering and embracing God everywhere in the world around us—in the soil, the water, the sky, in our homes and neighborhoods, and in the global commons. Faith is no longer a matter of mountaintop experience or institutional practice; instead, people are connecting with God through the environment in which we live. Grounded guides readers through our contemporary spiritual habitat as it points out and pays attention to the ways in which people experience a God who animates creation and community.

> religion (whether through revivals, priesthood, ritual, story, sacraments, personal conversion, or morality) is to act as a holy elevator between God above and those muddling around down below in the world.[101]

As a divorced person, I had trouble riding that elevator. Angry with myself as I saw my life unfolding with separations from Carol, my children, many friends, and my local parish, I sought refuge from my inner disappointments by walking away from life as I had known it. I visited other churches. None were restorative. I sat in the pews anonymously. At the same time, I looked beyond the church and all other apparent self-advancement programs. Knowing that I was wandering around in some sort of labyrinth or emotional corn maze, my first wife Carol in her love for me once recommended that I acquaint myself with "singles ministry" as sponsored by a local Episcopal church in Lexington, Kentucky. I went and found myself with a few men amid a small horde of eager-eyed women who introduced themselves without embarrassment. It was not for me. I needed time to sort things out. I enrolled myself in several group therapy sessions held at retreat centers. In one of them, everyone had to tell their story. When my turn came, I could do little more than cry and incoherently tell my tale. Mine was far from the worst, but nonetheless unmanageable. As I lived by myself in an upstairs three-room apartment with a kitchen floor so uneven that it felt as though I were living on the side of a hill, in and out of my teaching responsibilities, I thought a lot about what had happened to me on the lawn of OSU in the summer of 1976.

Buddhist awakenings

I began to consider my 1976 "lawn experience" a moment of "prevenient" grace" (to use a Methodist expression) that eventually led me to a more sustained and deeper continued life in God's Presence.

---

101 Diana Butler Bass, *Grounded: Finding God in the World, A Spiritual Revolution* (New York: HarperOne, 2015), 11–12.

It was something of a preview of what would arrive some fifteen years later after I left the church, entered academic life full-time, divorced my first wife, Carol, began an immersion in Buddhist practice, experienced the death of my son Krister, married Paula, adopted Chelsea, divorced Paula, returned to the church, and finally received the gift of contemplative prayer. Obviously, the "lawn experience" did not change me overnight or radically; it simply prepared me for what would later come. That coming took quite a while.

Paul Knitter's *Without Buddha I Could Not Be a Christian*[102] is the story of a now-married Jesuit priest's journey into a more profound understanding of his Christian faith with the help of Buddhist understandings about the mystery of life. That book has helped me to see Jesus as a living spiritual trailblazer who cannot be understood in Western thought forms alone. For anyone having difficulty with the dualist, paternalist, imperialist, and exclusivist nature of Western Christian orthodoxy, but who still thinks trying to be a follower of Jesus in today's world is worth an effort, I warmly recommend this book.

From my own experience, here in some detail is my telling as to how an exploration into Buddhist practice helped me live a more profound life in Christ. First, it's important to know that my conservative upbringing gave me an understanding as to how I was to practice praying: to pray is to think or speak words—words of repentance, words of thanksgiving, intercessory words, words of confession, entreaty, adoration, and request. As the writers of the Psalms show us, prayer may also include words of frustration, anger,

---

102 Knitter, a one-time professor at Xavier University and now teaching at Union Theological Seminary in New York, remains a churchman but one who is unflinchingly honest about the problems created for those who want to be followers of Jesus today—by what the Western Church has done over the centuries, with the life, example, and teaching of Jesus. In each chapter, Knitter spells out his own problems with one area of Christian orthodoxy, moves into what Buddhism offers in the corresponding area, and then brings back into his Christian self, what he has gained from immersion in Buddhism.

He brings to this book his own rich maturity in Christian faith and the fruits of his Buddhist insights, all of it honed by discussions with his students. The result—presented with freshness and humor—is a book as much a devotional and spiritual biography as an exercise in academic theology.

hatred, and disappointment—even disbelief. Prayers may be sung, done in community, or made privately. Prayer can be spontaneous, and it can make use of written texts.

I was taught from my earliest years that prayer is an "in-between" thing, an activity that takes two: me and God. Liturgically I was taught to pray to God the Father through Jesus in the unity of the Holy Spirit. As a boy, I was taught never to pray to saints. However, in seminary I learned that we can pray *with* them. By and large, prayer was a ritualized experience. I listened to how others prayed and prayed like them. Early on, I learned that Baptists like to use the word "just" in their prayers. For example, "Dear Lord, we "just" want to give you thanks." Sometimes my Baptist friends used the word "just" six or seven times in a one-minute prayer. Praying Baptists often mimic other praying Baptists just as Lutherans copy Lutherans. Sometimes prayers were answered; at other times apparently not. I quickly concluded that it's possible for there to be many different answers to prayer just as there are many ways to interpret an answer to a question, if in fact an answer comes along. As a young pastor, I prayed a lot, primarily using the Psalms as my underpinning. And, of course, I prayed the Lord's Prayer often as Jesus commanded Christians to do.

In all this, my basic problem was that I didn't know who I truly was when doing much of anything, much less when praying. My interior self was a mystery to me. Yes, I knew I was a sinner/saint, but I somehow managed to live on the surface of things, living by doctrines and teachings handed down to me. I often did not know why I acted as I did; I seemed to be habituated to many behaviors, living somehow at a stimulus/response level of mental activity. In all this, I was not adept at handling problems having to do with people who disappointed me. I experienced animosities, anger, resentments, indignations, and all sorts of irritations. Sexual impulses were at times difficult to manage. While publicly popular as a pastor and professionally successful as a professor, I knew that within all was not well. I was often begrumpled and piqued. Deep peace evaded me, and I longed for insights as to why my ego's functioning was so problematic. Forgiveness, even forgiving myself, didn't help much. I was stuck. In short, I wanted release from myself.

But how to find release? Intimations of possibilities came when EKU's chair of the Department of Humanities, Dr. Anne Brooks, asked me if I'd be interested in teaching a course in comparative religions. I jumped at the possibility and soon found myself reading Taoist, Hindu, and Buddhist scriptures, texts, and stories that opened new ways of seeing, thinking, and perceiving the world around me. At the same time, I applied for and received an Endowment for the Humanities scholarship, allowing me to attend a seminar at the John Hopkins University in Baltimore, Maryland, with no less a Milton scholar than Stanley Fish. He introduced me to Derridean thought and the constructive application of deconstructionist theory. I began to read differently, in-between and under the lines, allowing myself to descend into aporiae (those places of undecidability) present in nearly all texts, especially those having to do with religion, philosophy, and storytelling.[103]

The meditation center at Furnace Mountain Zen Center near Clay City, Kentucky

Serendipitously and with fortunate synchronicity, in Lexington, Kentucky, I attended classes in Tibetan and Zen Buddhism, eventually spending weekends at Furnace Mountain Zen Buddhist Monastery near Clay City, east of Richmond, Kentucky. It was there in the beautiful dharma room that I learned within the Korean Zen Rinzai tradition to quiet myself, sitting in zazen, a form of meditation asking one to sit upright with legs crossed for extended

---

103 My developing mistrust of language is evidenced by my presentation of "Deconstruction and George Herbert" at the Tenth Annual Meeting of the Kentucky Philological Association, March 3–5, 1983. The essay was published in the *KPA Bulletin* (Murray State University Printing Services, 1984), 33–51.

periods of time. My teacher, Dae Gak,[104] gave me koans, seemingly nonsensical or paradoxical questions (and sometimes stories), the answers and points to which came about when one entered the world of experiential wisdom. A satisfactory response to my first koan came only after several weeks of questioning, extended puzzlements.

What is it?

Once a day Dae Gak and I met privately, each of us sitting on a black cushion in a small room. One day after the usual formal acknowledgment of one another, Dae Gak placed a small bowl of water between us on the floor and requested that I do the following during zazen,[105] that is, while simply sitting on my cushion. When breathing in, I was to ask myself, "What is it?" And when breathing out, I was to respond, "I don't know." Then thereafter each day when I came for my interview, Dae Gak pointed to the bowl of water and asked, "What is it?" One answer was allowed each day. While I don't remember all the answers I gave, they ran along these lines: "a bowl of water," "H_2O," "H_2O in a clay pot," "liquid for drinking," "the essence of life," "a taste of the ocean," "the sweat of life," and all sorts of other rather quasi-logical articulations and imaginative figurings. Nothing worked. In fact, after each answer Dae Gak would take his teaching stick from his lap and gently strike me on my leg, look me in the eyes, and say, "Andrew, you are attached to forms and names.

---

104 Zen Master Dae Gak is an ordained monk and Dharma heir of Korean Master Seung Sahn. He has studied Zen since 1969 in both Japanese and Korean traditions. Dae Gak Sunim established the Lexington Zen Center in 1980, which led to the founding of Furnace Mountain, a retreat center near Clay City, Kentucky, in 1986. For many years Dae Gak has taught internationally and is the Guiding Teacher of centers in the United States and Australia. He currently leads a yearly Christian-Zen Retreat at the Abbey of Gethsemani. Zen Master Dea Gak holds a PhD of clinical psychology and is a practicing psychotherapist. Informative books describing his teaching include *Going Beyond Buddha: The Awakening Practice of Listening* (Boston: Charles E. Tuttle, 1997) and *Upright with Poise and Grace: Meditations on Entering into the Moment* (Frankfort, KY: Gnomon, 2012).

105 Detailed information on how to sit meditatively in Zen fashion is available at "Zazen Instructions," http://zmm.mro.org/teachings/meditation-instructions/.

Go back and sit again and then come back tomorrow to tell me what (pointing to the bowl of water) it is."

I finally came to know what the bowl of water is, a deep knowing that may fortunately come upon us all; knowing before thought, knowing prior to language, knowing as *sapientia experimentalis* (experiential wisdom) as Christian mystics often spoke of such knowing. That awareness fell upon me, imageless, without words, without thought, and I knew immediately—without the interference of thought—what water is. I had known all along, but I had forgotten. Now I was aware.[106]

Dae Gak gave me many koans (*kung'ons* as they are called in Korean), and I soon came to know a new way of living in the world, a way that began to take me away from binary awareness, my *this* and *that* thinking, the comparative mode of thinking that so blocked me off from what is true reality—true, foundational, worthy of attention.

Having learned to do zazen, I practiced diligently. Twice a day I'd close the door to my university office, pull out my zabaton (mat), place my zafu (round cushion) on it, anchor myself down with legs crossed in a half-lotus position, straighten my back, fold my hands in the "cosmic mudra," and begin practicing the breath, all the while working on a koan. I practiced zazen largely unnoticed by others, one lone exception being a beach zazen when a friend took a picture of me on the shoreline, the water lapping my legs. I was just a drop in the ocean.

---

106 If after looking at a glass of water and you still don't know how to tell me what it is, please don't do the following: don't tell me the definition as given in a chemistry book; don't tell me what the Bible tells us what it is; don't recite how it is defined in a dictionary; don't show me picture, and don't make me listen to a recording of the sound of Niagara Falls. All of that language and image stuff is not water. To know what water if, go take off your clothes and stand in a downpour of heavy rain (or take a shower in your bathroom) and actually experience water! When my Zen teacher asked me, "What is water?" I finally picked up the cup of water set between us and poured water on my head and when the cup was half empty, I threw the rest of the water directly onto his face. Dripping with water, my Zen teacher smiled because we had both experienced and knew what water really is! There's nothing quite like direct experience, is there? So also with God; experience God directly.

Frustrations nonetheless

As helpful as I found Buddhism, koan work, and zazen, I was also frustrated for several reasons. First, it was difficult for me to work within the Korean language and tradition. Much of the morning and evening chanting and the frequent use of Korean place names, tags, and common expressions proved themselves to be taxing. Aware that I was in a different culture (at that time the Americanization of Zen was just beginning), I knew I was missing much in terms of intonations, subtexts, the beauty of Korean poetry, proverbs, puns, innuendoes, and common assumptions. In spite of those difficulties, however, I hung in, hoping that eventually I'd fit in somehow.

But in 1993 I experienced a second difficulty. A hard one. A real blockage and bolt from the blue. My son Kris died, and sadly no one from the Furnace Mountain community said a word of consolation to me. Those at the monastery practiced day-by-day radical silence. They read no newspapers and knew nothing about his death. I did not know how Buddhists share a loved one's death and so said nothing. I screamed inwardly. Sometimes outwardly. I wept by myself, with my family and children, and on the shoulders of faculty friends at Eastern Kentucky University. Estranged from the Lutheran Church because of my refusal to sign the *Brief Statement* (see chapter 4) and just starting to attend a black Baptist church for my daughter's sake, I found myself largely without what I had known as the grace of God. It was no doubt my fault, and I frankly did not expect anyone from any local parish—Lutheran, Baptist, or otherwise—to stop by. No one from the Buddhist monastery put his or her arms around me. But miraculously, some others from far away got in touch with me, especially an old seminary friend who somehow found out that Krister had died.

Beloved Jon Kessler, severely disabled from a frightful lung disease that visited him while working as a missionary in India, reentered my life, and our friendship was renewed. As seminarians, Jon and I attended seminary classes together (reading the Psalms in Hebrew and Matthew in Greek). In a foursome we played tennis in the sweltering St. Louis afternoon heat. After graduating from the seminary, we had lost track of each other, but somehow there was enough spiritual glue between us that, after three decades, we rebonded quickly and with amazing mutual interests.

In India Jon came into contact with and was profoundly influenced by the Roman Catholic Benedictine Dom Bede Griffith, one of the church's finest contemplatives. The experience was life changing, and Jon became a Roman Catholic deacon (his wife, Judy remaining Lutheran). Upon returning to the States, Jon placed himself under the spiritual direction of Abbot Basil Pennington and so began a retired life, living on tanked oxygen, as a practitioner of centering prayer. With wholesale indebtedness to all in the Christian contemplative tradition (the number is staggering!), Jon and others of those who practiced what is now called Centering Prayer came to my rescue. What I had first tasted on the OSU grassy lawn and began to know more fully in the Furnace Mountain's dharma room now burst forth within me. I went to retreats with Jon at Lebh Shomea[107] in southern Texas and together in St. Paul, Minnesota, we spent numerous weekends with Basil Pennington. Surprised, I soon found the wisdom of Buddhism well within my own Christian tradition.[108]

---

107 Lebh Shomea (pronounced in Hebrew "lev show-mae-a") is a Christian community of men and women under the auspices of the Missionary Oblates of Mary Immaculate. Their lifestyle is contemplative-eremitical. Everyone at Lebh Shomea—guests included—participates in the contemplative-eremitical life of the House of Prayer. Moreover, there are hermits living in permanent hermitages situated at remote sites on the property. Guests who share the desert silence for indefinite periods are welcome year round. With the exception of meals and the celebration of the Eucharist each day, there is no predetermined schedule, no imposed structure, only the freedom and creativity of solitude. All guests are invited to share in the daily Eucharistic celebration, and members of the community are always available to listen heartfully to anyone seeking spiritual direction.

108 Today I'm even more convinced that the wisdom teachings of both Buddhism and Christianity have much to offer one another. In particular, I've found the following two books revelatory: Paul F. Knitter, *Without Buddha I Could Not Be a Christian* (Oxford: One World, 2011) and Brian J. Pierce, *We Walk Together: Learning from Thich Nhat Hanh & Meister Eckhart* (Maryknoll, NY: Orbis, 2005). In addition, one might wish to read Stephen Prothero, *God Is Not One: The Eight Rival Religions That Run the World* (New York: Harper, 2010), *Speaking of Silence: Christians and Buddhists on the Contemplative Way*, ed. Susan Walker (New York: Paulist Press, 1987), Daniel B. Clendenin, *Many Gods, Many Lords: Christianity Encounters World Religions* (Grand Rapids, MI: Baker 1995), Gerald R. McDermott, *God's Rivals: Why Has God Allowed Different Religions* (Downers Grove, IL: IVP Academic, 2007).

Jon Kessler, Fr. Basil Pennington, and me

I had first met M. Basil Pennington in the summer of 1999 when he came to visit me while I was living in a house on Leadmine Pond, near Sturbridge, Massachusetts.[109] I expected him to arrive from St. Joseph's Abbey in Spencer, Massachusetts, looking like a Cistercian monk in his religious habit, a white robe with a black overlay. He showed up in white summer shirt, wearing checkered shorts! We spent a most wonderful day together. After he took a swim in the lake ("pond" is not the right word for the fifty-seven acre, spring-fed tarn) and lay on the dock for a good sunning, we shared lunch and talked well into the afternoon. While I don't remember exactly what he said, I know I was so impressed with his spirit and generosity that I was determined to read all he had written. Eventually I did. Well, most of it. Before he left, he gave me some easy-to-follow instructions on how to practice centering prayer. Then, as I accompanied him back to his car, I asked him to bless me. What a blessing I got. This great, big, happy monk put both of his hands on my head and blessed me for five wonderful minutes. Then he hugged me, got into his car, and drove back to the monastery.

A few weeks later, I read this little essay in the *National Catholic Reporter*:

---

109 M. Basil Pennington entered the Cistercian Trappists in 1951 and was consecrated as a monk in 1956. After ordination he spent several years studying in Rome, and he assisted at the Second Vatican Council. Pennington is a spiritual father, retreat master, lecturer, and author of many books, including *Centering Prayer: Renewing an Ancient Christian Prayer Form*, *Vatican II*, and *Awake in the Spirit*. He died on June 3, 2005, the Feast of the Sacred Heart of Jesus, from injuries sustained from a car accident.

Love Does Things Like That

By M. Basil Pennington, O.S.S.O.
St. Joseph Abbey, Spencer, MA, USA

Friendship is one of the most beautiful things in God's creation. We might be slow to paraphrase St. John: God is friendship; but where there is friendship, there is love and there is God. It is always a wonderful thing when a new friend is welcomed into our lives.

A short time ago I received an e-mail from a friend of a friend and last week we got together for the first time. It was a wonderful day. Andy is a very special person. He had been formed in the richest and most conservative of Lutheran traditions. And for a time served in the ministry. He was near fifty when he met his wife, who herself was near forty. They sought to have a family in the usual biological way, but it proved too late. Then a beautiful little black girl came into their lives, almost directly from the womb. Andy first held her when she was only eight hours old.

As awareness of her surroundings began to dawn upon this little one, Andy became aware of a need. In the yellow pages he sought the nearest black Baptist church. And the next Sunday he was there with his little one in his arms. Andy chuckled as he related this: "In my seminary days I could never in my wildest dreams have imaged myself worshipping with Baptists, not to speak of black Baptists. But with his daughter, he and his wife have found a worshipping community among their black friends. Love does things like that."

I am not, of course, urging anyone to change their church to find a different liturgical experience. The richness of the Catholic Church is that it is truly catholic. It embraces all: rich and poor, people of all colors, and the whole spectrum of psychological, emotional, and ethnic needs. There are those who find the apt expression of their dedication to the Lord in fulfilling every jot and tittle of the law, from the divine and natural law down to the directives of the liturgical office and interpretations of these found in books, newspapers and magazines. At the other end of the spectrum there are those who believe that men and women are not made for the law but the law for men and women, even the divine law of Sabbath. They see law as guidelines that orient us in our doing. In the normal Catholic community there are these and everything in-between.

Now that the organization of the liturgy has in great part been returned to the responsibility of the local community, it is the challenge of the pastor and parish liturgical community to respond to the many and variant needs within their community. Where there is an abundance of talent, it is possible to offer a wide variety of liturgies: guitar and jazz masses, liturgies rich in the hymns of the English tradition, the spirituals of the south and Hispanic rhythms, Latin Gregorian, and even Byzantine chant. More often, the struggle is to find a parish liturgy that in some way fits in the middle and gives some adequate expression to all the members of the community.

Many of us could never have imagined ourselves singing and swaying, arms upraised in charismatic enthusiasm, or pulsating with the rhythms of Puerto Rico or Latin America. But love does things like that. In love we want all our sisters and brothers to find liturgy that is meaningful to them and we want to support them in the celebration. So we might well find ourselves singing: Kyrie...with rich Gregorian

> cadences, or "A Mighty Fortress is our God" with the whole-hearted devotion of a devout Lutheran.
>
> Love does things like that.
>
> [110]

Not only did Pennington write that article, but in the years to come he also let me know it is perfectly okay to ask questions, hard questions, even questions with no answers. In fact, as I was later to find out, it's also wonderfully okay to enter God's Presence without questions and without answers in what I now experience as prayer beyond thoughts, comprehensions, ideas and images--"unknowing prayer" described by Richard Rohr in Appendix B.

In referring to "a friend of a friend," Fr. Basil alludes to Jon Kessler, my old seminary buddy, whom I've already mentioned and will say more about in chapter 10. After meeting Father Basil, Jon and I made a number of retreats together to learn more about centering prayer. I soon became comfortable with Christianity's historic application of Jesus's encouragement to "go into a private room, close the door, and pray unseen to your Father who is unseen" (Matt. 6:6). Eventually Father Basil became my spiritual director and under his care, I entered Christianity's contemplative way of living. I listened to St. Paul when he says that "the Spirit welcomes you into God's own family. That's why we call out to Him, "Abba! Father!" as we would address a loving daddy" (Rom. 8:15). Encouraged by St. Paul, eighteen years ago I began to practice contemplative prayer (often called "centering prayer"). This kind of praying places a strong emphasis on interior silence. Most of those who write about it trace its roots to the contemplative prayer of the Desert Fathers of early Christian monasticism, to the Lectio Divina tradition of Benedictine monasticism, and to works like *The Cloud of Unknowing* and the

[110] On December 1, 2002, I was able to retrieve a copy of this little essay from www.lectiodivina.org/mbpLoveDoesThings.htm. Several years later the essay seems no longer to be available online.

writings of St. Teresa of Avila and St. John of the Cross.[111] Its recent popularization can be traced to numerous books published by three Trappist monks of St. Joseph's Abbey in Spencer, Massachusetts, in the 1970s: Fr. William Meninger, Fr. M. Basil Pennington, and Abbot Thomas Keating.[112]

> Concerning centering-prayer practice, Father Basil gave me these guidelines:
>
> First, sit comfortably with your eyes closed, relax, and quiet yourself. Enter the love of God with love for God.
>
> Then, choose a sacred word that best supports your sincere intention to be in the Lord's presence and open to His divine action within you (for example, "Jesus," "Lord," "God," "Savior," "Abba," "Divine," "Shalom," "Spirit," "Love," etc.).
>
> Let that word be gently present as your symbol of your sincere intention to be in the Lord's presence

---

111 Seeds of what would become known as contemplation were sown early in the Christian era. The first appearance of something approximating contemplative prayer arises in the fourth-century writings of the monk St. John Cassian, who wrote of a practice he learned from the Desert Fathers (specifically from Isaac). Cassian's writings remained influential until the medieval era, when monastic practice shifted from a mystical orientation to Scholasticism. Thus, it can be plausibly argued that contemplation was (one of) the earliest meditational or devotional practice of Christian monasticism, being later supplanted in dominance by the scholastic theologians, with only a minimal interest in contemplation.

112 I especially recommend two books by Basil Pennington: *Call to the Center: Gospel's Invitation to Deeper Prayer* (New York: Doubleday, 2003) and *Centering Prayer: Renewing an Ancient Christian Prayer Form* (New York: Doubleday, 2001). Many, as I do, consider the following by Thomas Keating indispensable: *Open Mind, Open Heart: The Contemplative Dimension of the Gospel* (New York: Continuum, 1992) and *Intimacy with God: An Introduction to Centering Prayer* (New York: Crossroad, 2003). William Meninger's *The Loving Search for God: Contemplative Prayer and The Cloud of Unknowing* (New York: Continuum, 1998) is best read with Carmen Acevedo Butcher's *The Cloud of Unknowing: With the Book of Privy Counsel* (Boston: Shambhala, 2009), a most excellent translation of the fourteenth-century classic, with superb notes.

> and open to His divine action within you. It is perhaps best that the word remain unspoken.
>
> Whenever you become aware of anything (thoughts, feelings, perceptions, images, associations, etc.), simply return to your sacred word, your anchor. Let it come down into your centering like a feather falling upon your heart.
>
> Then after you been centering for twenty minutes or so, gently re-enter your everyday visionary and thoughtful world by slowly opening your eyes. Perhaps you may wish to pray the Lord's Prayer and then go about your chores.
>
> Don't hesitate to center yourself more often throughout the day.
>
> Later in the day, enter again for another twenty minutes your centering prayer.

When I pray this way, I'm often given a space within where I'm more and more free from the business of thinking, thinking that frequently underscores the force of my ego, my attachments, and my preoccupations. With the help of the Holy Spirit, I am learning to let go and empty myself, often entering an "unknowing" stillness within the quiet Presence of God, the Ground of my being. I was and now am often out of the world of language, definitions, and dualities and into God.

Often (in Reality, all the time!) I am one with God. One'd.

And three'd

Yes, I was "one'd" on that bright lawn day in Oklahoma. And less dramatically, I've been one'd ever since. But with equal and perhaps more remarkableness, I've also been "three'd." God has also taken me to Thirdness. One'd and pulled out of the world of binary thinking (this and that, me and you, right and wrong, up and down, left and right, and so on), I was "three'd" and given the gift of the

Holy Trinity. Pulled out of judgmental binary thinking, I now realize that that One equals Three, and all twoness is gone. How that came about requires some telling. Let the music begin with a G-major chord! One sound, three notes! C for Christ, E for spiritual Energy, and G for God the Father.

But first a program note. While the word "trinity" is not in the Bible and doesn't become a part of our Christian vocabulary until Tertullian (c. AD 155–c. 240) coins it in the second century, the early Christian conviction that somehow God is Trinitarian marks a revelatory breakthrough in human consciousness about the Divine. God as mysteriously Trinitarian utterly undoes, does away with, and ultimately disallows all binary thinking. God isn't binary. God is one and trinary. In one blow of a single-axe handle with three iron heads (pardon the bad metaphor), God as Trinity disallows and dissolves racism,[113] class consciousness, sexism, any and all sense of binary privilege. The Holy Trinity as a realized presence totally and without embarrassment undoes everything our egos prefer, our culture endorses, and nearly all that our clergy love to teach, preach, and proclaim. Listen to what most binary-oriented preachers proclaim and you'll see how they do it. Often badly.

Preferring the power of a binary world view, the church has actually managed to make God as Trinity largely irrelevant. O yes, the church encourages everyone to mutter the word "triune" and sometimes make the sign of the cross "in the name of the Father, Son, and Holy Spirit," but churchy people do not live Trinitarian lives.

For most Christians the Trinity is simply a doctrine, not a lived experience. And if a Christian (sometimes unfortunately) becomes a theologian, she or he discovers that thinking about the Trinity is a skill difficult to master. A lot of big words must be learned: *hypostasis, ousia, substantia*, among others. Often it takes weeks and months for seminarians to master the so-called orthodox understandings of the Trinity. After all, it took the church three centuries to figure out who and what the Trinity is. And you can bet that the newly ordained

113 Richard Rohr, "How God as Trinity Dissolves Racism," *Sojourners*, August 25, 2016, available at https://sojo.net/articles/how-god-trinity-dissolves-racism.

seminarians will not use such learned language in a sermon or Bible class. It's just too complicated. Take, for example, how under Pope Benedict XVI's direction Roman Catholics now confess that they believe

> in one Lord Jesus Christ, the Only Begotten Son of God, born of the Father before all ages. God from God, Light from Light, true God from true God, begotten, not made, consubstantial with the Father.

Few practicing Catholics can tell you what they mean by "consubstantial." And even fewer Protestants can tell you much of anything about the Holy Trinity—except they baptize "in the name of the Father, the Son, and the Holy Ghost." Karl Rahner is quite right to observe that most believers "could drop the doctrine of the trinity tomorrow and it would have little or no practical effect on the lives of most Christians." Again, Rohr says it well:

> Unfortunately, for the majority of trinitarian Christians, we believed the doctrine of the trinity as some kind of strange riddle, a mathematical conundrum, but never let it call our addiction to Greek logic into question. The sweet Irish nuns who taught me wisely said "Don't think about it!" and held up the shamrock as a rather lovely natural symbol of the three-in-one. Even though the doctrine of the trinity was at the very centre of Christian faith, we did not allow it to change our consciousness. We just believed it to be true, and then shelved it, as we did most doctrines. Only the mystics tended to relate to God in a trinitarian way, and often passionately so (such as Augustine, Bonaventure, Julian of Norwich, and the Cappadocian Fathers). I am certain that the future of Christian mysticism will be strongly trinitarian which, perhaps surprisingly, also

> creates a huge opening for interreligious dialogue. Unfortunately, faith became a matter of believing impossible or strange things (which was supposed to please God, somehow), instead of an entranceway into a very different way of knowing altogether.[114]

Rohr is right. In my own life as a Christian, even as a seminarian and pastor, the Holy Trinity was mostly a doctrine and not a transformative Presence in and with whom I lived.

Is or is not

I grew up with a few ideas about the Holy Trinity that stayed with me until seminary. Mostly they came from Luther's *Small Catechism*, especially as depicted in an explanatory triangular diagram giving me ideas about who "is" and who "is not."

From that triangle I got the notion that God is three separate persons even though God himself is one God. Moreover, from the prayers ("collects" as we called them) in the Liturgy, we talked to God the Father, always through the Son, "who livest and reignest with the Father and Holy Ghost, ever one God, world without end." Somehow the Holy Trinity was more like a pyramid with the Father on top, the Son in the middle, and the Holy Spirit spread out as the base.

Let the divine dance begin

All this changed when I visited St. Gregory of Nyssa Episcopal Church in San Francisco, California. What I saw when I looked up startled, shocked, and surprised me. Whirling like dervishes up in the sanctuary were lots of people in a line dance, doing some sort of a hip-hop!

114 "Rohr on the Trinity," *Home*, August 5, 2011; available at http://www.home-online.org/2011/08/rohr-on-the-trinity/

Up there in the dome was Luther, kicking up his left leg and extending his hand to Thomas Merton! Luther's right hand rested on the shoulder of mathematician Paul Erda, who in turn was frolicking with Ghandi as all were led by Seraphim, a Russian mystic, who once fed a hungry bear because he loved all animals. As I circled myself under the dome to see everyone high stepping, especially Jesus Christ as the Great Dancer, I kept whispering to myself, "O my Lord! O my Lord." And amazingly, an hour later, when I participated in the liturgy, guess what? All of us joined the dance as everyone held one another's hands and jiggled around like old-time Shakers under the Dome of Dancers.[115] That's how I was introduced to the possibility of dancing with God.

But does the Trinity dance with us? I first began to think so when introduced to the Greek word *perichoresis* meaning "around" and *chorein* meaning "to rotate" or "go forward." To do *perichoresis* is to dance in a chorus. The term was first used to describe life within the Trinity by the Church Fathers. Today it's given currency by contemporary writers like Jürgen Moltmann, Miroslav Volf, John Zizioulas, and C. Baxter Kruger, among others. For me, Richard Rohr says it exceptionally well when he tells that in the fourth century Christian teachers emphasized that there's a flow within the Trinity that's like a "circle dance":

> And God is not just the dancer, God is the dance itself! The Incarnation is a movement—Jesus comes forth from the Father and the Holy Spirit to take us back with him into this eternal embrace, from which we first came (John 14:3). We are invited to join in the dance and have participatory knowledge of God through the Trinity.
>
> Trinity is the very nature of God, and this God is a circle dance, a centrifugal force flowing outward, and then drawing all things into the dance

[115] For a wonderful video of such a "Circle Dance," visit https://www.youtube.com/watch?v=l7_hLmim0Gs.

centripetally. If this God names himself/herself in creation and in reality then there must be a "family resemblance" between everything else and the nature of the heart of God.

Scientists are discovering this reality as they look through microscopes and telescopes. They are finding that the energy is in the space between the particles of the atom and between the planets and the stars. They are discovering that reality is absolutely relational at all levels. When you really understand Trinity, however slightly, it's like you live in a different universe. And a very good and inviting one![116]

Andrei Rublev, *The Trinity*
(also known as
***The Hospitality of Abraham*)**
Fifteenth Century

My initial understanding of the mystery of the Trinity ("is" and "is not") deepened when once teaching the history of art, I had opportunity to study Rublev's fifteenth-century icon, *The Holy Trinity*.[117] The icon takes as its subject the mysterious story wherein

116 Adapted from *The Divine Dance: Exploring the Mystery of Trinity*, disc 1 (CD, MP3 download); available at www.cac.org and https://danutm.wordpress.com/2014/08/20/richard-rohr-the-trinity-as-a-circle-dance/.

117 I first saw Rublev's *Holy Trinity* in H. W. Janson's *History of Art* (New York: Harry N. Abrams, 1969), Figure 288, as a black-and-white illustration. Janson, however, described the icon as anything but black and white:

> Although parts of it are poorly preserved—most of the background has disappeared—the [icon] reveals a harmonious beauty of design and a depth of lyrical feeling that vie with the most Classical products of the

Abraham welcomes three strangers as he camps by the Oak of Mamre. The aged monotheist serves them a meal. As the conversation progresses, Abraham realizes that he seems to be talking straight to God, as if these "angels" were in some way a visiting metaphor for a certain "Threeness" that later came to be known as the Trinity. Thus, on one level, it depicts a story from the Hebrew Scriptures. On another level, however, it is a dynamic visual expression of life within the Triune God. Reading the picture from left to right, we see the Father, the Son, and the Holy Spirit. As our eyes circle in and around the icon, we see Christ in the center looking to his right at the Father who looks across the table to the Holy Spirit, as he watches the Son's hand bless the cup. As we observe the Trinity in action, we notice that there's an open place for us to sit at the table across from the Son and between the Father and the Spirit. With wonderfully open body language (notice how the Father's and the Spirit's legs are not crossed), the Trinity invites us to walk over and sit down. We are invited to complete the circle, to join the dance, to share the movements of God by our own stepping forward. Rublev's *Trinity* is a quiet invitation to *perichoresis*.[118]

> Second Golden age. Rublev must have been thoroughly acquainted with the best Byzantine art had to offer...the most individual element—and also the most distinctively Russian—is the color scale, brighter, more complex, and different in key from that of any Byzantine work. In the hands of lesser masters, such combinations as orange, vermillion, and turquoise might easily have assumed a primitive garishness of the sort we often encounter in folk art; here, the controlled intensity of these tones becomes an essential part of the composition. (178)

After reading that, the next day I went to an Orthodox bookstore in St. Louis, Missouri, and bought a beautiful color print of the Holy Trinity icon mounted on a wood panel. It has been hanging in my home for more than forty years.

118 Although years ago I purchased a copy of Rublev's *Holy Trinity* that still blesses my study room in Barnesville, Georgia, it was not until late in 2016 that early in 2017 the fifteen or so of us in Theology on Tap began reading to one another, week after week, every page of Rohr's *The Divine Dance: The Trinity and Your Transformation* (New Kensington, PA: Whitaker House, 2016). With that wonderful book, I began to receive a truly big feel and understanding of the Divine Mystery we Christians are privileged to name "The Holy Trinity."

Such inviting may be likened to a continued outpouring of love, Trinitarian flowings of grace and effusions of mercy. Life within the Trinity is a flow of amity, amour, and ardor among those in the oneness of God. In *God for Us: The Trinity and Christian Life*, Catherine Mowry LaCugna paints her own verbal icon when she says, "The very nature of God, therefore, is to seek out the deepest possible communication and friendship with every last creature on this earth." About LaCugna's declaration, Rohr says:

> That's God's job description. That's what it's all about. The only things that can keep you out of this divine dance are fear, doubt, or self-hatred. What would happen in your life—right now—if you accepted being fully accepted?
>
> It would be a very safe universe.
> You would have nothing to be afraid of.
> God is for you.
> God is leaping toward you.[119]

God dances with all of us within the rhythm, music, and flow of banqueting love. Hanging on the wall behind my desk, Rublev's icon invites me to participate in the quiet dance, a special table choreography.

To help me dance and live within the river of such flowing Trinitarian love, on my desk I sometimes maintain a little three-storied fountain of water. As I move in and around my library and writing room, I hear the quiet sound of falling water, reminding me of the flow of the waterfalls at nearby High Falls State Park, some twenty miles away. These waters, splashing their way down fountain and falls, send sounds and sprays welcoming me to awareness that I'm always drenched with the flow of God's grace. Both fountain and

[119] Richard Rohr, "God is for Us," *Daily Meditation* (September 30, 2016), available at https://cac.org/god-is-for-us-2016-09-30/.

falls, like Rublev's icon, remind me that the love of the Holy Trinity is always flowing through my life. God is quietly roaring in my life.

But I have more than a fountain and nearby falls to help me participate in the life of the Trinity. The whole universe with its galaxies, dark holes, stars, and comets dancing around one another reminds me that the dance is everywhere, just as Gerard Manley Hopkins says it so well:

Thee God I come from,
To Thee go.
All day long I like fountain flow,
From Thy hand out,
Swayed about
Mote-like
In Thy mighty glow.

With God I flow and glow. When I take a shower. When I make my morning coffee by pouring boiling water over coffee grounds in my French press. When I water the flowers on the front porch. Whenever and wherever I watch life flow, I see, feel, breathe in, and am embedded within the Trinity. Driving down the highway. Walking in the park. Mowing the yard. All is participation in the Trinity, God's flow. I have moved from catechetical diagrams and ideas about the Trinity to participation in the Oneness of God, a Oneness overflowing into three Persons whom we have come to name as Father, Son and Brother, and Holy Spirit. The Trinity is everywhere, even in me. And in you in all you do.

Two decades after my son Krister's death and three years after my daughter Chelsea died, Jayne Mouchet gave me her used paperback copy of William Paul Young's *The Shack*. Yes, it's controversial in its presentation of the Trinity, but Eugene Peterson, whose edition of the Bible as *The Message* my pastor and I love, urged me to read it by saying, "Before you have read a dozen pages, you will know why we need to keep company with theologians." While slowly reading *The Shack*, I knew I needed this book. In its own very distinctive way, it plunged me into the life of the Most Holy Trinity. If, like me, you have suffered the loss of a child or someone you dearly loved, I urge you to read *The Shack*, a book of healing. And afterward, you may wish to read Randal Rauser's *Finding God in The Shack*, especially chapter 3, "The Mystery of Three in One."

For Further Consideration

Bourgeault, Cynthia. *The Holy Trinity and the Law of Three*. Boston: Shambala, 2013.

George, Timothy, ed. *God, the Holy Trinity: Reflections on Christian Faith and Practice*. Grand Rapids, I: Baker Academic, 2006.

Keating, Thomas. "Becoming Nothing." Available at https://integrallife.com/becoming-nothing/.

LaGugna, Catherine Mowry. *God for Us: The Trinity and Christian Life*. San Francisco: HarperCollins, 1973.

O'Collins, Gerald. *The Tripersonal God: Understanding and Interpreting the Trinity*. Mahwah, NJ: Paulist Press, 1999.

Pelikan, Jaroslav. *The Christian Tradition: A History of the Development of Doctrine* (100-600). Vol. I. Chicago: University of Chicago Press, 1973.

Rahner, Karl. *The Trinity*. New York: Continuum, 2001.

Rauser, Randel. *Finding God in The Shack*. Colorado Springs, CO: Paternoster, 2009.

Rohr, Richard. *The Divine Dance: The Trinity and Your Transformation*. New Kensington, PA: Whitake House, 2016.

Smith, Paul R. *Is Your God Big Enough? Close Enough? You Enough? Jesus and the Three Faces of God* (St. Paul, MN: Paragon House, 2017).

Young, William P. *The Shack: Where Tragedy Confronts Eternity*. Los Angeles, CA: Windblown, 2007.

Chapter 8

BEFRIENDING THE MYSTICS

"Theologians may quarrel, but the mystics of the world speak the same language."
—Meister Eckhart

"Mystical experiences do not necessarily supply new ideas to the mind, rather, they transform what one believes into what one knows, converting abstract concepts, such as divine love, into vivid, personal, realities."
—R.M. Jones

Mystical, mystic, mysticism

In *An Emptyful Chair*, I've not been afraid to use the word "mystical," along with the words "mystic" and "mysticism." The root meaning of these words is the Greek verb *muein* meaning "to close one's eyes or lips." Mystics are thus those who allow their experiences to go deeper than what's available by means of the five senses. They enter a reality beyond hearing, seeing, tasting, feeling, and smelling. Christian mystics are like Moses in Mount Sinai's great cloud when he experienced the ineffable Presence of God. When the suffix "–ism" is added to create the word "mysticism," we are referring to actions or practice that encourage such closing down of the five senses. It's the practice or discipline that Jesus recommends when he says:

> And *whenever* you pray, do not be like the hypocrites. Because standing in the synagogues and on the corners of the wide-roads, they love to pray so that they may make-an-appearance to people. Truly I say to you, they are receiving their reward in full. But whenever you pray, enter into your inner-room, and having shut your door, pray to your Father, the One in secret. And your Father, the One seeing in secret, will reward you. And while praying, do not babble as-indeed the Gentiles do. For they are thinking that they will be heard by means of their many-words. (Matt. 6:5–7, *Disciples' Literal New Testament [DLNT]*)

Notice the word *whenever*! This secretive way of prayer, Jesus tells us, is to be our regular, habitual way of coming before God, entering his Presence. Such inner-room praying with the door shut is to be done whenever we pray. As you probably realize, "your inner-room" is not to be taken literally (Jewish village homes had no "closets," as the KJV translates the Greek). Jesus has created a terrific metaphor to suggest a place and space beyond ordinary prayer that is beyond the living room, beyond ordinary living. It's a place you can enter inside or outside the house. It's a place one enters by closing one's eyes to let go of seeing images, wordy thinking, a head full of noise, the noise of life's business. It's a place of quietness, silence, and stillness. It's a responding to the God's recommendation in Psalm 46: "Be still and know that I am God." Or as the *Names of God Bible* translates: "Let go of your concerns! Then you will know that I am Elohim."

According to Scripture, inner and stilled experience is an essential and valid part of the Christian life, just as the Psalmist whispers a prayer all mystics murmur:

> Adonai, my heart is not proud, nor my eyes lofty, nor do I go after things too greator too difficult for me. But I have calmed and quieted my soul—like a weaned child with his mother, like a weaned child is my soul within me.
>
> (Ps. 131, Tree of Life Version)

Jesus: our Mystic Exemplar

Have you ever wondered what Jesus did before he was baptized by John the Baptist? I think Amos Smith gives us the best of answers when he explains how it was possible for Jesus to enter the desert and fast for forty long days and nights. Taking the forty-day fast at face value (all the Gospels refer to it), Smith wisely notes that

> The only way a person can survive a forty-day fast is years of training. If you or I were to attempt a forty-day fast without training we would be hospitalized or die of toxemia. The body needs to build up to a forty-day fast. The point is that Jesus trained rigorously. Jesus was a spiritual athlete. And his forty-day test and transformation in the desert didn't occur in a vacuum. Jesus lived for 33 years, and the Gospel only records two-and-a-half years of his ministry. What did Jesus do in those silent years? Many speculate about Jesus's biography, but one thing seems to be clear: Jesus spent a portion of those years in ascetic practice and training.[120]

120 Amos Smith, *Be Still and Listen* (Brewster, MA: Paraclete P, 2018), 40. For more thorough scholarly investigations, see Doloros Cannon, *Jesus and the Essenes* (Huntsville, AK, 1992); Simon J. Joseph, *Jesus, the Essenes, and Christian Origins: New Light on Ancient Texts and Communities* (Waco, TX: Baylor UP, 2018); and J. Rufus Fears, *Books That Have Made History: Books That Can Change Your Life* (The Great Courses Teaching That Engages the Mind), Lecture Six.

Smith strengthens his explanation by reminding us that Jesus very likely knew about and might well have lived among his Jewish comrades within the Qumran community before entering his public ministry. The Essenes were well known for their forty-days fasts. Moreover, the Essenes regularly fasted from physical activity, speech, and thoughts in order, as Smith says, "to eliminate all distractions and commune with God." It should be no wonder therefore as Smith reminds us that

> The new Testament often records that Jesus went to lonely places and prayed. Jesus was also known to "pray all night" (Matt. 1:35, Lk, 5:16, Lk. 6:122). This is the Christian tradition's epicenter. And it's from this root that we trace the lineage of Christian mysticism through the ages. "I will allure you into the desert and console your heart," as Hosea says 2:14 says.

Sharing life with the mystics

In the second half of my life, I have come to love living within the Christian mystical tradition. Don't get me wrong. I still live lots and lots of my life within my inherited faith, the life into which I raised as a child, the life I grew into as a teenager, young adult, seminarian, and middle-aged man. Sundays are special days in which, with others in the Body of Christ, I sing hymns, sing both tenor and bass in the choir, listen to conventional sermons, say the ancient creeds, and receive the living Jesus in Holy Communion. I cannot do without all the church provides: the songs, words, and images all Christians treasure and enjoy.

But also in the second half of my life, I also love, enjoy, and live in a deeper reality, the moment-by-moment Presence of God, the God of everywhereness, whose Presence is in trees, stones, oceans, little creeks, dandelions, corn fields, glaciers, deserts, the core magma of Mother Earth, and the outer reaches of universe which only the

Hubble Telescope sees a wee bit. I love, enjoy, and live in the deep reality of God present in elephants, worms, bumblebees, lizards, snakes, and my Pomeranian companion, Ringo, to whom book is dedicted. This is why I am a communicant within a church that welcomes everyone and all within God's Presence.

Whom do we mystics welcome into the mystical life?

The mystics welcome you! Like the Christians at Grace and Glory Lutheran Church in Goshen, Kentucky, they greet you with these words:

Grace and Glory Lutheran Church Goshen, Kentucky

> We extend a special welcome to those who are single, married, divorced, gay, filthy rich, or dirt poor. We extend a special welcome to those who are crying new-borns, skinny as a rail or could afford to lose a few pounds.
>
> We welcome you if you can sing like Susan Boyle or can't carry a note in a bucket. You're welcome here if you're "just browsing," just woke up, or just got out of jail. We don't care if you're more Lutheran than Martin Luther, or haven't been in church since your great uncle's funeral.
>
> We extend a special welcome to those who are over 60 but not grown up yet, and to teenagers who are growing up too fast. We welcome soccer moms, NASCAR dads, starving artists, tree-huggers, latte-sippers, vegetarians, junk-food eaters. We welcome those who are in recovery or still addicted. We welcome you if you're having problems or you're down in the dumps, because we've been there too.
>
> If you blew all your offering money at the dog track, you're welcome here. We offer a special

> welcome to those who think the earth is flat, work too hard, don't work, can't spell, or because grandma is in town and wanted to go to church.
>
> We welcome those who are inked, pierced or both. We offer a special welcome to those who could use a prayer right now, had religion shoved down your throat as a kid or got lost in traffic and wound up here by mistake. We welcome tourists, seekers and doubters, bleeding hearts.
>
> And if you don't find yourself anywhere on that list, come and introduce yourself! There is a place for you too![121]

Yes, there's a place for everyone in the contemplative and mystical life. Everything and all are within the Presence.[122]

Daily I live among my mystic friends because they, like my dance teacher Bill Shaffer, help me dance within the love of God. They keep me living within the vast, deep, wide, boundless, and rhythmic flowing of the Presence of God. There are, of course, many ways by which one may live among mystics—going on retreats, entering special friendships, participating in Centering Prayer meetings, connecting with a spiritual director, joining a special book club, and reading book like Carl McColman's *Christian Mystics: 108 Seers, Saints, and Sages,* among others.

---

121 This gracious welcome is the website embrace of Grace & Glory Lutheran Church in Goshen, Kentucky. Its open-arms welcome is not only available at the parish's website (http://graceglory.weebly.com/who-is-welcome.html) but also comes with hugs of welcome at the front door and within the lives of everyone at Grace & Glory.

122 To see if you are a mystic, visit "Are You a Mystic: 10 Sign You are . . ." at https://mommymystic.wordpress.com/2009/02/18/are-you-a-mystic-10-ways-to-know/

The mystic revival

Thankfully, Christian mysticism is experiencing a revival throughout the church, in all denominations.[123] Within my own tradition, Lutherans are now realizing that Luther was deeply influenced by Christian mysticism. For Luther salvation by faith is not so much an arguable point of doctrine, an idea one must have to be saved; faith is, above all, an inner experience, an inner *savoir faire*, struggle, or *Erfahrung*, as Luther would say. It's being in love with God; the mystic is God's bride in the most intimate way of being and loving. Here's how Luther in his *The Freedom of a Christian* (1520) describes our relationship with God:

> The third incomparable grace of faith is this, that it unites the soul to Christ, as the wife to the husband; by which mystery, as the Apostle teaches, Christ and the soul are made one flesh. Now if they are one flesh, and if a true marriage—nay, by far the most perfect of all marriages—is accomplished between them (for human marriages are but feeble types of this one great marriage), then it follows that all they have becomes theirs in common, as well good things as evil things; so that whatsoever Christ possesses, that the believing soul may take to itself and boast of as its own, and whatever belongs to the soul, that Christ claims as his.
>
> If we compare these possessions, we shall see how inestimable is the gain. Christ is full of grace, life, and salvation; the soul is full of sin, death, and condemnation. Let faith step in, and then sin, death, and hell will belong to Christ, and grace, life, and salvation to the soul. For, if he is a husband, he must take himself that which is his wife's, and, at the same

123 See, for example, *Meister Eckhart, The Return of the Mystic*, available at http://www.abc.net.au/radionational/programs/spiritofthings/meister-eckhart-the-return-of-the-mystic/3370420.

> time, impart to his wife that which is his. For, in giving her his own body and himself, how can he but give her all that is his? And, in taking to himself the body of his wife, how can he but take to himself all that is hers?[124]

As Philipp Stoellger points out, in Luther's Latin text upon which our English translation is based, Luther does indeed use the image of marital copulation between husband Christ and his Christian bride as an apt metaphor to describe the mystical union.[125] What unites [*copulate cum* = copulates with] the soul with Christ as a bride and groom is faith and love. It comes as no wonder that for mystics throughout the ages, spousal love shared between a man and a woman—especially when beautifully erotic—was a favorite unfolding of the contemplative and mystical life. For more than two thousand years, mystics have loved the Bible's Song of Songs.[126] Metaphorically speaking, Christian mystics dare to say they enter into "bed-love" with Christ. Like David they are unafraid to lose themselves in dancing for and with the Lord. Jon Zuck puts it this way:

---

124 *The Freedom of the Christian* (1520). The text is available at http://sourcebooks.fordham.edu/mod/luther-freedomchristian.asp.

125 Philipp Stoelinger, "Martin Luther on Faith," *Oxford Research Encyclopedia on Religion* (March, 2017), available at http://religion.oxfordre.com/view/10.1093/acrefore/9780199340378.001.0001/acrefore-9780199340378-e-331?rskey=xNeY-D4&result=1.

126 See, for example, *Bernard of Clairvaux on the Song of Songs*, vol. 1–4, trans. Killian Walsh (Kalamazoo, MI: Cistercian Publications, 1971). As Christopher Pramuk notes, "Perhaps no interpretation of the Song of Songs has exerted a greater influence on Western Christian spirituality than that of St. Bernard of Clairvaux, whose commentary86 sermons composed over a period of 18 years is rightly revered as the masterpiece of medieval monastic literature. Like many others before and after him, Bernard saw the song as a sublime allegory on the love of God that can be experienced through contemplation. It was the paradigmatic text for monks, because its poetry vividly describes the pursuit that is the basis for the whole program of monastic life: love's union with God, of which the monk may enjoy a sweet foretaste here below." ("Sexuality, Spirituality, and the Song of Songs," *America: The Jesuit Review*, October 31, 2005).

> When Jesus declared "I and the Father are one," (*Jn.* 10.30) he proclaimed in himself the union of God and humankind, and he offers it to all who follow him (he gave the power to become sons of God to all who believe. (*Jn.* 1.12). From there, the mystic heart is seen in the letters of the apostles: Paul reached the divinized state of losing his "self": *I no longer live, but Christ lives in me!* (*Gal.* 2.20) James wrote that every good and perfect gift comes from the Father of Lights, in whom there is no variation nor shadow of turning. (*Jas.* 1.17) Peter proclaimed that Christ even descended to hell to liberate imprisoned souls, (*1 Pet.* 3.19) and John understood the most sublime truth of God's essence: God is Love! (*1 Jn.* 4.8,16). This is only the beginning. Every century has been influenced by Christian mystics—from apostles and martyrs, Church Fathers and Desert Mothers, to monks and nuns of religious orders, to the lay mystics—men and women and boys and girls in every century, in every denomination, in every walk of life.[127]

"Mystics," Zuck truthfully observes, "range the gamut of walks of life, from intellectual priests such as Frs. Pierre Teilhard de Chardin and Matthew Fox, to laywomen like Bernadette Roberts, Katherine Nelson, and the remarkable Jarena Lee.[128] The mystic way is old, but timeless—it is alive and ever new for each one who chooses it. It

---

[127] Jon Zuck, "What is Mysticism? The Wild Things of God," available at http://www.frimmin.com/faith/mysticismstart.php.

[128] Jarena Lee was a pioneering nineteenth-century African-American preacher and mystic whose powerful conversion experience inspired her to travel the country, overcoming both the gender and racial barriers of the time. She was also the first African American woman to publish an autobiography, *Religious Experience and Journal of Mrs. Jarena Lee, Giving an Account of Her Call to Preach the Gospel,* an eloquent account of her spiritual and preaching. For more information, visit https://mommymystic.wordpress.com/2015/05/21/women-mystics-series-jarena-lee-19th-century-african-american-preacher/.

invites you to an adventure of divine transformation and discovery. The life of a mystic is open to all. Even you!

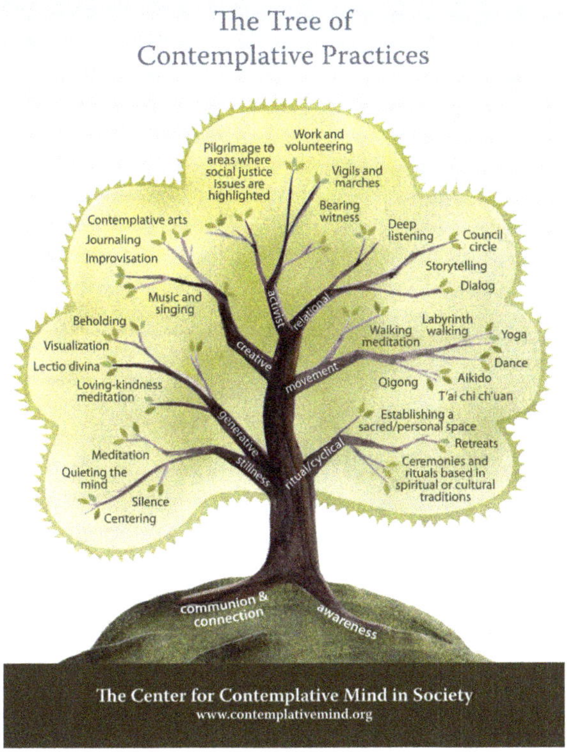

"Mysticism—Christian or otherwise," as Carl McColman tells us, "comes in many flavors. Some mystics are very withdrawn and profoundly silent, almost zen-like in their practice. Others are much more engaged in the world (even if they are monks or nuns). Some are "head" mystics, with a strong bent toward philosophy, theology, and academic scholarship, while others are more "heart" mystics with an emphasis on devotion, worship, and simple adoration.[129] As you know by now, my little branch and practice is located on the lower-

[129] Carl McColman, "How to Find a Mystical Teacher," available in two postings at http://www.patheos.com/blogs/carlmccolman/2017/11/find-mystical-teacher/#B-w3P5uhM8QyvDDvj.99.

left side of the tree, hanging close to the ground as Centering. That's the fruitful branch of the contemplative tree that I hope you will reach up to grab and explore. The fruit is delicious!

So if you wish to live a life that lets Christ pray within you, consider becoming an ordinary centering mystic! After all, it is not you who lives but Christ in you. Take advantage of his hidden interior prayerful Presence in your life. Be still and become intimate with God who lives within.

For Further Consideration: A Selected Bibliography

Bauerschmidt, Fredereick. *Why the Mystics Matter Now*. Notre Dame, IN: Sorin Books, 2003.

Campolo, Tony, and Mary Albert Darling. *The God of Intimacy and Action: Reconnecting Ancient Practices, Evangelism, and Justice*. San Francisco, CA: Jossey-Bass, 2007.

Cole, David. *The Mystic Path of Meditation: Beginning a Christ-Centered Journey*. Vestal, NY: Anamchara Books, 2013.

Chu-Cong, Joseph. *The Contemplative Experience: Erotic Love and Spiritual Union*. New York: Crossroad Publishing, 1999.

Fanning, Steven. *Mystics of the Christian Tradition*. London: Routledge, 2001.

Fox, Matthew, ed. *Christian Mystics: 365 Readings and Meditations*. Novato, CA: New World Library, 2011.

Griffin, Emilie. *Wonderful and Dark Is This Road: Discovering the Mystic Path*. Brewster, MA: Paraclete Press, 2004.

Happold, F. C. *Mysticism: A Study and Anthology*. New York: Penguin, 1970.

Harmless, William. *Mystics*. Oxford: Oxford University Press, 2008.

Hollywood, Amy, and Patricia Z. Beckman, eds. *The Cambridge Companion to Christian Mysticism*. New York: Cambridge University Press, 2012.

Johnston, William. *Mystical Theology: The Science of Love*. Maryknoll, NY: Orbis, 2000.

King, Ursala. *Christian Mystics: The Spiritual Heart of the Christian Tradition*. New York: Simon & Schuster, 1998.

Kruschwitz, Robert, ed. *Mysticism: The Christian Reflection Project*. Institute for Faith and Learning. Waco, Texas: The Center for Christian Ethics, 2005.

Marion, Jim. *Putting on the Mind of Christ: The Inner Work of Christian Spirituality*. Charlottesville, VA: Hampton Road, 2011.

McColman, Carl. *Answering the Contemplative Call*. Charlottesville, VA: Hampton Roads Publishing, 2015.

———. *The Big Book of Christian Mysticism: The Essential Guide to Contemplative Spirituality*. Charlottesville, VA: Hampton Roads Publishing, 2010.

———. *Christian Mystics: 108 Seers, Saints, and Sages*. Charlottesville, VA: Hampton Roads Publishing, 2016.

McGinn, Bernard. *The Essential Writings of Christian Mysticism*. New York: Random House, 2006.

______. "Mystics Invite Us to Imagine: Selected Excerpts." Shalem Institute for Spiritual Formation (August 2018 eNews), available at https://shalem.org/2018/07/31/

mystics-invite-us-to-imagine/.

Peterson, Christiana N. *Mystics and Misfits: Meeting God through St. Francis and Other Unlikely Saints*. Harrisonburg, VA: Herald Press, 2018.

Rohr, Richard. *Everything Belongs: The Gift of Contemplative Prayer*. New York: Crossroad Publishing, 1999.

———. *The Naked Now: Learning to See as the Mystics Do*. New York: Crossroad Publishing, 2015.

———. *What the Mystics Know: Seven Pathways to Your Deeper Self*. New York: Crossroad Publishing, 2015.

Smith, Amos. *Be Still and Listen: Experience the Presence of God in Your Life*. Brewster, MA: Paraclete Press, 2018)

Tuoti, Frank X. *Why Not Be a Mystic?* New York: Crossroad, 1995.

Underhill, Evelyn. *Mysticism: A Study in the Nature and Development of Spiritual Consciousness*. Mineola, NY: Dover, 2002.

Wolpert, Daniel. *Creating a Life with God: The Call of Ancient Prayer Practices*. Nashville, TN: Upper Room Books, 2003.

Chapter 9

CULTIVATING CONTEMPLATIVE PRAYER

Only through poverty of spirit do humans draw near to God; only through it does God draw near to humans. Poverty of spirit is the meeting point of heaven and earth, the mysterious place where God and humans encounter each other, the point where infinite mystery meets concrete existence.
—Johannes Baptist Metz, *Poverty of Spirit*

I have a need of such a clearance
as the Savior effected in the temple of Jerusalem
a riddance of the clutter
of what is secondary
that blocks the way
to the all-important central emptiness
which is filled
with the presence of God alone.
—Jean Danielou, "Such a Clearance"

The mind that is the prisoner of conventional ideas, and the will that is the captive of its own desire, cannot accept the seeds of an unfamiliar truth and a supernatural desire...I must learn therefore to let go of the familiar and the usual and consent to what is new and unknown to me. I must learn to "leave myself" in order to find myself by yielding to the love of God.
—Thomas Merton, *New Seeds of Contemplation*

"Lord, help me lose myself in You."
—a prayer the Holy Spirit gave to me
during Holy Communion, July 5, 2015

The Christian of the future will be a mystic
or he will not exist at all.
—Karl Rahner

Learning from my Buddhist friends

I came to learn this way of praying from several friends, but most importantly from Jon Kessler, a seminary friend who has since gone to sleep in the Lord. Jon reentered my life after Kris died, at a time when I was reconsidering my commitment to Buddhism. As a *westerner*, I found it difficult to assimilate myself to the Korean ambience of Zen Buddhism at Furnace Mountain Monastery. I deeply appreciated the discipline of sitting with koans,[130] the serenity of zazen, and my newfound ability to pay attention to everything without the clutter of judgments and commentaries. After my decision to divorce Carol (I should never have done that), I became simultaneously unhappy with myself and with the church. No one came to visit or talk with me. I entered something of a divorce with nearly everyone. Finding myself quietly angry and frustrated, I was at the time teaching several courses in the Department of Humanities at EKU. It was then that I began to read many world scriptures, especially the Hindu Vedas and

[130] Koans are paradoxical anecdotes or riddles, used in Zen Buddhism to demonstrate the inadequacy of logical reasoning and to provoke enlightenment.

the Buddhist Sutras. Buddhism began to take on meaning for me. It made sense not only because Thomas Merton wrote enthusiastically about it as a helpful clarification of Christian contemplative living, but also because it presented me with the possibility of introspection beyond what I had already experienced as a father, husband, and pastor. I wanted and needed to know myself, genuinely and truly. I wanted to know why I was who I was, not in the abstract but by a profound knowing that was deeply experiential and practical. I wanted to know who I was and am, my "self." Buddhism and the practice of quiet sitting with the guidance of a Buddhist teacher provided me with such a path, a way of exploration.

Before I encountered Buddhist meditation, I thought I knew myself, my inner, private world, what I was tempted to regard as my real "self," but what in fact is not. This became clear to me when I started a serious practice of sitting still in meditation. Cyprian Smith describes such sitting well:

> The kind of meditation I am talking about is not meditation upon anything or about anything; it consists simply of sitting still for a lengthy period and simply watching the various thoughts and emotions which arise in the mind; not trying to resist them, drive them out, or change them, but simply watching them without identifying with them or being engulfed by them. This is not, strictly speaking, a religious exercise; it is not prayer, and it has nothing to do with God; in fact it is possible to practice without believing in God at all. Nevertheless, it is an extremely useful exercise; so much so that certain Buddhist schools make it their basic spiritual practice. Why? Because if we watch our emotions and thoughts for long enough, we may eventually become aware of something within us which is not these emotions or thoughts. If I am watching something, then I must be different and distinct from what I am watching. The fact that I am able to watch my thoughts means

> that they are different from me; I am not them. I am, indeed, none of those things which I am accustomed to regard as "myself"; I am not my body, nor my mind, nor my emotions, nor am I all these things taken together. So what am I? What is "me"?[131]

Buddhism helped me learn to see who I am not. Many Christians, like me, have learned such unlearning from our Buddhist sisters and brothers. We need not be afraid of such blessed learning. Vietnamese Buddhist monk and peace activist Thich Nhat Hanh often likes to remind us that we Christians have nothing to fear about Buddhists:

> There is a misconception that Buddhism is a religion and that [we Buddhists] worship Buddha. Buddhism is a practice, like Yoga. You can be a Christian and practice Buddhism. I met a Catholic priest who lives in a Buddhist monastery in France. He told me that Buddhism makes him a better Christian. I love that.[132]

One of my favorite books is Paul F. Knitter's *Without Buddha I Could Not Be a Christian*.[133] Knitter boldly reminds us, as so many Christians imagine, that we are not our thoughts, feelings, and emotions. For this new awareness to take place, I learned how to do zazen, a Buddhist practice involving work with koans and engage in

---

131 Cyprian Smith, *The Way of Paradox: Spiritual Life as Taught by Meister Eckhart* (London: Darton, Longman, and Todd, 1987), 47.

132 Qtd. Ethan Nichtern, *The Dharma of the Princess Bride*, "November 30, 2016, available at https://www.facebook.com/EthanNichtern/posts/10154716356887296.

133 Paul F. Knitter, *Without Buddha I Could Not Be a Christian* (London: Oneworld Publications, 2009). Honest and unflinching, Knitter narrates the spiritual dilemmas he struggled with and explains how a Buddhist world view has allowed him to resolve each one. From the "petitioning" nature of Christian prayer to how Christianity views life after death, Knitter argues that a Buddhist standpoint can help inspire a more person-centered conception of Christianity, where individual religious experience comes first, and liturgy and tradition second. The latest edition comes with a new postscript in which Professor Knitter reflects on and reevaluates his position as a double-belonger.

interviews with a Zen master. At the same time, I read everything I could find about Buddhism, all sorts of Buddhism: Mahayanna, Theravidian, Zen, and Tibetan, books by many Buddhist teachers, nearly all the recognizably authoritative speakers and writers whose books I could find in libraries or purchase. What I found was remarkable, helpful, and life changing. At my university I began to teach classical Buddhist texts so well that many of my students thought I was the real thing: the first Buddhist they had ever met. I spent weekends at various dharma houses and eventually took first vows as a Buddhist initiate at Furnace Mountain Monastery in Kentucky. Here is the gift of a poem, which I received that day. Originally, written in Korean, it translates this way:

Revelation

Good and evil have no self-nature; "Holy" and "unholy" are empty names. In front of the door is the land of stillness and light. Spring comes; the grass grows by itself.

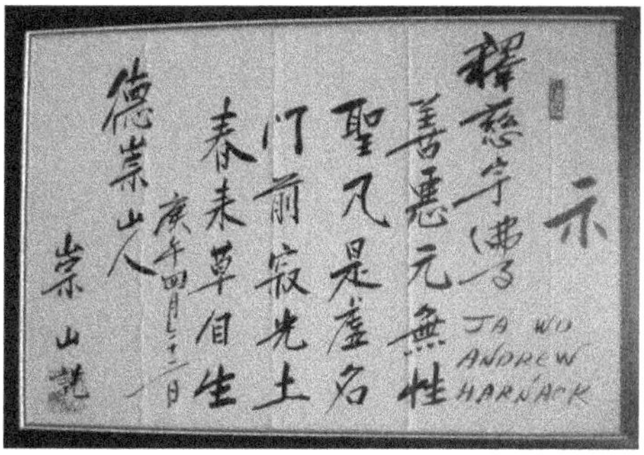

This poem, signed by Zen Master Seung Sahn on April 22, 1990, still hangs framed on my library wall next to my desk. On the back of the frame is the envelop that originally contained the poem. In Korean calligraphy Seung Sahn also gifted me with this Zen wisdom:

The tip of the needle falling from heaven
touches the mustard seed.

I treasure this poem as a gift from the East because it reminds me that I must always be aware of the conceptual inadequacies of human language. That's a word of wisdom that time and again my

Eastern Orthodox Christian brothers and sisters have also spoken to me. Unlike many in the Western Church, they warn me about taking words too seriously. Daniel B. Clendenin describes their observations about "God language":

> [Eastern theologians] point to texts in the Old Testament that remind us that no person can see God and live. Though acknowledging that God spoke to Moses face to face, as a man speaks with his friend, they point out that when Moses asked to see the glory of the living God, he responded, "You cannot see my face, for no one may see me and live." So it was that as he passed by, God covered the face of Moses so that Moses would see only his back and not his face (Exod. 33.11, 18–23).
>
> Other examples include Isaiah, who feared death because of his vision of God; even the seraphim shielded their eyes from his very presence (Isa. 6.1–5). Isaiah also saw a radical abyss between the mind of God and our minds: as the heavens are higher than the earth, so are his ways and thoughts higher than ours (55.8–9). Gideon and Manoah feared death at the sight of God (Judg. 6.22; 13.22). And when God appeared to Elijah, the prophet covered his face with a mantle (I Kings 19.13). The Psalms, Eastern thinkers point out, are filed with references to the utterly transcendent God. "Clouds and thick darkness surround him" (Ps. 97.2), a theme that perhaps recalls the experience of Moses at Sinai. The very name of God is majestic and wonderful (Ps. 8.1), causing Gregory of Nyssa to observe that "God's name is not known; it is wondered at."[134]

134 Daniel B. Clendenin, *Eastern Orthodox Christianity: A Western Perspective* (Grand Rapids, MI: Baker Academic, 2003), 58–59.

The New Testament also often emphasizes the radical incomprehensibility of God:

> Oh, the depths of the riches both of the wisdom
> and knowledge of God!
> How unsearchable are His judgments
> and unfathomable His ways!
> For who has known the mind of the Lord,
> Or who became His counselor?
> Or who has first given to Him
> that it might be paid back to him again?
> For from Him and through Him and to Him
> are all things.
> To Him be the glory forever. Amen. (Rom. 11:33–36)[135]

This is one of the most beautiful statements on the incomprehensibility of God in the New Testament. The Apostle Paul makes it the doxological climax to his discussion of election, predestination, God's sovereignty, and human responsibility in Romans 8–11. The Apostle Paul calls us to worship a God who is beyond our capacity to comprehend in either his being or his works. This God is *unsearchable* and *unfathomable*. No one will ever *know* all the *ins and outs* of the mind of the Lord. If someone could, he would "become His counselor," for he who can understand God would be as great or greater than God.

St. Paul is emphatic about what we can and cannot know: "The love of Christ which surpasses knowledge" (Eph. 3:19). Paul prays that the saints might "comprehend" and "know" the love of Christ (vv. 18–19). But while they can have a finite but true knowledge of such things, they cannot exhaustively comprehend the Lord Jesus Christ or His love. Christ is God as well as man. He is infinite in His being and love. We will never be able to understand the "whys," "hows," and "wherefores" of his love for sinners.

135 See also John 1:18, I Timothy 6:16, and 1 John 4:12.

Theological limitations

In a wonderful chapter titled "Talking about God," William Shannon gives all of us who presume to think theologically this reminder as to who we are and what we can do:

> There is a miracle story narrated in the seventh chapter of Mark's Gospel (vv. 31–37) that tells of the cure of a deaf man who is described as having a "speech impediment." The words "he had a speech impediment" are actually a translation of one single word in Greek. It is the Greek word *mogilalos* accurately translated as "having a speech impediment." It could also be given a one-word translation: "stammerer." The Gospel story can be seen as a picture of all of us. As we stand before the mystery of God revealed in Christ, we are all *mogilaloi*; we are all "stammerers." That might be a good definition of theologian: "he/she is a 'stammerer' in the face of the reality of God." Jesus was able to cure the deaf man of this physical impediment, but it is only the direct vision of God that could possibly cure us of the speech impediment we have in talking about God.
>
> A good theologian understands this. He knows that all he/she says can never approximate the experience. So much is lost between the experience and the articulation. Theological words and definitions and treatises are like matches lighted by our experience to help us look at the sun. The fact is that we can look at the matches, but we cannot, without losing our sight altogether, look at the sun. That means that when we want to talk about God or think about God, we have no other choice: we have to use matches.
>
> But when we have the experience, when we are fully aware, when we look at the Sun, we not

> only cease "stammering" because we have nothing to say; we also no longer use the matches. We can't even see them (nor do we have any desire to), for the brightness of the Sun blinds us by its brilliance. We really see because we can't see. We really are silent, for we have no words (and no desire for any). But when the inner eyes of the mind are darkened and I am no longer thinking about or trying to talk about God, then the inner eyes of the heart are opened and I am able to grasp God (or rather be grasped by God) in the embrace of love.[136]

"In practical terms," as Kenneth Leech observes, "the beginning of contemplative prayer will mean that it becomes progressively more difficult and perhaps impossible to think about God or to use many of the traditional methods of 'saying prayer.'"[137] I never conceived of such a possible outcome within the progress of my prayer life. Unthinkable. My Lutheran background had led me to suppose that the more we thought about God, the better we understood him. Words, whether in prayer, books, sermons, liturgies, or commentaries, were a great way to *get* God. We orthodox (lower case "o") and evangelical Christians had figured God out, written Him down, and published Him. Years of theological education with hours spent in Biblical languages assured me that I knew God quite well. My brand of theology, conservative Lutheran, encouraged me to take an ordination oath by which I swore that my ideas about God were superior to those of my Roman Catholic, Baptist, and Presbyterian friends. I had a lock on God. And I was not alone. As did the "Papists" (just so we Lutherans loved to label Roman Catholics), so do my Baptist and Presbyterian friends. We all shove God into various boxes, some labeled Lutheran, others Southern Baptist, among hundreds of other denominational names.

---

136 *Silence on Fire: Prayer of Awareness* (New York: Crossroad, 2000), 97–98.

137 *True Prayer: An Invitation to Christian Spirituality* (San Francisco, CA: Harper & Row, 1991), 46.

Saying "Amen" to prayer

We *western* Christians—hard at thought and fascinated with logic—surely had and have a decided tendency to make idols out of our words, sentences, and books. We codify interpretations of God. But the truth is that all who read and talk about God wear special theological glasses and speak in a denominational dialect. And that truth complicates prayer.

Yes, it's best to put a stop to a lot of traditional praying. Especially those long, windy, self-advertising prayers preachers like to spout off so often. Jesus himself warned us against such praying (Matt. 6:7). Try praying without thoughts and words. At least listen to Luther when he says, "The fewer the words, the better the prayer." I know that's a radical statement, a paradox, a conundrum, a real enigma, and puzzlement, that at first blush poses a contradiction to logical minds forfeiting resolution. To make sure that you thoroughly grasp and digest the severity of this unorthodox confession, Baptist Pastor Theodore R. Clark shares my conviction this way:

A PRAYER?

I

I do not believe in prayer.
Why should I?
I have never known one to be answered.
If I ever could be sure
That a prayer had been answered,
I could never believe in God.
For God would have to be "there,"
Would have to be listening,
Would have to be waiting
For my words to reach Him.
For me to pray
Would presuppose that God had "ears,"
Ears on the side of His Head,

Ears with little hairs on the lobes.
Also, if God heard my words
When I speak,

He could not hear me
When I did not speak.
By my silence
I could make Him wait,
Wait for me, for my word.
He would be my listener,
My slave.
So, I do not believe in prayer,
Because I do not believe in a God
Who "hears" my prayer and answers it.
If He did answer it
I could argue with Him
Whether He answered it right or not.
My conclusion then is that he who prays is deceived,
Because he can only pray to one
Who is less than God,
Or no god at all.

II

But yet I do pray, as I am doing now,
Even though I do not believe in prayer.
Why?
Because it is not I who am praying.
If "I" pray
Then I "do not" pray;
For my prayer is nothing but words
That God cannot understand
As I understand,
In thoughts connected in time and space.
So I do not pray
For to pray would be the end of prayer.

How can I hear while I am talking?
Not to pray is prayer.
For when I do not pray,
I am praying most truly.
Lord, teach me now <u>not</u> to pray.[138]

Clark wonderfully perceives and articulates what it's like to ponder the problems that metaphors, images, and words present to wordy, "literalistically minded" people. Assuming with considerable arrogance that their words say it all, all that can be said, enclosing everything, including truth and reality, they do and don't pray. They simply aren't aware of the inadequacies of language.

Increasingly aware of such arrogance on my part, late in my life I came to know another way to live with God, as the way of wordless prayer was given to me as a gift. Christian friends suggested that in addition to my more usually *wordy* praying, I might learn to reduce my need for language. So it happened that more than twenty years ago, I began practicing what some call "wordless" prayer, Prayer of the Heart, Centering Prayer, and Silent Prayer. Becoming a minimalist, I choose only one little word ("Abba") to serve as my heart's murmured desire to be within God's mysterious, be-clouded presence.

Here's how many enter into God's mystical Presence

Self Portrait
Acrylic on board, 1995
Andrew P. Buglass

Find a quiet place. If necessary, leave the house and go into your workshop for this way of praying. There's a chair there. Sit in it. Read some Scripture, meditate on what you've read, offer a few intercessions, spiritually rehearse what you have done and left

[138] *Herald of "The Total Event"* (Edinburg, TX: New Santander Press, 2004), 86–87. For emphasis, Clark has underscored the words "not," "did," and "my."

undone, and enter into forgiveness and grace. Then sit comfortably, your back as straight as possible for the sake of awareness; close your eyes. Enter God's presence quietly. When you find yourself engaging in some kind of thinking (plans for day, memories of whatever, pious thoughts about God or whomever, shadowy reflections of past wrongs, or whatever), silently say your sacred word or phrase (for example, "Be," "Only This," or "Abba." Let the Spirit release yourself from the following of thoughts and all commentaries on images and feeling. After all, you don't simply want to think about God or to hear about him; you want to be with Him, in his Presence, entering into the mystery of his Divinity so that together you become one, heart to heart, just as Jesus was "one with the Father," just as Jesus prayed for us to be one with the Abba Father. What happens is a gift from God; words disappear, thoughts fall away, images evaporate, and the Presence becomes everything. If this is not realized, that is all right, okay. If it does happen, that too is all right, okay. Sometimes you'll be in the Presence only briefly, sometimes longer; often you can't tell. Only this you know: you are either on the verge of being "one'd" or you are "one'd," and that is enough, very much enough, sometimes too much; either way the happiness is sufficient for the day. After a while, rise from your chair with God in your heart. You have been with God, the Christ within. As you stand, see him everywhere, in all whom you meet, in everything that comes your way. It is no longer you who live, but Christ lives in you.

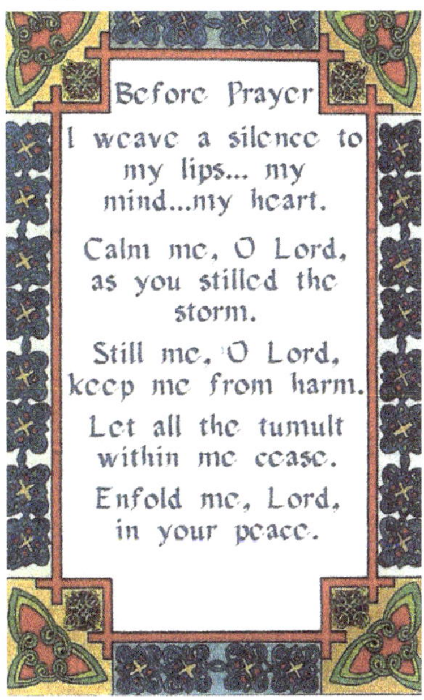

For more encouragement, see Appendix A: The Method of Centering Prayer.

It's the gentlest of all prayings. Within this prayer I let go of thoughts, preoccupations with body sensations, feelings, images, and reflections. I empty my "self" (that's with a small *s*) so that I might be filled with God's Self (that's with a big *S*), God's presence, his loving presence. I let go and let "be." Luther was right when he said, "The fewer the words, the better the prayer." More often than not, for example, if I'm interceding for someone, I simply mention the person's name and let the sound of it sink it for reflection. Both God and I know what I'm asking for. There's little need to belabor things.

Richard Rohr narrates what happens, and I don't hesitate to quote him at length:

> In our regular contemplative "sit" (time of silent prayer) we are actually practicing being awake. Religious teachers, including Jesus, the Buddha, as well as many Hindu sages, are always telling us to wake up—to be alert, alive, awake, attentive, or aware. You might call it the AAAAA recovery program! But how can you do that? What does being awake actually mean?
>
> Being conscious or aware means:
>
> 1. I drop to a level deeper than the passing show.
> 2. I become the calm seer of my dramas.
> 3. I watch myself compassionately from a little distance, almost as if "myself" is someone else.
> 4. I dis-identify with my own emotional noise and no longer let it pull me here and there, up and down.
> 5. I stop thinking about this or that and collapse into pure or "objectless awareness" of nothing in particular. I don't get there; I fall there.
>
> At first, it does not feel like "me." It is unfamiliar territory because up to now I thought that my thinking was "me," yet now my thinking has ceased. I believe this is the meaning of Jesus' teaching on "losing oneself to find oneself" (see Luke 9:24).
>
> This new and broader sense of "me" gradually, over time, began to feel like my deepest and truest

> self; it seems solid and unchanging. At this point, God, consciousness, I, silent emptiness, and fullness all start to feel like the same wonderful thing! This is what spiritual teachers mean by growth in holiness.
>
> This deeper self is what most traditions refer to as "the soul" or the True Self and what psychology might call "the collective unconscious." When I live here I am somehow "shared" and participating in something Larger. I am not doing it; it is being done to me, with me, through me, and as me! Paradoxically, this pure consciousness is usually described as the "unconscious" because, in a sense, I am not at home here at all, and I am surely not in control. So you see why we fight it.[139]

There is indeed a certain contemplative "logic" (pardon the expression) of such praying. Realizing that I can't put a stop to the chattering monkey in my head, I allow myself just one sound—a single word. That word may not have any special philosophical, theological, sociological, academic, epistemological, or semantic significance. It's simply an indication that I want to be in God's presence. Quite frankly, the single syllable "O" will work as well as "Abba," "Jesus," or "Be"—words that other contemplatives have chosen as expressions of their quiet intention to be in God's silent presence. Our minds want to think abstractly about God, to find answers to life's questions, and often enough, to compose grocery lists. Quietly to all those efforts, we let all such musings (even the most pious ones) go by allowing ourselves a wee tiny word that will help us enter God's lovely silence and presence.

Within contemplative prayer, the fewer the words, the better. One word will do lots. Again, a little more contemplative logic. Words for us are vehicles that take us somewhere—to another person,

---

139 "Being Awake," Richard Rohr's *Daily Meditation*, February 9, 2017, available at www.cac.org; adapted from *The Naked Now: Learning to See as the Mystics Do* (New York: Crossroad, 2009), 134–36.

to an idea that we want to explore, to a clarification of some sort. In contemplative prayer, however, we don't need to go anywhere. Here's how one contemplative said it six hundred years ago:

> Spiritually speaking, heaven [that is, God] is as close down as up, and close behind as before, as quickly reached from one side as the other. In fact, anyone who longs for heaven [God] is already there in spirit. The highway to heaven is measured by desires, not by feet. Our longing is the most direct route.[140]

Words work over telephone wires, by way of digital impulses, via satellites, and from mouth to ear. Such is not the way contemplative prayer works. God is everywhere, closer to us than we are to ourselves, as St. Augustine once famously said. We can let go of words because heaven (i.e., God) is everywhere.

Like a drop of water falling into the ocean, we let our thoughts, images, and preoccupations drop away. We can let go because an Inner Someone does our praying for us. That Someone, the Holy Spirit, Paul says "makes you God's children, and by the Spirit's power we cry out to God, 'Abba! my Abba!' ('Father! my Father!'). God's Spirit joins himself to our spirits to declare that we are God's children" (Rom. 8:15–16). Paul goes on to say that when our prayers are inadequate, stunted, and feeble, "the Spirit helps us in our weakness; for we do not know how to pray as we ought, but that very Spirit intercedes with sighs too deep for words." Too deep for words. Beyond words. Free of and on the far side of words. Wordless prayer.

140 *The Cloud of Unknowing* (Boston: Shambhala, 2009), 137.

Heeding Paul's realization, for years I've taken "Abba" as the sacred or love word I silently mutter in the Presence as an echo, knowing that the Spirit is always muttering "Abba" inside me. I know that every time my heart beats, that Inner Someone is breathing "Abba." The Holy Spirit is telling the Father that She loves him. By quietly echoing the Spirit's "Abba," I simply enter the expressive love and inner voice of the Holy Trinity. In this kind of contemplative prayer, I pray not to God as an object; I simply enter the Presence and am within the Divine.

Embracing one's shadow self

When we quiet ourselves in prayer, such stillness not only ushers one into God's presence, but it also often leads to an awareness of one's interior dark self, the shadow self, introduced in Chapter 6. Bruce Sanguin describes the archetype of the shadow this way:

> These are elements of oneself that from which we are so dissociated that when they rise up to bite us in the butt, we can hardly believe it has anything to do with us. This is obviously because when these feelings, thoughts, or images first surfaced there was no apparent way to integrate them and own them. We shoved them down into the basement of our psyches, there to function outside the realm of our conscious control. Usually, these elements are what society regards as unacceptable—rage, murderous inclinations, the desire to dominate the other, jealousy, sexual energy, ambition, etc. but the shadow can also be positive qualities that threatened our early environment, such as passion for life, deep intelligence, enjoyment of beauty, and

> even happiness—if our home was depressive, our happiness would threaten the equilibrium.[141]

One effective way of dealing with the shadow self is for us to quietly observe what characteristics and behaviors of others we respond to judgmentally. We may, for example, see another's financial success as a mark of his or her greed. We might note a man's manner of adorning himself with fine clothing as a sign of his vanity. What is it in others that irritates us? As Sanguin notes, "When we find ourselves receiving information from the outside world, and interpreting it negatively, we are very possibly in the realm of our own shadow."

As you become aware of your shadow self, you may wish to enter what Richard Rohr calls "The Shadowlands," walking through the valleys of your life.[142] It can be a humiliating but good journey. Walking hand in hand with your shadows and getting to know them intimately may well mean that eventually you are no longer bewildered, ambushed, or bushwhacked by their dark presence. You will no longer, as Rohr says, be "so totally humiliated by your humiliations!"[143] Remembering that your persona or your shadow is neither evil in itself nor so damnable that you must get rid of it, you simply allow yourself to hold hands with who is in the basement. Most of your close friends can see your shadow, so it's crucial that you acknowledge what everybody else knows about you—except yourself.

Rohr is quite right to say that "the closer you get to the Light, the more of your shadow you see" and for this reason "truly holy people are always humble people":

> Christians could have been done a great service if [their] shadow had been distinguished from sin. Sin and shadow are not the same. We were so encouraged to avoid sin that many of us instead avoided facing

---

141 "From Shadow-Boxing to Shadow-Hugging," *Evolving Mystics*, available at http://brucesanguin.com/from-shadow-boxing-to-shadow-hugging/.

142 Rohr, *Falling Upward*, Chapter 11.

143 Ibid., 131.

> our shadow, and then we ended up "sinning" even worse—while unaware besides! As Paul taught, "The angels of darkness must disguise themselves as angels of light" (2 Corinthians 11.14)...The shadow self invariably presents itself as something like prudence, common sense, justice, or "I am doing this for your good," when it is actually manifesting fear, control, manipulation, or even vengeance.[144]

When we courageously go down in the cellars of our lives and explore the dark underside of who we are, we are spelunkers who intimately know the terrain of what is beneath us when we come out into the daylight. Exploring the caverns with headlights on our helmets, we map out interior territories that sometimes make walking upright upstairs difficult. Realizing that others also have dark places in their lives, we will be less judgmental, simon-pure, and unctuous in the presence of others. We come to know the wisdom of Jesus's advice: "Judge not, lest you be judged," and know better how to respond to his question: "Why do you look at the speck of sawdust in your brother's eye and pay no attention to the plank in your own eye?" (Matt. 7:3). Knowing the crucial importance of shadow work, it becomes a part of our day-by-day contemplative life.

What to do with thoughts and images

As everyone (including me), however, soon finds out, in contemplative prayer thoughts do arise. We are accustomed to thinking about God rather than simply being in his presence. For this reason, we often find it necessary to give privilege to one word that will nicely stall and halt heady traffic of thinking. Yes, thinking has its place in our lives as when, for example, we want to compare house prices or talk to an attorney. But that said, there are times, holy

144 Rohr, 132–33.

and special times, when thinking is best left alone. When entering contemplative prayer, we are within special times, timeless times.

Of course, even in timeless times, we may experience all sorts of thoughts. Whatever are we to do with them? Cynthia Bourgeault answers that question with force:

> When I teach Centering Prayer introductory workshops, the hardest part of the training for most people is the instruction that during the prayer time every thought must be let go: including messages from God and mystical experience. Thomas Keating's teaching around this point is humorous but blunt: If the Blessed Virgin herself should appear to you during prayer time and offer to pluck that wound from your flesh, the answer is "Not now, Dearie, I'm doing my Centering Prayer." Ouch!!! Many people, trained to use silence as a backdrop for receiving messages, rail against this teaching and positively refuse to follow it. But Thomas Keating is correct here, and in holding the line on this difficult and counterintuitive point again clears the way that leads from mystical experience to unitive perception.[145]

We will experience thinking about thinking! It is the experience of all contemplatives that we are bombarded with thoughts—thoughts about all sort of things—a beautiful face, a terrible tragedy, a joke we remember, a courtesy we hope to give someone, a regret, a painful memory, a pious saying we recently heard, a resolve we wish to make, and so on. Within one's special and hopefully intimate twenty minutes with the Divine Presence, we may need to use our little one word a thousand times. But, as Keating reminds us, by a thousand "one-wordings" we nevertheless direct ourselves to God

145 "Mystical Experience or Unitive Seeing?," *Spiritual Paths*, December 20, 2009, available at, http://www.spiritualpaths.net/mystical-experience-or-unitive-seeing-by-cynthia-bourgeault/.

a thousand times, creating with the Spirit within the wordless and pathless way to God's already-present presence.

If you're like me, sometimes you may find that poets and artists help us see the mystery of it. Here, for example, is how poet Scott Cairns gives voice to mystic Meister Eckhart, creating "The Prayer of a Heart Detached":

> What is the prayer of a heart grown calm
> in the peace of God?
> From such a purity one no longer prays
> as we are wont to pray.
> From such a purity one is free from asking
> any further gifts of God, and is free
> also from asking that anything
> be taken away.
> A heart in calm detachment asks
> for nothing, nor has anything
> it would wish to shed.
> Its prayer is finally only for uniformity
> with God. This is its entire prayer.[146]

Three doorways

As I've practiced centering prayer over the years, subtle but important developments have presented themselves within my morning and evening quiet times. Not knowing how best to describe my interior progression, it's with gratitude that several years ago Martin Laird came to my assistance. Laird's *Into the Silent Land: A Guide to the Christian Practice of Contemplation* has helped me remember and

[146] Scott Cairns, *Love's Immensity: Mystics on the Endless Life* (Brewster, MA: Paraclete, 2007), 99–100. For books on Eckhart, I especially recommend James M. Clark, *The Great German Mystics* (New York: Russell and Russell, 1970); Matthew Fox, *Breatkthrough: Meister Eckhart's Creation Spirituality* (New York: Doubleday, 1980), Jeanne Ancelet-Hustache, *Meister Eckhart* (London: Longman, 157); and Richard Woods, *Eckhart's Way* (London: Darton, Longman and Todd, 1987).

trace the path in which I've been sitting. Perceptively Laird suggests that there are three doorways through which contemplatives pass as their practice matures.

Going through the first door, we find it necessary to make sure that we are following instructions: where and how to sit, how to mark out twenty minutes, how to decide on a sacred word, and so on. New to the practice, we want to do it right. We soon, of course, find it quite difficult or next to impossible to sit down and be physically still for twenty to thirty minutes. We are restless, busy with thinking. We acknowledge the importance of our sacred little word and learn to use it again and again when necessary. Our little word becomes a shield protecting us against a barrage of feelings, thoughts, imaginative flights, floods of memories, and cranial wonderments.

As time passes and our practice develops, we begin to move toward a second doorway. Like a dancer within the dance or a weaver with her or his loom, we eventually learn how to become one with our prayer word. Establishing our practice, with increasing effectiveness we let our prayer word be the release from our preoccupation with following thoughts. We enter simple awareness, and more and more we sense physical and emotional benefits that often accompany our practice. We discover a certain wisdom settling into our day-to-day lives as we let go of attempts to control what everybody else ought to be thinking, saying, and doing. Learning to let go of interior dialogs, we find ourselves letting go of other unnecessary conversations, especially those that give our egos privileges over others. We find ourselves in a deepening interior silence that makes it easier to give ourselves to the praying of the prayer word, even after our time for formal contemplative prayer is complete. Moreover, we realize quite deeply that this going through the second doorway is a gift from God. We are learning how effortless it is to observe and then let go of the elaborate commentaries we make about other people and their lives. Quietly our use of the prayer word is altered; no longer a protective shield against thoughts, it is more and more an invitation to stillness. More and more we are meeting thoughts with simple detachment.

And more than once, we find ourselves waiting for the third doorway to open. Without surprise we are aware that a shift is occurring. We are moving from being aware of a thought to an awareness of our being aware. More and more we enter "aware-ing" itself. Often we enter a vastness, a kind of unknowing characterized by depth, spaciousness, quietness, calmness, and one-ing. We encounter what the prophet Jeremiah imaginatively calls "our self before we were born, somewhere known by God from all eternity."[147] We are where Paul says we are—"in Christ," that is, not living our own lives but living the life of Christ who lives in us (Gal. 2:20). Sitting in darkness, our eyes closed with our little word of desire, we are in a luminous darkness with God who shines within our closeted self, "closer to us than we are to ourselves."

After some practice (for some almost immediately, for others several months, for others perhaps years, and for a few like me—within the last decades of their lives), praying in the *unknowing* gently leads one into letting go of unnecessary attachments, the gradual loss of a strident ego, and a growing openness to the Divine Presence and the needs of others. With the Spirit of God praying within, by spiritual osmosis I practice taking on the mind of Christ, his self-emptying, his sacrificial love for all creation, all people.

Centering Prayer and supportive friends

When we started meeting, there were only five or six of us in our Centering Prayer group. Now that we've been meeting for at least two hours weekly on Tuesdays for more than eight years, we've grown, and the care we give to one another is something to behold. Together we've read through and shared, sentence by sentence, Keating's *Open Heart, Open Mind*, Cynthia Bourgeault's *Centering Prayer and Inner Wakening*, *The Cloud of Unknowing* (a fourteenth-century masterpiece by an anonymous mystic), Martin Laird's *Into the Silent Land: A Guide to Christian Contemplation*, and Amos

[147] "Before I shaped you in the womb, I knew all about you" (Jer. 1:5).

Smith's *Be Still and Listen: Experience the Presence of God in Your Life*, among many others. I'm not sure what we'll do next, but whatever it is, you can be sure it will bind us even further together in mutual support as parish contemplatives.

It's okay to pray in different ways.

Someone recently asked Carl McColman, one of my favorite teachers, if contemplative Christians may practice more than one type of prayer.[148] It's very good question. Here's how Carl answered:

> Christian spiritual practices are different in some ways from other contemplative traditions, like various schools of Buddhism. I think it's common in eastern spiritual traditions to have a more structured discipline of meditation—in other words, more of an emphasis on following the instructions of your teacher, and of keeping a consistent practice—one specific technique of meditation, or not changing the mantra, that sort of thing.
>
> In the Christian tradition, an emphasis on structure is found more in the liturgy than in individual prayer or meditation practice. There's a "right way" to pray the Daily Office, which is usually done in a community setting. But when it comes to private practices, like lectio divina or various forms of "mental" or contemplative prayer, there seems to be more latitude.
>
> As one of my monastic teachers was fond of saying, "pray as you can—not as you can't."
>
> So that said, I know of no Christian teacher of prayer or meditation who requires his or her students

[148] I have edited Carl's response; for his full response, see "Two Questions on the Practice of Silent Prayer," available on Carl's blog at http://www.patheos.om/blogs/carlmccolman/2018/09/two-questions-on-the-practice-of-silent-prayer/

to only practice one type of prayer. I myself am regularly engaging in both silent or "apophatic"[149] centering" forms of prayer, but also more content-rich, imaginative, "Ignatian" exercises. Of course, I'm a Lay Cistercian who works for the Jesuits, so naturally both of these approaches to prayer are a big part of my world!

Yes, it's possible to engage in different types of prayer or meditation. Whether it is useful to do so is another question, and since everyone is different and everyone has different needs or concerns at different points in life, it's impossible to address that issue through a blog post. This is why having a spiritual companion or spiritual director is so valuable. Being able to discuss our unique needs and challenges with a trusted guide is really essential for a maturing spiritual life.

Now, about focusing on the breath. Centering prayer, as a practice, involves using a repeated prayer word to calm and focus our attention—but there is a recognition that sometimes, the prayer word will "fall away" and the person who is praying will simply rest in the silence of the Divine Presence.

Clearly, our breath does not "fall away." But I think it is possible that our attention on our breath might open up to a more subtle, more gentle resting in a non-focused awareness of silence and presence. We still our breathing, of course; but our awareness is not focused on the breath.

---

149 Apophatic theology, also known as negative theology, is a form of theological thinking and religious practice which attempts to approach God, the Divine, by negation, to speak only in terms of what may not be said about the perfect goodness that is God. The apophatic tradition is often, though not always, allied with the approach of mysticism, which aims at the vision of God, the perception of the divine reality beyond the realm of ordinary perception

> In my experience, such graced moments of non-focused awareness seem timeless, so it's hard to say how long they last. A few seconds? Maybe longer? I'm sure it varies. But what usually happens in my prayer is that eventually my "inner commentator" will chime in, usually with some variation of "Isn't this wonderful!?!"
>
> And at that point, I realize that I am distracted, and so I return to resting my attention on my breath.

My own practice is much like Carl's.

Want to begin?

If you'd like to begin or find support for practicing contemplative prayer and don't know where to start, see Appendix A: The Method of Centering Prayer. Also try visiting Contemplative Outreach, Ltd. at www.contemplativeoutreach.org and click on Getting Started. You'll find a wealth of resources, listings of workshops and retreats, an online course, an in-home training package, and lots of information about local Centering Prayer support groups. You'll also discover that Contemplative Outreach, Ltd. provides four free Centering Prayer Online contemplative communities for those interested in entering Centering Prayer and for those already practicing it as taught by Fr. Thomas Keating OCSO and Contemplative Outreach, Ltd. Those interested may apply at any time. Experienced Centering Prayer practitioners moderate each group.

For Further Consideration

Haas, Peter Traben. *A Beautiful Prayer: Answering Common Misperceptions about Centering Prayer.* ContemplativeChristians.com, 2014.

Heuertz, Phileena. *Pilgrimage of a Soul: Contemplative Spirituality for the Active Life.* Downers Grove, IL: InterVarsity Press, 2017.

Houselander, Caryll. *Essential Writings: Selected with Commentary by Wendy M. Wright.* Maryknoll, NY: Orbis Books, 2005.

Hunt, John D. *Centering Prayer: Journey to Divine Union and Healing.* Colorado Springs, CO: Upper Gate Publishing, 2017.

Huston, Paula. *A Season of Mystery: 10 Spiritual Practices for Embracing a Happier Second Half of Life.* Chicago, IL: Loyola Press, 2012.

Smith, Paul R. *Is Your God Big Enough? Close Enough? You Enough? Jesus and the Three Faces of God.* St. Paul, MN: Paragon House, 2017.

Soering, Jens. *The Way of the Prisoner: Breaking the Chains of Self through Centering Prayer and Centering Practice.* New York: Lantern Books, 2003.

Rapsas, Tom. "A 4-step guide to the prayer that's 'better than meditation'." *Wake Up Call*; available at https://www.patheos.com/blogs/wakeupcall/2018/05/a-4-step-guide-to-the-prayer-thats-better-than-meditation/

Thibodeaux, Mark E. *Armchair Mystic: Easing into Contemplative Prayer.* Cincinnati: St. Anthony Messenger Press, 2001.

Chapter 10

LIVING CONTEMPLATIVELY

The mind that is the prisoner of conventional ideas,
and the will that is the captive of its own desire,
cannot accept the seeds of an unfamiliar truth
and a supernatural desire . . . .
I must learn therefore to let go of the familiar and the usual
and consent to what is new and unknown to me.
I must learn to leave myself in order to find
myself yielding to the love of God.
—Thomas Merton, *New Seeds of Contemplation*

Appreciating, honoring, and integrating the first half of life

I'm now in what Richard Rohr calls "the second half of life." I no longer think, act, believe, and love as before. I'm different, changed, and moving on. That being so, whatever do I do with what I've left behind, that is, my inherited identity, the first half of my life?

Today I do three things. First, I appreciate all that happened to me when I inherited my family, religious, and communal identity. My parents, church, and many friends sacrificed themselves to make sure that I was raised as a conservative Lutheran. May God bless Mom and Dad, the Lutheran Church-Missouri Synod, and everybody who started me out on life. Much of that inheritance I still keep and treasure. Sue Monk Kidd tells us why:

> There's an old Carolina story I like about a country boy who had a great talent for carving beautiful dogs out of wood. Every day he sat on his porch whittling, letting the shavings fall around him. One day a visitor, greatly impressed, asked him the secret of his art. "I just take a block of wood and whittle off the parts that don't look like a dog," he replied… In spiritual whittling, though, we don't discard the shavings. Transformation happens not by rejecting these parts of ourselves but by gathering them up and integrating them. Through this process we reach a new wholeness. Spiritual whittling is an encounter with Mystery, waiting, the silence of inner places—all those things most folks no longer have time for.[150]

I have not rejected or discarded my inherited identity; it is still with me. But I have integrated it so that it is part of a new wholeness.

Second, while appreciative of my spiritual inheritance, I'm thankful that I have been given opportunities to be critical of it. Like Sue Monk Kidd, I have been moved to think about my world and ask her question:

> If all souls developed in cookie-cutter fashion, we would have spirituality by duplication rather than by waiting and transformation. Yet the tendency exists among Christians to want everybody to be at the same place at the same time. You know how it goes. Everybody should be actively ministering. (But even

---

150 *When the Heart Waits: Spiritual Direction for Life's Sacred Questions* (New York: HarperCollins, 1992), 49.

> Jesus had seasons of waiting as well as ministering.) Everybody should be happy. (But even Jesus was at times sad, anguished, and in pain.) Everybody should be relating to God in the same way. (But even Jesus related to God in different ways—sometimes inwardly, sometimes outwardly.) What would happen if we allowed people to unfurl their wings and move into the fullness of being each in her own time and way?[151]

When I discovered that my inheritance was inadequate to the task of living with honest answers to difficult questions, my wings were unfurled. Thoughtful teachers, both Christian and otherwise, helped me fly down "the road less traveled," as Scott Peck calls it.[152] I learned, for example, that the Bible contains errors, prescientific curiosities, contradictions, and unsolvable conundrums that we would surely expect from a library of books written and gathered together nearly two thousand years ago. During my seminary years, I learned that there are in fact "terrible texts" in the Bible: numerous atrocities—rapes, murders, genocides—either performed or endorsed by "God." Moreover, when I spoke to other Christians outside the Lutheran tradition, I saw firsthand how the Bible can be interpreted in a thousand significantly different ways by non-Lutherans. And then I discovered that even Lutherans know how to split themselves into sometimes angry, warring interpretive factions. So I had to make some decisions. I saw it was necessary for me to distinguish between the whole Bible (however you define that) as the so-called inerrant word of God and the grace-filled, nonviolent ministry of Jesus as

151 Ibid., 183.

152 M. Scott Peck's *The Road Less Traveled: A New Psychology of Love, Traditional Values and Spiritual Growth* (New York: Touchstone, 1985) surely asks us to remember the last lines Robert Frost's narrative poem, "The Road Not Taken." Recent commentaries suggest that the latter is perhaps one the most misunderstood poem in our American heritage. See, for example, Karl Smallwood's "Robert Frost's Commonly Misinterpreted 'The Road Not Taken' and the Role It Played in the Death of His Best Friend," Today I Found Out, September 15, 2015, available at http://www.todayifoundout.com/index.php/2015/09/robert-frost-poem-killed-friend/.

the "Word of God": the Story of God. To put it bluntly, only Jesus is exclusively the Word of God for me. As I'll explain later in this chapter, I'm a "Red-Letter Christian."

I've decided to let God give me a newer and more extensive identity. Some call it "progressive"; others "liberal." Inasmuch as I am a paradox (simultaneously conservative and liberal), I prefer to see myself as one who has moved beyond all self-serving binary thinking. Thus, I honor the first half of my life and live fully in a wider, deeper, and more extensive second half.

Finally, I encourage others, including you, to live in what many call the way of "unitive consciousness," the "One-ing" lived by Jesus. This chapter tells you how I walk such a way—call it "contemplative," perhaps even "mystical."

Contemplative living within a Christian community

That said, I do not wish to give anyone the impression that my developing a contemplative life is somehow divorced or separate from my day-to-day life within a Christian community, mine being Lutheran. Communal living and contemplative living are inseparable. Knowing how involved I am in my local parish, in the spring of 2015, my pastor asked me to write the following article for our local newspaper:

> Representing everyone at Saint John Lutheran Church, located at 1689 Martin Luther King Jr. Parkway (next door to Ingles and across from McDonalds), I wish to thank the *Griffin Daily News* for this opportunity to tell you about our congregation, its many ministries, and its witness to the love of God.
>
> First, let me say upfront that we emphasize hospitality as a special gift to everyone. We welcome all people no matter their backgrounds, orientations,

and origins. We embrace with love every person whom we meet. As you enter our multinational, multiracial, and radically open parish, you will be embraced with the love of Christ, the gift of friendship, and the warmth of a community marked with its wall-to-wall diversity and inclusion without exception. When we say, "We welcome all, we mean 'ALL!'."

Second, with us you will personally experience the grace of God. Sharing the love of God is our special and yet very ordinary and ever-present gift to you and the world. We will present God's love to you in whatever way works best for you. If you like music, come listen to us sing. Come and hear our choir chant, belt out, purr, and make melody to the Lord and to you. Come and listen to one of Griffin's most gifted preachers, our Pastor Katie Pasch. Come and enjoy our parish breakfast every Sunday. Come for Wednesday suppers at 5:45 p.m. each Wednesday. And then stay for Evening Prayer and/or Holy Communion and Bible study.

Third, we do all to the glory of God and in many different ways. As a liturgical church, we are never stuffy or stiff; no, indeed. With us you'll find it's easy to join in the ancient and ever-new worship centered on good preaching and Holy Communion every Sunday. Yes, we are the church of Johann Sebastian Bach and large European cathedrals, but we also strum guitars and hear a harmonica now and then. All of which means that we love good liturgy, robust singing, reverence at all times, hugs and handshakes, love for children, nicely pressed vestments, a processional cross, lots of candles, beautiful art in the sanctuary, organ music, some kneeling, times for confession of sins and the ever-ready announcements of forgiveness to all, everyone, and to you. We sing hymns, spirituals, and songs that are sometimes ancient and medieval; then too we sing with joy to Hispanic melodies, German pub tunes, and Irish folk rhythms. Musically, we are universalists.

Four, we are a missional and ecumenical church supporting world-wide ministries of help for orphans, homes and food for the homeless, clothes for the nearly naked, and visits to those in hospitals, hospices, prisons, and refugee camps. Belonging to the Evangelical Lutheran Church in America and the world-wide network of Lutherans in hundreds of countries, we believe it is always God's work among us that strengthens our hands to reach out in mercy, compassion, and justice among all peoples. Our ministries are both local and global (as we say, "GLOCAL"). You find us hunting for the homeless in Griffin, opening our facilities to Alcoholics Anonymous, encouraging organizations like the Boy Scouts to meet in our fellowship hall, and helping small churches like the Seventh Day Adventists to grow and build. With more than a dozen other churches we annually serve some 1500 Thanksgiving meals to those in need of November love. At 6:00 p.m. every first and third Tuesday evening we work with Jesus in "Theology on Tap" in the upper pub room at Montego Bay Seafood House.[153] Any and all are welcome to come and explore questions of faith in a completely free ranging discussion. This year our young people will join some 35,000 other Lutheran teens in Detroit as together our national church reaches out to that city and community with God's love and our helping hands.

Finally, we are a praying church, praying for you and all people. Realizing that prayer is an offering

153 As of this printing we are now meeting at Margo's Mediterranean Cuisine in Griffin, GA, at 1:00 p.m. every Tuesday.

not only to God but also to one another, we unite ourselves in the Lord's Prayer during every service. We chant easy-to-sing litanies and make specific intercessions as our lay leaders voice our concerns during each Sunday's Holy Communion. We pray contemplatively and open ourselves to silence, the first and ever-present language of God. On Tuesdays at 10 a.m. our Centering Prayer group has been gathering together for over three years to practice wordless prayer and learn about the world and listen insightfully to the Word of God.

Well, there you have it for now. I could tell you more, but I'd like for you to discover the "more" for yourselves. Here's what I say to everyone I meet:

> Come and be with us on Sunday mornings at 8:15 and/or 11:00 am. At 9:30 we are students learning to be disciples in Sunday School and the Adult Formation classes. Breakfast is served at 9:15 am. On Wednesday evenings we share supper from 5:45 to 6:30 and then gather with our youth for worship, Scripture study, and choir practice. If you would like to be loved as you are and wish to grow in Christ, come and be with us whenever you can. Our doors are open. And we are waiting.[154]

As I hope you can tell, I've been profoundly blessed as a communicant within the community of St. John Lutheran Church.

---

[154] "Saint John Lutheran Church," *The Griffin Daily News*, April 30, 2015.

Reading the Bible as a Red-Letter Christian

As a contemplative Christian, I read the whole Bible; in fact, my Bible includes the Apocrypha, and I read it too. But it's likely that I read the Bible differently than most other Christians. Most Christians tend to think that one page in the Bible is just as good as another page somewhere else. After all, the Bible is inspired. What's written in the Book of Judges is thus on equal footings as what's written in the Gospel of Mark. Inasmuch as all the words in most Bibles are printed in black, we can call such readers "black-letter Christians."

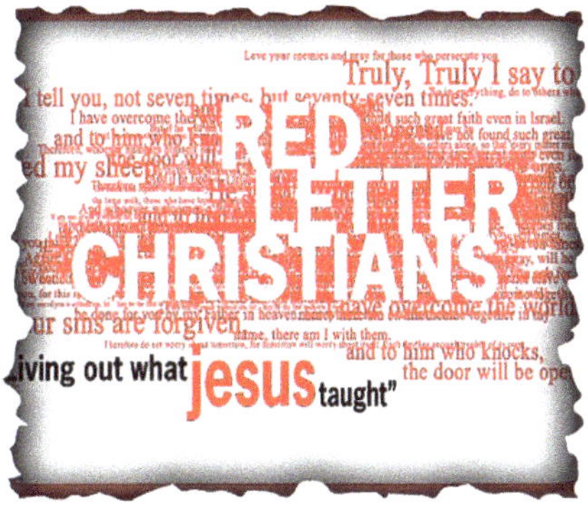

Unlike most Bibles, the words in my Bible are printed in two colors: red for the words of Jesus and black for everything else. Using such a Bible daily I, along with a growing number of other Christians, now call ourselves "Red-Letter Christians" (RLC). Why? Because the red-printed words of Jesus are the most important words ever uttered from the mouth of a human being. What Jesus says is definitively the Word of God.

Jesus often tells us that not everything in the Hebrew Scriptures is "God's word." For example, Jesus says:

> You're familiar with the command to the ancients, "Do not murder." I'm telling you that anyone who is so much as angry with a brother or sister is guilty of murder. Carelessly call a brother "idiot!" and you just might find yourself hauled into court. Thoughtlessly yell 'stupid!' at a sister and you are on the brink of hellfire. The simple moral fact is that words kill. (Matt. 5:21, *The Message*)

Words printed in the Bible's black ink are not as spiritually reliable, and trust worthy as the words spoken by the Living Word. In his Sermon on the Mount, Jesus talks not only about anger but also about adultery, retaliation, and love for one's enemies. In addition to openly criticizing what was supposed to be God's word, Jesus by his many actions demonstrates his opposition to what his co-religionists thought was God's thinking. At times he doesn't obey the Ten Commandments, especially the one about keeping the Sabbath holy. When he upsets the tables in the Temple, he commits civil disobedience. He transgresses religious boundaries and praises heretics like the Samaritans for their God-pleasing behavior. He declares the clergy of his day a bunch of phonies. Through his life, Jesus avoids recriminations and violence. When he becomes a victim on the cross, he refuses to condemn his executioners.

Jesus practices radical, nonviolent love. He tells us that violence is counterproductive: "Those who chose to live by the sword will die by the sword." When a woman gets caught in bed as an adulteress, Jesus comes to her rescue and forces her heavy-handed persecutors to lay down their stones. On one special High Holiday, when he's asked to read from the Scriptures, he edits the reading so as not to include what people expect—God's endorsement of retribution and violence. The story is in Luke 4, and here's the retelling:

Early in his wandering ministry, during a visit to Nazareth, his hometown, Jesus steps inside the local synagogue and is asked to be the Scripture reader. He agrees to be the lector; and when the time comes, after picking up a scroll containing the words of Isaiah, Jesus reads these verses:

> The Spirit of the Lord is on me, because he has anointed me to preach good news to the poor. He has sent me to proclaim freedom for the prisoners and recovery of sight for the blind, to release the oppressed, to proclaim the year of the Lord's favor.

He then rolls up the scroll, hands it back to an attendant, sits down, and makes a one-sentence statement saying, "Today this text has been fulfilled in your hearing."

What happens next is strange. It appears that his audience initially likes what Jesus says. But Jesus doesn't smile or say he's glad they liked what they heard. Instead, he sarcastically quips and reminds everybody to remember the outlandish behavior of Elijah and Elisha. Here's how Luke tells us what happened:

> I suppose you're going to quote the proverb, "Doctor, go heal yourself. Do here in your hometown what we heard you did in Capernaum." Well, let me tell you something: No prophet is ever welcomed in his hometown. Isn't it a fact that there were many widows in Israel at the time of Elijah during that three and a half years of drought when famine devastated the land, but the only widow to whom Elijah was sent was in Sarepta in Sidon? And there were many lepers in Israel at the time of the prophet Elisha but the only one cleansed was Naaman the Syrian.

It is at this point that the crowd gets hostile. They get angry and want to take him out and kill their hometown young man by throwing him off a cliff.

To make sense of what's going on, take a good hard look at what Jesus does when he opens up his "Old Testament" Bible. He decides to read Isaiah 61:1–2, one of the most popular passages among the Jews. Cited in the *Dead Sea Scrolls* and in lots of rabbinic literature, those verses were popular and memorized; Michael Hardin asks, "Have you ever seen a football game where after a touchdown somebody holds up a sign in the end zone seats that reads John 3:16?" If they had played football in Jesus's day that sign would have read "Isaiah 61:1–2."[155]

---

[155] Michel Hardin's *The Jesus Driven Life: Reconnecting Humanity with Jesus* (Lancaster, PA: IDL Press, 2010), especially Chapter 2: How Jesus Read His Bible, provides a

Isaiah 61:1–2 was popular because it's a lectionary passage for the Year of Jubilee, a kind of hoped-for Jewish Fourth of July. This was a grand text that expressed Israel's passionate desire for liberation from the bondage not only of spiritual dis-ease but also from political and economic oppression. Isaiah's verses were loaded with political dynamite. They were revolutionary, full of hope for insurrection and military rebellion.

But notice what Jesus does and doesn't do! Jesus sits down and doesn't read what everybody was expecting—Isaiah's additional verse, Isaiah's most important verse, a verse that blesses violence. Here, in full, is how Jesus should have quoted the opening verses of Isaiah 61:

> The spirit of the Lord God is upon me,
> because the Lord has anointed me;
> he has sent me to bring good news to the oppressed,
> to bind up the broken-hearted,
> to proclaim liberty to the captives,
> and release to the prisoners;
> to proclaim the year of the Lord's favour,
> ~~and the day of vengeance of our God.~~

Notice the strikethrough! Jesus omits the line verse about vengeance! He doesn't express God's hatred, anger, and vengeance against Israel's oppressors, the brutal Romans who are victimizing the Jewish people. It's no wonder the townspeople get up off their benches with a desire to throw Jesus off the cliff. Jesus is saying no to vengeance, killing, and war.

When we read Scripture as "Red Letter Christians," the words and actions of Jesus stand out forcefully in bold relief.[156] We begin

---

more thorough explication as to what happened after Jesus gave his inaugural sermon in the synagogue at Nazareth.

156 If you are interested in finding out why you too might want to become a Red Letter Christian, be sure to read Shane Claiborne and Tony Campolo, *Red Letter Revolution: WHAT IF JESUS REALLY MEANT WHAT HE SAID* (Nashville: Thomas Nelson, 2012). The book will change the way you listen to the Word of God, transforming your life.

to see and learn how Jesus redacts and edits the Hebrew Scripture regarding issues such as church worship, racism, civil disobedience, politics, hell, women, homosexuality, war and violence, reconciliation, and missions. Quite remarkably we begin to take on, as St. Paul say, "the mind of Christ."

If you would like to give special attention to the "red-lettered" voice of Christ, you don't have to buy a "Red Letter Bible." Save your money by taking whatever Bible translation you prefer or use, put a red felt-tip pen in your hand, and highlight for yourself the words of Jesus as you read them. You'll be surprised at the transformation that will take place in your thinking as you "put on the mind of Christ"!

Just a typical parishioner

None of this is to let you imagine that I'm more than an ordinary communicant at Saint John Lutheran Church. I'm not. Many in our parish put much more time and talent into the workload of Jesus. Some gather and distribute food and meals for the homeless; others maintain the lawns and buildings, and others teach classes. Others serve on the parish council. Three or four play guitars to accompany our singing Holden Evening Prayer on Wednesdays.[157] Opportunities abound, and many who understand discipleship as a life of service place themselves under the lordship of Jesus. At the end of every Sunday service, at the sanctuary door we gather under the large "I AM the Way" icon to remind one another:

> Assistant: We are called by the Holy Spirit.
> Congregation: We are called to equip saint and sent
> to proclaim Christ.

[157] *Holden Evening Prayer* was written in 1985–86 while Marty Holden was the musician-in-residence at Holden Village, a Lutheran retreat center in Washington State. This lovely setting of vespers follows the traditional form while using contemporary and inclusive language. For more information, visit GIA Publications, Inc. at giamusic.com.

Assistant: Go in peace. Proclaim God's love in Christ
to all people.
Congregation: Thanks be to God!

For Further Consideration

Campolo, Tony. *Red Letter Christians Guide to Faith & Politics.* Ventura, CA: Regal, 2008.

Claiborne, Shane, and Tony Campolo. *Red Letter Revolution: What if Jesus Really Meant What He Said.* Nashville: Thomas Nelson, 2012.

Cyzewski, Ed. *Flee, Be Silent, Pray: An Anxious Evangelical Finds Peace with God through Contemplative Prayer* (2017).

Finey, James. *The Contemplative Heart.* Notre Dame, IN: Sorin Books, 2000.

Laird, Martin. *Into the Silent Land: A Guide to the Christian Practice of Contemplation.* Oxford: Oxford University Press, 2006.

Marion, Jim. *Putting on the Mind of Christ: The Inner Work of Christian Spirituality.* Charlottesville, VA: Hampton Road, 2011.

McColman, Carl. *Answering the Contemplative Call: First Steps on the Mystical Path.* Charlottesville, VA: Hampton Roads Publishing Company, 2013.

Chapter 11

SHARING GOD'S MYSTICAL PRESENCE

Beautiful are the youth
whose rich emotions flash and burn,
whose lithe bodies filled with energy and grace
sway in their happy dance of life;
and beautiful likewise are the mature
who have learned compassion and patience, charity and wisdom, though they be rarer far than beautiful youth.
But most beautiful and most rare is a gracious old age
which has drawn from life the skill to take its varied strands: the harsh advance of age, the pang of grief,
the passing of dear friends, the loss of strength,
and with fresh insight weave them
into a rich and gracious pattern all its own.
This is the greatest skill of all,
to take the bitter with the sweet and make it beautiful,
to take the whole of life in all its moods,
its strengths and weaknesses,
and of the whole make one great and celestial harmony.
—Terry Weston, "Most Beautiful"

Pastor Katie's encouragement to share

Pastor Katherine Pasch

As St. John parish's recent materfamilias, Pastor Katie was our shepherd for more than twenty-five years. Gentle, firm, quiet, and outspoken when necessary, Katie wrote out all her sermons, delivered them with charming life-changing effectiveness, and managed a multitude of programs designed to promote justice and compassion for all people wherever possible. A quiet liberal who was fully aware that she shepherds lots of conservatives, Pastor Katie chooses her words carefully, seldom compromised, and was well into the practice of introducing good liturgical innovations without calling attention to undue pomp and circumstance. Always available, her workweek was easily in the fifty-plus hours. If there is ever a woman worthy of the cloth, Katie is at the front of the line. Pastor Katie's parish within The Evangelical Lutheran Church in America (ELCA) promotes, endorses, and encourages the radical proclamation of the Gospel, genuine hospitality to everyone, the possibility of same-sex marriages, ordinations of qualified straights and GLBTQs, and social ministries designed to help the poor, especially the homeless. We are so blessed to have experienced her love, witness, and leadership as our parish pastor. Pastor Katie laid the solid foundation for all that our congregation is now building--strong relationships with all people.

Our GLBTQ friends

Like many older folks in our congregation, as a young Lutheran boy and well into my twenties, I was taught that it was necessary to condemn all people who identify themselves as "lesbian, gay, bisexual, transgendered, or questioning" (LGBTQ). I avoided them because we were told such folks are a disease in society. Until I was in my mid-thirties, I thought that way. But after some fifty years of research and study (especially Biblical study), I became convinced that my conservative Lutheran way of approaching homosexual realities was no longer acceptable. Many books, conversations, and testimonies have confirmed my evolving understandings.[158]

Yes, I am aware that the word "abomination" is used in some Bible translations to describe the sexual propensities of our LGBTQ friends and neighbors. That's true enough. But it is also true that the Hebrew words translated as "abominations" (for example, *toevah* pronounced to'eváh)[159] occurs over a hundred times in the Hebrew Bible. Lots and lots of things in the Bible are "abominations." Proverbs 6 tells us that "There are six things that the Lord hates, seven that are an abomination to him: haughty eyes, a lying tongue, and hands that shed innocent blood, a heart that devises wicked plans, feet that make haste to run to evil, a false witness who breathes out lies, and one who sows discord among brothers."

---

158 Peter Gomes' five-star *The Good Book: Reading the Bible with Mind and Heart* is number one on my list. I also recommend Gary David Comstock's *Gay Theology without Apology* (Cleveland, OH: Pilgrim Press, 1993). Comstock finds God's liberating connection in body experience. He shows that only in taking our lives seriously can we be lovers of the world. These essays are both a judgment on church oppression and a charter of hope for gay/lesbian/bisexual and transgendered Christians on the edges of the church. His critique of heterosexism in the Bible leads to a creative search for meaning in the lives of those struggling for wholeness and new life in community. He makes a persuasive case for the richer, more erotic, more just, and loving humanness of every one of us.

For Lutheran Christians, I recommend *A Study of Issues Concerning Homosexuality: Report of the Advisory Committee of Issues Relating to Homosexuality Lutheran Church in America* (1986). Members of my parish's church council have consistently found this resource a helpful study guide. For information on how a Lutheran congregation becomes an Reconciling in Christ (RIC) parish, visit https://www.reconcilingworks.org/get-involved/become-an-ric-congregation.

159 The term *toevah* (and its plural, *toevot*) occurs 103 times in the Hebrew Bible, and almost always has the connotation of a non-Israelite cultic practice. In the Torah, the primary *toevah* is *avodah zara*, foreign forms of worship, and most others flow from it. The Israelites are instructed not to commit *toevah* because other nations do so. A close contextual reading of the term *toevah* suggests that while something is permissible in one group, it is forbidden in anther another group. Quite often *toevah* means simply means that something is "taboo." For further clarification, see Bill Fowler, "What Does the Bible Label as an Abomination? Available at http://yellowstonetheology.org/bible-label-abomination/

Many Christians, however, don't realize is that in addition to idolatry and sowing discard among brothers, the following are also labeled as abominations:

a) Wearing clothes of the opposite sex (Dt. 22:5)
b) Having sexual relations with a menstruating spouse (Ezek. 18:6)
c) Eating pork (Is. 66.17)
d) Having tattoos placed on your body (Lev. 19.28)
e) Eating shrimp or shellfish (Lev. 11:9-12)
f) Sowing fields with two kinds of seed (Lev. 19.19)
g) Wearing clothing made from mixing two kinds of fabrics (Lev. 19.19)

As lovers of shrimp, lobster, and Cajun crayfish, we can't believe that eating fried shrimp on our plates at our favorite restaurant is a *toevah*, an abomination. Neither do we chastise our wives and daughters when they wear what used to look like men's pants. No do we declare them abominable when they go to the tattoo parlor and come home with images on their arms, legs, and elsewhere. Although such habits and practices are common among us, we don't see Christians in an uproar over eating bacon, catfish and shellfish, and ordering chocolate-covered grasshoppers from amazon.com a problem.[160] Are our men's prayer breakfasts and catfish fries in jeopardy? What about our desiring the carved images of gold and silver in the world around us (Deut. 7:25)? Shouldn't we be declaring the Academy Awards to be an abomination? Is it possible that our coveted sports trophy on the mantelpiece is an abomination to the LORD as well?

I and others in my local parish are aware that what we once as a nation considered good and/or bad has undergone radical change in our thinking as time goes by. For almost two thousand years, many Christians found it impossible to image anything wrong about owning African-Americans as personal property. Christians

160 See Deut. 14:3-19.

owned slaves, sold slave children, and impregnated slave women without any feelings of guilt. After all, they argued, there is not a word against slavery anywhere in the Bible. It took a Civil War between the North and the South to get us where we re today. And still today, many Christians still think it's unbiblical and wrong for churches to have women as pastors. Who's right? Why the changes in our thinking? Can we also undergo change in our understanding of sexual orientations? Can our understanding of the Bible about sexual orientations undergo re-evaluation?

We now know that no one chooses to be gay. Sometimes babies are born as hermaphrodites, without clear and definite gender identities.[161] Yes, those opposed to homosexuality regularly describe being gay as a choice, despite all evidence to the contrary.[162] What is never explained is why people would make this choice in the first place. Sexual orientation--as scientists, physicians, psychiatrists, psychologists, therapists, and councilors now tell us--is a spectrum with many possible manifestations.

Many Christian churches world-wide now welcome people from the LGBTQ community as fellow Christians and dear friends.[163] Among many in the United States are congregations of Baptist, Episcopalian, Lutheran, Pentecostal, and Presbyterian persuasion. Among Lutherans there are now 865 Reconciling in Christ (RIC) congregations with 385 Lutheran Faith Communities on their

---

161 A hermaphrodite is an individual who is born with variations of both male and female reproductive sex organs. However, usually one set is not fully developed. This occurs in about 1.7 percent of all human births.

162 So-called "conversion therapy," sometimes known as "reparative therapy," is a range of dangerous and discredited practices that falsely claim to change a person's sexual orientation or gender identity or expression. Such practices have been rejected by every mainstream medical and mental health organization for decades, but due to continuing discrimination and societal bias against LGBTQ people, some practitioners continue to conduct conversion therapy. Minors are especially vulnerable, and conversion therapy can lead to depression, anxiety, drug use, homelessness, and suicide.

163 A "List of Christian denominations affirming LGBT" is available at https://en.wikipedia.org/wiki/List_of_Christian_denominations_affirming_LGBT.

journey to becoming RIC congregations.[164] Lutheran churches identifying themselves as RIC welcome the LGBTQ community!

Finally, we know what Jesus the Christ says about the LGBTQ among us as he lived in a country under Roman rule and populated with LGBTQ living with and around him.[165] Jesus says not a word about LGBTQ people. They were and are simply part of the general population. Although Jesus repeatedly criticizes those who divorce their spouses, he is quiet about people who identify themselves at LGBTQ. We might well be quiet too.

A wonderful confirmation came in the fall of 2011 while June and I were vacationing in Santa Fe, New Mexico. On Monday evening, October 31, I made this entry in m y journal:

> After arriving at our resort on Saturday afternoon, June and I wanted to attend worship on Sunday, and I found directions to the Christ Lutheran Church in the Yellow Pages. We called the parish and got a recording listing the time of services. Although we had no idea what to expect, we decided to go. On Sunday morning we got dressed, had breakfast, and drove over to participate in the Eucharist. What a wonderful surprise! Upon entering the church, I looked up and read this large four-by-eight-foot notice, so colorful that I photographed it right away. Take a look!

164 For more information, visit https://www.reconcilingworks.org/ric/

165 For a description of homosexuality as practiced by the Roman rulers and soldiers living in the Holy Land, read "Homosexuality in Ancient Rome," available at https://en.wikipedia.org/wiki/Homosexuality_in_ancient _Rome

Christ Lutheran Church is a "Reconciling in Christ" (RIC) parish, one of some six hundred Lutheran churches that publicly welcome lesbian, gay, bisexual, and transgender believers. After completing a program of education, discussion, and mutual discernment, a congregation, synod, or other organization joins the program in one of several ways: by having its council (or equivalent body) approve the "Affirmation of Welcome" or by having a vote of the whole congregation. This "Affirmation of Welcome" must state "lesbian, gay, bisexual, and transgender," "LGBT," "people of all sexual orientations and gender identities."

For a Lutheran congregation to become a RIC parish is not without its difficulties. No one congregation that I know of claims that every person in the congregation is in full agreement with everyone else. Yet beyond reservations and disagreements, a transcendent and agapeic love for one another in the church binds everyone together in Christ. My Lutheran congregation in Griffin is now in the process of exploring the possibility of becoming a RIC parish. We're on the way, but not there yet. I'm praying that someday my little church, St. John Lutheran Church in Griffin, Georgia, soon we'll join hands with Christ parish in Santa Fe, New Mexico, and openly welcome our LGBTQ friends, visitors, and neighbors.

With the Divine Presence who introduced us to four Haitian young men in 2009!

Those of us who went on a mission trip to the small mountain village of Ranquitte in northern Haiti in January, 2009, were blessed to meet four young men as our translators: Johnson and John-Smith Deshommes, Stevenson Dimanche, and Andronic Hillaire. As young upper-level high school students, each spoke four languages: Creole, French, Spanish, and English! We all admired them immensely. And before we left to fly back to the States, we promised to help them educationally. Eventually with God's help that happened.[166] After years of university education in Haiti and the United States Johnson and Stevenson are now licensed physicians, Andronic will soon be certified, and John-Smith now oversees an orphanage in Port-au-Prince. What's truly wonderful about these four men is that they are committed to staying in Haiti as professional citizens of a country that deeply needs their professional ministries. Yes, they might well come to the United States and eventually become citizens, working somewhere in the States. But they have chosen to serve their own nation, their own people. And in doing so they are helping, as Jesus put it, "the least of these," their Haitian brothers and sisters.

166 Read how it all happened in Pat Mundt's historical sketch, available at http://www.gracemissionsinc.org/aboutgm.aspx

January 2009

University Students

Dr. Johnson Deshommes

Dr. Andronic Hillaire

Dr. Stevenson Dimanche

John - Smith Deshommes

With our Haitian sisters at *Chez Moi*

Pat Mundt and Marie Major

Delette Matheus

It's been an exceptionally wonderful pleasure to know two Haitian-born women—Marie Major and her daughter, Delette Matheus. Their love for "the least of God's children" in Haiti has changed the direction of so many lives. Here's the back story. While on our way home from Ranquitte, where a team of us with Christian Flights International[167] had been building small concrete-block, two-room homes for the poorest in the village, we went walking one afternoon in a section of Port-au-Prince called Bon Repos. Along the way, we noticed an orphanage and school filled with little girls. Inquisitive, we knocked on the gated door and were welcomed by Marie Major, the foundress of the Grace Orphanage. We soon became friends; months later Marie visited us in Kentucky several times even as we began traveling to her home, staying in her large guest house.[168]

Then it happened: on January 12, 2010, a magnitude 7.0 Mw earthquake not only killed an estimated 240,000 Haitians, it also destroyed the orphanage, nearly everything Marie had built to house, feed, and educate some thirty orphan Haitian girls.

---

[167] For information about Christian Flights International, visit http://christianflights.org/cgi/wp/.

[168] For more of what God did and updates visit http://www.gracemissionsinc.org/history.aspx.

Before the earthquake

After the earthquake

During the earthquake the girls and staff escaped the collapsing building without injury, and temporary accommodations were found for the survivors. In the spring of 2012, Delette moved the girls to a rented property in a better location. In early 2014 under Delette's guidance, a small ecumenical group of Christians we organized ourselves as Grace Missions, Inc., a registered 501(c) 3 non-profit Christian charitable organization incorporated in Barnesville, GA. In the summer of 2014, a team visited Haiti searching for property to purchase. We wanted a building that was structurally sound with room for possible expansion, a place we could renovate to meet our future needs. We found a 3,000 square-foot home on one acre and purchased it, enabling us to offer our girls a safe place with a large steel-gate, surrounded with twelve-foot high concrete block walls. Known as *Chez Moi* (French for "My Home") it now provides comfortable quarters for thirty young orphaned girls, along with beds for visiting mission teams. In 2017 students and from the University of Kentucky under the leadership of Professor Bruce Swetnam visited *Chez Moi*, made wonderful improvements, and initiated detailed plans for further expansions. Today the girls, headmaster Renal Ochasmar and his wife Gina, along with three staff adults live in the home and on the property at 17 Ruelle de la paix Lilavois 1, Bon Repos, Port-au-Prince, Haiti. It's our hope that in the coming decade we'll be able to continue to build on the property and eventually house some seventy girls.[169]

[169] If you would like to help, go to www.gracemissionsinc.org and let us know how we can work together.

Chez Moi (French meaning "My Home")

With other Christians and other religious traditions

The Presence in the Midst
J. Doyle Penrose, 1916

I like to be with Christians in traditions other than my own. On the first and second Sundays of each month I drive down to Macon to be with a small group of my Quaker friends. In afternoon meetings at a Unitarian church, we sit quietly for about thirty minutes, greet one another with a handshake and then discuss books like Pink Danlion's *The Quakers: A Very Short Introduction.*

Recently I've been invited to attend the Friday gatherings of my Muslim friends in Griffin. To be honest, I don't understand a lot of what is said and done because many of the prayers and reading are in Arabic from *The Qu'ran*. But slowly the fifty or so attendees and I are becoming friends. Dr. Mahmood Ahmed, a Griffin physician and the local imam at Griffin's Islamic Center, generally gives a twenty-minute talk. After prayers, we share greetings and responses to questions as I try to understand what it means to be a Muslim in the Sunni tradition.

Dr. Mahmood Ahmed, friend Basil, and me

The impetus for such a relationship came about a year ago when a dozen of us in Theology on Tap worked our way through Brian D. McClaren's *Why Did Jesus, Moses, the Buddha, and Mohammed Cross the Road?* And, of course, it helped that while teaching at EKU, I shared parts of The *Qu'ran* with the help of my Muslim students in college literature classes. Years earlier in the mid-80s, the witness of Thomas Merton jump-started it all when I read how he described an important part of his prayer life to Abdul Aziz:

Strictly speaking I have a very simple way of prayer. It is centered entirely on attention to the presence of God and to His will and His love. That is to say that it is centered *on faith* by which alone we can know the presence of God. One might say this gives my meditation the character described by the Prophet as "being before God as if you saw Him." Yet it does not mean imagining anything or conceiving a precise image of God, for to my mind this would be a kind of idolatry. On the contrary, it is a matter of adoring Him as invisible and infinitely beyond our comprehension and realizing Him as all. My prayer tends very much toward what you call *fana.* There is in my heart this great thirst to recognize totally the nothingness of all that is not God. My prayer is then a kind of praise rising up out of the center of Nothing and Silence. If I am still present as "myself,"' this I recognize as an obstacle about which I can do nothing unless He Himself removes the obstacle. If He wills, He can then make the Nothingness into a total clarity.

I do not ordinarily write about such things and ask you therefore to be discreet about it. But I write this as a testimony of confidence and friendship. It will show you how much I appreciate the tradition of Sufism. Let us therefore adore and praise God and pray to Him for the world which is in great trouble and confusion. I am united with you in prayer during this month of Ramadan and will remember you on the Night of Destiny. I appreciate your prayers for me. May the Most High God send His blessing upon you and give you peace." [170]

Reading those words from Merton to Addul Aziz was my first introduction to centering prayer. And in visiting the Islamic Center in nearby Griffin, GA, I've come to appreciate what Barbara Brown Taylor shares in her *Holy Envy: Finding God in the Faith of Others.*[171] The title of her book comes from Biblical scholar Krister Stendahl (after whom I named my second son), who proposed three rules of religious understanding:

---

170 Letter from Thomas Merton to a Pakistani Sufi scholar, Abdul Aziz, written in 1966, from *The Hidden Ground of Love: The Letters of Thomas Merton on Religious Experience and Social Concerns,* ed. William H. Shannon (New York: Farrar Straus Giroux, 1985), 63-64. Reprinted in *Light from Light: An Anthology of Christian Mysticism,* 2nd edition, revised and updated, ed. Louis Dupre and James A Wiseman, OSB (New York: Paulist Press, 2001), 455-456.

171 (New York: HarperCollins, 2019).

1. When trying to understand another religion, you should ask the adherents of that religion and not its enemies.
2. Don't compare your best to their worst.
3. Leave room for holy envy.

When with my Muslim friends on Friday afternoons, I have indeed experienced holy envy, especially when realizing how often they pray every day. Observing *salat,* the second of Five Pillars,[172] they pray at each day's dawn before sunrise, at midday after the sun passes it highest, at the late part of the afternoon, just after sunset, and finally between sunset and midnight. It's not the length of the prayers that matters; it's pausing five times every twenty-four hours to live within their relationship with God. And if a Muslim prays without the proper attitude, it is as if he had not bothered to pray at all. After all, the *Qur'an* says, "Woe to those who pray, but are unmindful, or who pray only to be seen by people" (107.4-6). That sounds a lot like what Jesus say in Matthew's Gospel (6.6). My Muslim friends in prayer encourage me to be in prayer with God as they are: often.

My Muslim friends have also given me several books to read: Abdul-Rahman Alsheha's *The Key to Understanding the Kor*an, among others. All of which means that I am now reading the Muslim's holy book more than before, especially *The Qur'an: with References to the Bible,* translated by a team of two: Safi Kaskas (a Muslim) and David Hungerford (a Christian), along with several commentaries. May God keep my friendship with my Islamic neighbors beautiful to behold.

I am what I am: a universalist

What I will say next may come as a surprise, perhaps even a shock to some of you. It comes, however, after more than twenty

[172] The Five Pillars of Islam are five basic rules that all Muslims are urged to follow: : *shahādah*, the Muslim profession of faith; *ṣalāt*, or prayer, performed in a prescribed manner five times each day; *zakāt*, the alms tax levied to benefit the poor and the needy; *ṣawm*, fasting during the month of Ramadan; and hajj, the major pilgrimage to Mecca, if financial and physical conditions permit.

years of a "one'd" life with God. It has come upon me as an awareness of my "one'd" life with all life in its entirety. It's not a particularly idiosyncratic view of life, for it has been the vision of many before me, especially the vision of many Christians who have come to live beyond their own institutional boundaries, especially if those boundaries have been drawn by narrow-minded authority figures as is so often the case in organizations both secular and religious.

I say it bluntly (and hope you will stick with me). I am a universalist in that I know, living in the mystery of God's presence, that God in Christ refuses to be bordered or his grace hemmed in by doctrines, traditions, bookish notions, or religious teachings. The New Testament quite openly says so, as William Barclay[173] reminds us:

> First, there is the fact that there are things in the New Testament which more than justify this belief. Jesus said: "I, when I am lifted up from the earth, will draw all men to myself" (John 12:32). Paul writes to the Romans: "God has consigned all men to disobedience that he may have mercy on all" (Rom. 11:32). He writes to the Corinthians: "As in Adam all die, so also in Christ shall all be made alive" (1 Cor. 15:22); and he looks to the final total triumph when God will be everything to everyone (1 Cor. 15:28). In the First Letter to Timothy we read of God "who desires all men to be saved and to come to the knowledge of the truth," and of Christ Jesus "who gave himself as

[173] Barclay is a Scottish author, who was a radio and television presenter, Church of Scotland minister, and Professor of Divinity and Biblical Criticism at the University of Glasgow. He's known especially for his New Testament commentaries that are housed in thousands of church libraries of every denomination, especially within Baptist churches. Out of a lifetime of scholarship, Barclay has explained every verse in *The New Daily Study Bible*, a seventeen-volume set commentaries on the New Testament. Barclay knows the New Testament as well as anyone, and his overall conviction is "in the end all men will be gathered into the love of God."

> a ransom for all" (1 Tim 2:4–6). The New Testament itself is not in the least afraid of the word *all*.[174]

In fact, we are already one! Surely, Richard Rohr is right when he posted these announcements online in a *Daily Meditation*:

> There was no place in the universe that was separate from the originating power of the universe. Each thing of the universe had its very roots in this realm.
>
> —Brian Swimme and Thomas Berry

> There is only Christ. He is everything and he is in everything.
>
> —Colossians 3:11

Surprisingly, it was a Roman Catholic priest who first proposed the Big Bang theory of the origin of the universe. Georges Lemaître, a Belgian priest, astronomer, and physics professor, not only proposed the theory of the expansion of the universe, he was the first to note in 1927 that the expanding universe might be traced back to a single point of origin called a singularity. As Ilia Delio describes, "Science would say it appeared like a little quantum size blip on the screen [creatio ex nihilo] and inflated rapidly like a balloon and since that time, it has been expanding." I'll let Delio, a scientist, explain the implications for this cosmology—our story of the universe:

> Every human person desires to love and to be loved, to belong to another, because we come from another. We are born social and relational. We yearn to belong, to be part of a larger whole that includes not only friends and family but neighbors, community, trees, flowers, sun, earth, stars. We are born of nature and are part

174 This and all the following quotations are from Barclay's "I Am a Convinced Universalist," available at www.auburn.edu/~allenk/barclay1.htm.

> of nature; that is, we are born into a web of life and are part of a web of life. We cannot know what this means, however, without seeing ourselves within the story of the Big Bang universe. Human life must be traced back to the time when life was deeply one, a Singularity, whereby the intensity of mass-energy exploded into consciousness. Deep in our DNA we belong to the stars, the trees, and the galaxies.
>
> Deep within we long for unity because, at the most fundamental level, we are already one. We belong to one another because we have the same source of love; the love that flows through the trees is the same love that flows through my being...We are deeply connected in this flow of love, beginning on the level of nature where we are the closest of kin because the earth is our mother.
>
> We began as one and our goal is oneness. Studying evolution, Teilhard de Chardin found that increased complexity and increased consciousness ironically lead to greater unity at a much higher level—which we would call love. We must always be reminded, it seems, that unity is not the same as uniformity. Not at all! With increased complexity, there is actually greater diversity and a greater enjoyment of that very diversity, which is the fruit of love. As Teilhard says, "Everything that rises must converge." We are in the midst of that convergence today—and seemingly at an accelerated pace—both in terms of good and resistance to the good.[175]

Having referenced the New Testament's and God's inclusive love for all and everyone, it should not come as an additional surprise that I no longer believe in hell in any traditional sense. I'm not sure I ever did.

175 Qtd. Richard Rohr, "We Are Already One," *Daily Meditation* (November 4, 2015), available at http://www.cac.org.

Even when I was a Lutheran pastor, years ago, I don't ever remember saying a word about it, not in the pulpit, not anytime, anywhere. Yes, of course, you say, the Bible mentions it. Yes. And it mentions a whole of other things I no longer believe in any literal manner. But back to hell. Here's what I think about it as again Barclay speaks for me:

> One of the key passages is Matthew 25:46 where it is said that the rejected go away to eternal punishment, and the righteous to eternal life. The Greek word for punishment is *kolasis*, which was not originally an ethical word at all. It originally meant the pruning of trees to make them grow better. I think it is true to say that in all Greek secular literature *kolasis* is never used of anything but remedial punishment. The word for eternal is *aionios*. It means more than everlasting, for Plato—who may have invented the word—plainly says that a thing may be everlasting and still not be *aionios*. The simplest way to out it is that *aionios* cannot be used properly of anyone but God; it is the word uniquely, as Plato saw it, of God. Eternal punishment is then literally that kind of remedial punishment which it befits God to give and which only God can give.

All of which means that it's impossible to stuff the grace of God in any kind of a box and nail it shut. It's impossible, as Barclay says "to set limits to the grace of God. I believe that not only in this world, but in any other world there may be, the grace of God is still effective, still operative, still at work. I do not believe that the operation of the grace of God is limited to this world. I believe that the grace of God is as wide as the universe." With Barclay, I believe that when all is said and done, God, whom St. John defines as "love," will triumph completely when as St. Paul says, "all things will be subject to him, and God will be everything to everyone" (1 Cor. 15:24–28):

> If one man remains outside the love of God at the end of time, it means that that one man has

> defeated the love of God—and that is impossible. Further, there is only one way in which we can think of the triumph of God. If God was no more than a King or Judge, then it would be possible to speak of his triumph, if his enemies were agonizing in hell or were totally and completely obliterated and wiped out. But God is not only King and Judge, God is Father—he is indeed Father more than anything else. No father could be happy while there were members of his family forever in agony. No father would count it a triumph to obliterate the disobedient members of his family. The only triumph a father can know is to have all his family back home. The only victory love can enjoy is the day when its offer of love is answered by the return of love. The only possible final triumph is a universe loved by and in love with God.

Of course you may ask what in the world do we do with those words of Jesus in John's Gospel when he says, "I am the way, and the truth, and the life; no one comes to the Father, but through me" (John 14:6). Please pay attention. When Jesus says those words, it's of utmost importance to remember that he is sitting around a big table with the disciples in a private moment, getting them ready for the time when he will leave them, and telling them to follow him where he is going. They ask, "But how will we know the way?" To this question regarding direction, Jesus answers, "I am the way." Please notice that Jesus is not preaching to the world here; he is simply giving brotherly comfort and guidance to his close friends who are afraid of becoming lost without him: "Remember what I've shown you, fellas, stick with it, and you'll be fine." Thus "I" in the upper room means "what you've seen me do is the path." The "I" of Jesus is the way he gives himself as a model of compassion, forgiveness, a means of reconciliation, all of which he personifies, exemplifies, and puts into action. Jesus is using a metaphor to tell us that it's really his manner of life that is going to prove truthful. In short, when we walk the Jesus Way, then by faith we have Jesus, life in abundance, a life that guides and takes us into the truth of living with God.

This is my understanding of Jesus's announcement, and I am not alone. Scholars and theologians tell us that in the early centuries of Christian faith and life, most Christians were not only in love with Jesus, but they were also walkers in the Way and universalists. They saw God's grace in Jesus and God's grace at work throughout the whole world. Influential Christian leaders like Clement of Alexandria (150–220), Origin (185–254), Macrina the Younger (324–80), Gregory of Nyssa (335–94), among others, were keenly aware that God was at work everywhere and in everyone. Johannes Scotus Erigena (815–77), Meister Eckhart (1260–1328), John of Ruysbroek (1293–1381), Julian of Norwich (1342–1416), along with many Anabaptists and Moravians, were universalists, convinced that the grace of God is universally everywhere. And in our own times, we know that many like Barclay in the United Church of Christ, many in the Disciples of Christ Church, and lots of Christians in the Evangelical Lutheran Church of America openly teach the salvation of all.[176]

---

176 If you wish to more fully explore the nature of God's radical grace and inclusion, read Phillip Gulley and James Mulholland, *If Grace Is True and If God Is Love* (New York: HarperCollins, 2003). Gulley as a Quaker and Mulholland as an American Baptist work together interdenominationally to send one message with one voice: God will save every person. I highly recommend this book for people questioning or recovering from fundamentalism.

For more concerning God's realized grace for all, see Thomas Allin and Mark T. Chamberlain, *Every Knee Shall Bow: The Case for Christian Universalism* (Maitland, FL: Xulon, 2005); Stephen Prothero, *God is Not One: The Eight Rival Religions that Run the World* (New York: Harper, 2010); Finally, consider reading Bradley Jersak, *Her Gates Will Never Be Shut: Hope, Hell, and the New Jerusalem* (Eugene, OR: Wipf & Stock, 2009). Jersak works toward answering these questions: Would the God of love revealed by Jesus really consign the vast majority of humankind to a destiny of eternal, conscious torment? Is divine mercy bound by the demands of justice? How can anyone presume to know who is saved from the flames and who is not? Who are the damned? Who are the saved? These questions have a way of provoking controversy, often quite heated. Knowing the lines of argument expressed by all interpreters, Jersak endeavors to reconsider what the Bible and the church have actually said about hell and hope, noting a breadth of real possibilities that undermines every presumption. He tells us that the polyphony of perspectives on hell and hope offered by the prophets, apostles, and Jesus should humble our obsessive need to harmonize every text into a neat theological system. Surely, he contends, they but open the door to the eternal hope found in Revelation 21–22: the City whose gates will never be shut; where the Spirit

Scott Cairns, an Orthodox poet whose love of Christ is never in doubt, is one of my favorite contemplatives, a genuine mystic. Cairns was raised a Baptist and became a Presbyterian during his college years. In 1998, he became Orthodox Christian, receiving, at his conversion, the name Isaac, after St. Isaac of Syria, whose Ascetical Homilies were key to Scott's embracing Orthodox Christianity. The title of the poem is "Gehenna, Its Duration":

> Even in the matter of afflictions
> —the judgment of Gehenna, say—
> there bides a hidden mystery, whereby
> the Maker has taken as a starting point
> our patent willfulness, using even Hell
> as a way of bring to perfection
> His greater dispensation.
> If the world to come proves entirely the realm
> of mercy, love, and goodness,
> how then a final state that claims
> requital for its measure?
> That we should think that hell
> is not also full
> of love and mingled with compassion
> would be an insult to our God.
> By saying He will deliver us
> to suffering without purpose, we
> most surely sin. We blaspheme also if we say
> that He will act with spite or with a vengeful purpose,
> as if He had a need to avenge Himself.[177]

Yes, all and everything and everyone will be "one'd" with God. You too.

---

and Bride perpetually invite the thirsty who are outside the city to "Come, drink of the waters of life." No less than Eugene H. Peterson and Walter Brueggemann recommend Jersak's *Her Gates Will Never Be Shut: Hope, Hell, and the New Jerusalem*. Readers will be greatly instructed by this thoughtful book.

177 *Love's Immensity: Mystics on the Endless Life* (Brewster, MA: Paraclete Press, 2007), 78.

For Further Consideration

If you're still hesitant about finding out more about the Christian response to various sexual orientations, other religious traditions, exploring opportunities in Haiti, and entertaining the possibility of universalism, perhaps a little more reading will convince you everything is worth an exploration. Dip into one or more of these books:

Allen, Thomas, and Mark T. Chamberlain. *Every Knee Shall Bow: The Case for Christian Universalism.* Xulon Press, 2005.

Bidwell, Duane R. *When One Religion Isn't Enough: The Lives of Spiritually Fluid People.* Boston, MA: Beacon Press, 2018.

Burleson, Blake W. *A Contemplative Approach to Understanding World Religions: C. G. Jung as Phenomenologist of the Soul.* New Orleans, LA: Spring Journal, Inc., 2014.

Burnfield, David. *Patristic Universalism: An Alternative to the Traditional View of Divine Judgment.* 2nd ed. Columbia, SC: CreateSpace Independent Publishing, 2016.

Gulley, Philip, and James Mulholland. *If Grace Is True: Why God Will Saved Every Person.* San Francisco, CA: HarperCollins, 2003.

Taylor, Barbara Brown. *Holy Envy: Finding God in the Faith of Others.* New York: HarperCollins, 2019.

Chapter 12

CONTEMPLATIVELY POLITICAL

My political mentor

Jesus is my teacher and example as to how to be contemplatively political. Time and again in the Good News, he shows us how it's done. In my Bible I've underscored dozens of instances, some of which follow. In Mark 1:23–26, Jesus undoes a deeply disturbed man with a nasty spirit who screams at him in a Jewish synagogue. Shocking everybody, Jesus dramatically unpacks and throws out the man's violence. Several verses later, 40–42, Jesus goes against traditional piety and disobeys a well-respected sanitary custom, actually touching an ugly "untouchable" leper creeping along on his knees, asking for help. By doing so, Jesus himself also becomes unsanitary, unclean, and marginalized. In chapter 3, Jesus, not giving a damn, wraps himself with the smell of lower-class street people: sinners, tax collectors, prostitutes, the sick, the destitute and dying, the hungry, widows, women, fishermen, and children. Unembarrassed, he goes for total union with the poor and oppressed. By eating with people from the Southside Bowery, Jesus breaks nice people's rules and publicly embraces all who were excluded by societal laws. He even seems to prefer working and healing on the Sabbath in direct violation of Mosaic Law (Deut. 5:12–15). Engaging in civil disobedience, he encourages his disciples to illegally pluck and harvest grain for a snack (Mark 3:1–6). He goes out of his way to heal some bloke with a withered hand (Luke 13:10–17) and then proceeds to heal an unsightly bent-over and twisted woman. For Jesus, mercy and human needs preceded regulation and rule.

There is more outrageous behavior. In Matthew 8:28–34, Jesus addresses the economy of militarism, the business of war allowing the imperialistic forces of Rome ("legion") to control people. Jesus calls for the economic conversion from profits and oppression to justice and disarmament. Then, as always, Jesus's message is scandalous and radical. He unhesitatingly goes after the clergy, the "Reverends," challenging the religious leaders by breaking the legalized religious dietary codes used to manipulate and oppress (Mark 7:1–23). Not washing his hands before eating is supposed to result in self-condemnation and social ostracism. But not with Jesus. He calls for a return to the basics of justice and mercy (Luke 11:37–43). His language is exceptionally strong, and he doesn't let the lawyers escape his condemnation (Luke 11:45–46).

And can you imagine? Jesus is constantly fraternizing with his country's enemies even though such behavior is dangerous, subversive activity. Yet it is the hallmark of Jesus's teaching and life. During his life the enemies are the Romans, Samaritans, Gerasenes, and Greeks (John 4:4–43). When crucified by enemies, he prays, "Forgive them!"

And what about that show of street theater with the donkey ride into Jerusalem? Jesus deliberately stages it as outrageous satire, targeting the military parades of the empire (Luke 19:29–40).[178] Jesus demonstrates how a real liberator acts: in humility, nonviolence, and simplicity. The procession is public and political, like Gandhi's Salt March to the sea or King's march from Selma to Montgomery.

As his climax of nonviolent direct action, Jesus lets everyone see him on what today would be TV at the temple. At the public center of the Jewish Roman system, which kept the people subdued

178 For a wonderful reading of this episode, see "Palm Sunday," Marcus J. Borg and John Dominic Crossan, *The Last Week: A Day-by-Day Account of Jesus's Final Week in Jerusalem* (San Francisco, CA: HarperCollins, 2006).

and oppressed, he wrecks the tables so that birds can escape. Jesus symbolically throws over the imperial and religious domination (Mark 11: 15–18). He quotes Isaiah and Jeremiah who regularly condemned the Temple-state system and called for justice and peace. Following the Temple action, Jesus continues to stress radical obedience to God. High on his list is not paying taxes to Caesar, a revolutionary declaration (Mark 12:13–17). The meaning of his words is clear as Dorothy Day notes, "Once we give to God what is God's, there is nothing left for Caesar." If the people follow Jesus in voluntary poverty and radical obedience to God, Caesar loses his power. Recognizing the political nature of Jesus's divine obedience, the authorities arrest and kill him (Luke 23:2).

God approves! God raises Jesus from the dead and the resurrection to stage the ultimate act of nonviolent civil disobedience! According to God, suffering love and truth telling (not the empire's law) always lead to resurrection and life. Thomas's "my Lord and my God" is an act of faith and an expression of love for Jesus. Thomas's outcry, with his index finger exploring Jesus's wounded side, is an act of political "blasphemy" because the emperor alone wants to be declared God. Thomas puts a big red slash mark across that billboard. The resurrection inspires disciples to practice nonviolent civil disobedience as a way of life toward the ruling authorities of the day.

Barnesville, GA

All the above noted and declared, here now is the context in which I write as witness against brute force, turbulence, and political "callitrumpery"[179] wherever and whenever it occurs. Living in Barnesville, Georgia, what I say next is spoken within a big blended family wherein political views espousing some political notions are

179 My own neologism, combining the root of *callithumpian*, denoting a band of noise-makers on New Year's Eve from the British dialectic *gallithumpians*, "disturbers of order at Parliamentary elections, probably equivalent to the word gally, to frighten (as in *gallicrow* scarecrow; akin to Old English agælwan to scare). And, of course, a wee embedding of the name Trump.

not popular. My neighbors, many family members, and a good many friends are almost all politically and religiously conservative: far-right Republicans, some alt-right, religiously fundamentalist, and decidedly not comfortable with my Jesus-inspired political outlook. The local newspaper speaks for nearly everyone in Barnesville, Kentucky, and it rarely if ever speaks editorially for radical nonviolence. The editor by personal example encourages the citizens of Barnesville to arm themselves with guns and assault rifles. It finds living under the lordship of a nonviolent Jesus anathema.

With others in Barnesville and surrounding counties, I often feel a need for finding traveling companions and spiritual communities open to alternatives. As you might imagine, I gravitate toward folks in the local NAACP, the nearby Lions Club, a Spirituality Book Club, and progressive political gatherings like the Coffee Party.[180] We draw energy, inspiration, and support from one another as we quietly share wine, caffeinated tea, and political musings. I find that almost all of us have come to agree on the following eight convictions, beautifully articulated by Kimberly Broerman in nearby Atlanta:[181]

- As people called to be light, we have to keep our own lights trimmed and burning. For me this means, I have

180 The Coffee Party USA is an American political movement that was initially formed in January 2010, as an alternative to the Tea Party movement. Coffee Party spokesman Cameron Moore, Republican, says that the movement is neither liberal nor conservative, and even Tea Partiers are welcome to crash their party. Addressing issues directly, the Coffee Party USA is not liberal, centrist, progressive, or conservative. It's best described as a grassroots movement calling on all Americans to become active citizens. The party's members and leaders nationwide have diverse orientations, affiliations, and political experience so that no single person's previous participation or expression reflects the entirety of the organization. Civility when sharing ideas, facts, and opinions is a core value of the Coffee Party. For more information, visit http://www.coffeepartyusa.com.

Closely related to the mission and values of the Coffee Party is Living Room Conversations, an organization that espouses "a simple way that anyone with an open mind can engage with their friends in a friendly yet meaningful conversation about topics we care about. These conversations increase understanding, reveal common ground and allow us to discuss possible solutions." Visit www.LivingRoomConversations.org for further information.

181 Available at http://www.kimberlybroerman.com.

to engage in prayer, silence, reading and reflection, life-giving community—to keep my light burning, without being seduced by all the darkness. Too much news, and not enough prayer, and we are toast.

- We are one small part of a great whole. We have power to do good. We also have limitations of time, energy and resources. I have to listen for what is uniquely mine to do—what aligns with my God-given gifts and limitations, and trust others to do the same.
- Seeing and listening and caring about what we see and hear matters. We cannot do something about every single injustice and suffering we witness, especially since our technology allows us to see it 24-7 from all corners of the earth. But letting some in, allowing it to soften and break our hearts toward more empathy and compassion, is I believe, part of how God is present in and healing us and our world.
- While we need to stay informed, we also have to discern how much news we can take in without becoming poisoned or incapacitated by it. Fatigue, burnout, and cynicism will serve no one.
- We cannot afford to spend too much energy on the detractors, haters, and critics. We think of Jesus's own teaching and life, offering himself and speaking truth to those with ears to hear, eyes to see, hearts to receive. Like the seed in the parable of the sower, we must sow our lives, our words and actions into the world, trusting some will find welcome soil, and praying God will continue to cultivate the hard, barren, thorny places.
- At the same time, we must try to refrain from judgment of others, and with humility and compassion, keep focusing on our own lives as works in progress. We all stand in need of so much grace and mercy. We are all responsible for our hearts, our words, and our actions, and others are responsible for theirs. As much as we would maybe like to fix or change or heal others, and they us, we mostly can't.

And in my experience, it's love and mercy that change us, not contempt and judgment.

- We need to find ways out of our own bubbles and echo chambers, to speak with and more importantly to listen to, folks who live and think and believe differently than us. These are hard conversations and best undertaken in person, not on social media, which leaves out so much that is vital about human communication.
- We also need safe spaces where we can vent and process what we're really thinking and feeling. In the tradition of the Psalms, expressing our full range of rage, lament, confusion, fear, gratitude, and supplication in prayer should be our first resort. Having a few deep friendships that can bear that fullness is also critical.
- We cannot get so consumed with all that is wrong and broken and scary that we lose sight of all that is good and beautiful and right. We want to live in gratitude for this wondrous life, and not let these present challenges sour me, or rob me of the joy and beauty that are in every single day.[182]

Personally

Well said, Kimberly. It's important to stay connected with those providing help and with those whom we can help. For those reasons, I personally support the Southern Poverty Law Center, an organization that tracks hate groups and backs the Center's petition calling on our political leaders to disavow bigotry. In addition, I support the ACLU, Lutheran Refugee Services, and The New York Times Neediest Cases Fund that enables the International Rescue Committee to work for refugees.

At the same time, I resist dwelling in a private echo chamber. I have and will continue to follow intelligent people with whom I

182 Kimberly Broerman, "Wading In," February, 2017; available at http://www.kimberlybroerman.com.

disagree on Twitter and Facebook. I listen to views on Fox News, subscribe to Reason, the Libertarian house organ, and read articles in *The Nation*. By greeting Muslims with love, I fight Islamophobia and volunteer help for the Council on American-Islamic Relations. I periodically visit the local mosque in Griffin, Georgia, and subscribe to *Muslim News* and other newspapers that help keep me informed about Islamic thoughts, practices, and events.[183]

I try to avoid demonizing people who don't agree with me about a recent election, recognizing that it's wrong to stereotype people. I avoid Hitler-ish metaphors, recognizing that they stop conversations and rarely persuade. I remind myself that no side has a monopoly on truth and that many supporters of opposing thoughts are good people who want the best for the country. The left already has gotten into trouble for condescending to working-class people. Insulting the opposition as racists simply magnifies that problem.

As a citizen in Georgia, I regularly call and write Senators Isakson (202-229-3643) and Perdue (202-224-3521) to express my opposition to mass deportation, cutting millions people off health insurance, and nominating people who are unqualified or bigoted, reducing access to contraception and cancer screenings. And, when possible, I attend my representative's town meeting and put him or her on the spot.

I will not lose hope. I will keep reminding myself that politics zig and zag and that I can do more than shout in the wind. I can fight for my values even between elections, and even at the micro-level, I can mitigate the damage to my neighbors and attempt to heal a social fabric that has been rent.

The Civility Pledge

As we contemplatively work within political contexts, it's important to practice civility, taking specific steps to engage others with diverse political views to promote civility and respect. To do so,

[183] For full listing of Islamic newspapers, magazines, and blogs, visit http://www.world-newspapers.com/islam-magazines.html.

I've found it helpful to take what many call "the civility pledge."[184] Here is the pledge I take when about to attend a political meeting, walk or march in a political demonstration, find myself about to write a letter to a congressman or senator, or make a phone call to a politician in Atlanta or Washington, DC:

To help revive civility and respect in my community, I will make a conscious effort to:

1. Seek out a variety of reliable news sources with different perspectives in order to learn more about the forces that divide—and also unite—our country.
2. Listen respectfully to people who have views different than my own, be mindful to avoid stereotyping and not use language that is insulting or derogatory.
3. Encourage and support efforts to bring people of different points of view together in our community to have civil and respectful conversations
4. Invite other people to join me in the Initiative to revive civility and get involved in helping to connect people across political divisions.

Pro-life, but also *consistently* so

I sometimes disagree with my liberal friends. I am pro-life and support Democrats for Life of America (DFLA)[185] In fact, I am so pro-life that I enthusiastically support with prayer and financial contributions an even more radical group: the Consistent Life

[184] Promoted, for example, by the nonpartisan National Institute for Civil Discourse, a non-partisan institute based at the University of Arizona's School of Social and Behavioral Sciences dedicated to addressing incivility and political dysfunction in American democracy by promoting structural and behavioral change. For more information, visit https://www.revivecivility.org/about-initiative-revive-civility.

[185] Democrats for Life of America offers this statement about its pro-life commitment:

We believe in the legal protection of unborn life and a comprehensive approach to reducing the number of abortions in America and around the world. We believe in supporting women and children and strengthening families and communities.

Network: Voice for Peace and Life, an organization that endorses life far beyond (but including!) fetal protection.[186]

At the same time, there is much to value from other organizations, which some pro-lifers perceive as unworthy of support. For example, many pro-lifers were angered at what happened on January 21, 2017, when the Women's March on Washington sent a bold message to the new Trump administration on their first day in office. Streamed live on YouTube, Facebook, and Twitter, the march drew at least five hundred thousand people, and worldwide participation has been estimated at five million.[187] That march was a worldwide protest advocating legislation and policies regarding human rights and other issues, including women's rights, immigration reform, healthcare reform, the natural environment, LGBTQ rights, racial equality, freedom of religion, and workers' rights.

You ask: How could a pro-lifer like myself participate in such a march? Pro-lifer Meryle Angelicola Lee tells why. She marched in solidarity with women, some of whom who disagreed with her pro-life convictions, for many reasons:

> We believe in the elimination of the death penalty, euthanasia, and embryonic stem cell research, but support the life enhancing promise of adult stem cell research.
>
> In representing pro-life Democrats within the true "big tent" party, DFLA works across a broad spectrum of life ethics. We recognize that people of good faith have different approaches to these issues; therefore, we refuse to use a single issue as a "litmus test" to exclude those who would otherwise seek common ground with us on the expansion of human rights. We encourage all people committed to the common good to work together to protect human life at all of its stages.

Available at http://www.democratsforlife.org/index.php/about-us.

186 Go to http://www.consistentlifenetwork.org to become a supporter. Be pro-life beyond being antiabortion.

187 According to Wikipedia (https://en.wikipedia.org/wiki/2017_Women's_March):

> At least 408 marches were reported to have been planned in the U.S. and 168 in 81 other countries. After the marches, officials who organized them reported that 673 marches took place worldwide, on all seven continents, including 29 in Canada, 20 in Mexico, and one in Antarctica. In Washington D.C. alone, the protests were the largest political demonstrations since the anti–Vietnam War protests in the 1960s and 1970s, with both protests drawing in similar numbers. The Women's March crowds were peaceful, and no arrests were made in Washington, D.C., Chicago, Los Angeles, New York City, and Seattle, where an estimated combined total of 2 million people marched.

I am a pro-life Christian who participated in a local march in support of the women's march on Washington. One reason I am proud to have marched in the protest is because of that fact, not in spite of it.

I believe life begins at conception and I want to see fewer women choose abortion. I grew up in church and was always told that voting republican meant saving babies and voting democrat meant the opposite. A few years ago, I got curious and decided to study the CDC statistics for myself. What I learned basically blew my mind…abortion rates decline at the same rate or faster when a democrat is in office (chart below, if you want to take a look). So that got me thinking…can we really call it the pro-life party if it doesn't save more babies than the pro-choice party? Something isn't working.

Make no mistake, it breaks my heart that millions of women choose abortion…and you know what? Many of their hearts are broken, too. Do you believe anyone actually wants to see abortion increase? I don't think so.

God says they will know we are Christians by our love, but we can't get close enough to love these women when we're standing on the sidelines and calling them murderers instead of what God calls them: His beloved.

Because even if they wanted the abortion and felt relief when it was over, it wasn't easy. What they needed was someone to embrace them while they felt that fear and pain, while they weighed their options. But our arms weren't available…we were too busy with our picket signs. Our arms were crossed and our fingers were pointed while we lectured others about their selfishness and posted pictures of aborted babies on social media. We should have been embracing them. How many babies would have been

> saved if the pro-life party was known for offering a listening ear to the scared pregnant woman, instead of for pushing legislation and protests outside of the abortion clinics?
>
> I marched because many of the women who choose abortion are living in poverty, struggling with addiction or facing the realities of being a single parent. They walk into the clinic because they have no idea how they are going to provide for the child growing in their belly. Neither does the pro-life party. Instead, the party cuts the very programs that would help her. She can barely afford to feed herself, much less a child. But she should just work harder, right? What should she do when she racks up thousands in medical bills after she goes into labor because she can't afford insurance? The pro-life party can't answer that, either. How can she work without paid maternity leave, or without affordable childcare? The answer is that she can't. How many babies would have been saved if the pro-life party was known for fighting to help these women instead of lobbying to cut the programs that do?

In her lengthy explanation,[188] Lee lists more reasons and, fully aware that her explanation was going to be controversial, Lee concludes with these words:

> I marched because I am not interested in forcing anyone to believe what I believe or making people "follow the rules." But I am interested in saving babies, showing genuine love and helping to shoulder the burdens of my fellow (wo)man. That's what is actually going to change things. At the end of the

[188] Posted by Meryle Angelicola Lee, January 22, 2017, on her Facebook page.

> day, isn't that what God did for us? He gave us free will and won us over with his love.

You can imagine how delighted I was to discover that several women in my own big family—my wife included!—agreed with Lee's outspoken love for those who disagree with her.[189]

And how delighted I am to know that Pope Francis in August, 2018, declared that the death penalty is wrong is all cases—unconditionally wrong! It is so good to see that the spiritual head of the Roman Catholic Church is solidly a pro-life and consistently so.[190]

Pro-choice from a Christian vision

I agree with Catholic Sister Joan Chittister when she explains why being against abortion doesn't necessarily mean you're really pro-life:

> I do not believe that just because you're opposed to abortion that that makes you pro-life. In fact, I think in many cases, your morality is deeply lacking if all you want is a child born but not a child fed, not a child educated, not a child housed. And why would I think that you don't? Because you don't want any tax money to go there. That's not pro-life. That's pro-birth. We need a much broader conversation on what the morality of pro-life is.[191]

189 In addition to June's approval, her granddaughter Sara Beth Stout and my daughter Lisa Simonds posted appreciative responses. And in response to Lee's posting, many more said, "Yes."

190 For more information, see Elisabetta Povoledo and Laurie Goodstein, "Pope Francis Declares Death Penalty Unacceptable in All Cases," *The New York Times*, August 2, 2018.

191 "A Catholic Nun on What It Really Means to Be Pro-Life," available at https://billmoyers.com/story/what-pro-life-means/.

I hear you and agree, Sister Joan! Moreover, as a pro-lifer—and "consistently so" as I have explained—I also listen attentively to others who encourage us to be even more nuanced in our thinking, more progressive and open to a variety of Christian understandings. For these reasons, I have learned much from Christian women who urge us to judge compassionately those who find if necessary to choose abortion as an existential option. Two books in particular—Rebecca Todd Peter's *Trust Women: A Progressive Christian Argument for Reproductive Justice* and Kira Schlesinger's *Pro-Choice and Christian: Reconciling Faith, Politics, and Justice*—offer compelling presentation for possibly becoming pro-choice from a Christian perspective.[192]

Schlesinger's *Pro-Choice and Christian* explores the biblical, theological, political, and medical aspects of the debate in order to provide a thoughtful Christian argument for a pro-choice position with regard to abortion issues. As an Episcopal priest, she considers relevant Scriptures, the politics of abortion in the United States, and the human realities making abortion a vital issue of justice and compassion. Importantly, by examining choice from a Christian perspective, Schlesinger provides a common vocabulary for all of us to discuss faith and reproductive rights. Rebecca Todd Peters, a Presbyterian minister and social ethicist, argues in *Trust Women* that our shaming and judging those who have had abortions reflects a deep, often unspoken patriarchal and racist assumptions about women and their sexual activity. These assumptions are at the heart of what she calls the "justification framework," which so often governs our public debate about abortion and disrupts our ability to have authentic public discussions about the health and well-being of women and their families. Abortion, for Schlesinger and Peters, isn't the unique social problem we should be focusing on. The problem is more truly our inability to trust women to act as rational, capable, responsible

---

192 Other books well worth examining include Charles Camosy's *Beyond Abortion, Wars: A Way Forward for a New Generation* (Grand Rapids, Eerdmans, 2015), *Liturgies and Prayers Related to Childbearing, Childbirth, and Loss: Enriching Our Worship 5* (New York: Church Publishing Inc. 2009), and Bromleigh McCleneghan's, *Good Christian Sex: Why Chastity Isn't the Only Option—And other Things the Bible Says about Sex* (New York (HarperCollins, 2016),

moral agents who must weigh the concrete moral question of what to do when they are pregnant or when there are problems during a pregnancy.

Ambitious both in method and scope, Schlesinger and Peters skillfully interweave political analysis, sociology, along with ancient and modern philosophy, Christian tradition, and medical history as ground and foundation for their analyses in the material reality of women's lives and their often painful decisions about sexuality, abortion, and child-bearing. As Christians we need to listen to them.

Contemplatively gunless

Should Christians arm themselves with guns? That question is not easy to answer. Nevertheless, after working through various responses, I have come to know that as a Christian, I cannot and will not arm myself with a gun.

Here's why. First, Jesus is my Lord. He shows me how to live a nonviolent life. He did not arm himself with any weapon of violence. In fact, he did just the opposite. He allowed others to kill him and prayed for God to forgive them.

Second, because Jesus is my model for life, I want to have "the mind of Christ" as St. Paul recommends. This means that, like Christ, I need to empty myself of ego, status, and privilege for the sake of others.

Third, from a strictly pragmatic point of view and unbeknownst to most people, I am reasonably safe as a citizen living in the United States. I don't really need a gun. Recent statistics on homicides indicate that I am safer today than I was in 1965 inasmuch as the murder rate in the United Sates is at a fifty-year low.[193] I did not own

[193] The rate at which Americans commit suicide with guns has been increasing for several years, even as the rate of gun homicides has declined. Research shows that the increase is correlated with higher gun ownership. Public health experts say ready access to firearms makes it easier for people to act on suicidal thoughts. And about 85 percent of suicide attempts that involve guns are successful, compared with less than 3 percent of those involving drug overdoses. Over all, guns were used in about half of the forty-one thousand suicides in 2013, the latest year for which there is data

a gun in 1965 and do not need to do so now. Of course, if I lived in other countries such as Canada, Australia, Norway, or Germany, I would be considerably safer.

Fourth, I am a missionary for Jesus. If I kill someone with a gun, that person may not come to know the love of God. That is why I am opposed to the death penalty. As Christians we want to give everyone an opportunity, no matter when or how, to live in oneness with God.

Fifth, "we are not fighting against human beings," as St. Paul says (Eph. 6:12), "but against the wicked spiritual forces in the heavenly world, the rulers, authorities, and cosmic powers of this dark age." I am aware that the *spiritual forces* of our culture—-newspapers, magazines, radio, movies, books, and television—promote a fascination with violence so massive that we have become mentally and psychologically preoccupied with vengeance, killings, and mass murders. Our culture encourages us to think about and participate in violence, so much so that citizens in the United States own 44 percent of all the guns in the world. In downtown Barnesville, for example, I can easily buy an American-made AR-15, a military-style assault rifle, and purchase dozens of magazines loaded with forty rounds of .223 ammunition as though I were purchasing a peashooter.[194] I can also easily buy an AR-15 online.

But some Christians want to arm themselves!

Not a few Christians, including members of my family, present the following two major arguments for owning guns. First, they say they have a Second Amendment right to own guns. And second, Jesus says, "Take up your swords" (more about that verse in a page or two). Therefore, God wants us to own and shoot a gun defensively.

---

from the Centers for Disease Control and Prevention as Ian Reifowitz reports in *The Huffington Post*, December 15, 2015, available at https://www.huffingtonpost.com/ian-reifowitz/we-are-more-afraid-than-e_b_8740750.html.

194 As of late 2015, I could buy a Spike's Tactical's "Christian" AR-15 (ironically named the Crusader) for $1,400.

As the paterfamilias (the oldest living male my family), I do not believe these two basic arguments—one cultural, the other biblical—are as good as the witness of Jesus.

Yes, in the United States, a person has the right to own guns for defensive purposes. But Jesus specifically taught the contrary. He taught nonviolence. I ask you to ask yourself this question: would Jesus own and use a gun? I don't think so. Listen to what Jesus says: "If someone strikes you on one cheek, turn the other" (Luke 6:29). Here, Jesus is teaching you to give up your right of self-defense. He does not say to hit people back. It's interesting to note that Jesus never resisted his persecutors. When the police came to arrest him and his buddies, Jesus told them to put away their swords. And not resist illegal arrest.

If someone shot at Jesus, do you really think he would have shot back? He says, "Love your enemies and pray for those who persecute you, so that you may become the children of your Father in heaven" (Matt. 5:44). I have asked many gun-owning Christians if they would shoot an intruder who had broken into their house. Most of them say, "Yes, I would." But what would Jesus do? He answers that question this way: "If anyone asks you for anything, give it to them without question" (Matt. 5:42). "If someone steals from you, don't try to get it back" (Luke 6:30). "If someone hits you, invite them to do it again" (Matt. 5:39). "If you lose a lawsuit, give more than the judgment" (Matt. 5:40). "If someone forces you to walk a mile, walk two miles" (Matt. 5:41). These sayings do not sound as though Jesus was a man with a gun. If someone broke into his house, he would simply let them steal.

Of course, Jesus did not care a whole lot about material possessions anyway and suggests that his followers act likewise. Shocking! Very shocking! Jesus says, "Don't become wealthy" (Mark

10:21–25). Sell everything you have and give it to the poor" (Luke 12:33). Ask a Christian: "Would you shoot someone trying to harm your family?" In answering that question, Jesus says, "Do not resist evil." He also says, "And every one that has forsaken house, or brethren, or sisters, or father, or mother, or wife, or children, or lands, for my name's sake, shall receive a hundredfold, and shall inherit everlasting life" (Matt. 19:29). So, if you forsake your children and wife, allowing them to be killed in order to follow Jesus's teachings of nonviolence, then our Lord says you get a hundred times what you had and everlasting life. Again, shocking! Very shocking!

Scripturally disarming ourselves

That, of course, may be a bit too much for most Christians. After all, taking Jesus seriously can be appalling. To lessen the shock of Jesus's teaching, lots of Christians like to visit the front part of our Bible, the Old Testament. But even there, we must be careful. Turning to the Hebrew Scriptures, Benjamin L. Corey clarifies why we Christians may elect not to arm ourselves even when quoting from our inherited Jewish tradition:

> As one who teaches that Christians are under Christ's command to love their enemies and refrain from violence against them (Luke 6:27–36, Matthew 5:38–48), I have heard every counter-argument in the book. The paradigm of nonviolent enemy love does not align with the type of Christianity many of us are born into, and out of that tension we're often forced to try to explain away what Jesus taught on the matter.
>
> It is impossible to justify violence against enemies using the teachings of Jesus (though there's a frequent attempt to misuse Luke 22:26. Since one cannot justify being a pistol-packer from Jesus himself, many turn to the Old Testament for validation. However, even

grossly misapplying the stories of the Old Testament, one still cannot arrive at a solid argument for individual Christians being armed to the teeth with guns. The closest one can get is an argument for jihad—because [that sort of] religious war is really the bulk of what we see in the OT.

However, folks certainly do try to justify Christians and guns from the OT, and they'll often turn to Exodus 22:2 to do so. Let me quickly explain why this simply doesn't work. First, as Christians we do not turn to the Law of Moses to find our ethical standards for living—we are under the Law of Christ, not Moses. Furthermore, the works of Jesus brought a complete end to the law and all of its regulations. Even Paul himself called out followers of Jesus who still taught we were to follow the Law of Moses and said either every regulation is still in full effect, or none of it is (Gal 5:3). Thus, when someone appeals to the OT to skirt around something Jesus said, they're not only wrong but it shows they've missed the entire point of Scripture itself (John 5:39).

However, even if appealing to the Law of Moses were a valid argument, Exodus 22:2 still doesn't work to justify American style armed self-defense. Let's look at the verse:

> If a thief is caught breaking in at night and is struck a fatal blow, the defender is not guilty of bloodshed.

At face value, that certainly seems to justify lethal violence in self-defense—but it just so happens that Exodus 22:2 is only part of that law, which is precisely why those who misuse it do not continue the full quote. The second half, found in the next verse says:

> But if it happens in daylight, the one who killed the thief is guilty of murder.

This verse was written to ancient nomads living in tents in the desert, and covers two scenarios: one where you're startled by an intruder in your tent when it is complete darkness, and one where you can fully see them in daylight. The concession of verse 22 is clearly pointing to being startled in the darkness by an intruder, and the intruder accidentally ends up dead.

When people are scared in the dark and try to get away, bad things can happen even though the individual doesn't intend it. For example, if you're grabbed while walking on a dark path and shove the attacker to get away, but the attacker falls and dies, it would be disingenuous to say that lethality was an actual intent. This verse made room for those kinds of incidents when lethality was clearly not the intention.

However, the verse then switched to daylight—when you can actually see the intruder in your home. In this scenario, any kind of violent response that would lead to death is not only condemned, but also considered murder. In these cases, the one who used lethal violence against a day-time intruder would themselves be put to death.

While often used by gun-slingers to justify shooting a home intruder, verse 3 actually backfires on the one making the argument. If we were to apply verse 3 to the modern world, we'd see that for guns to be used properly they must be precisely aimed. One can only aim at a target if there is enough light to actually see the target. If there were enough light to see the target and formulate the intent to kill the intruder, such scenarios would be considered murder and punishable by death if we were to actually apply the full passage.

> Appealing to Exodus 22 not only fails to win the theological argument, but actually shows that Christians who'd use a gun to kill an intruder would suffer death by stoning under the Law of Moses.[195]

Corey also unpacks one of the most abused passages in all of Scripture, that time when Jesus says, "But now if you have a purse, take it, and a bag; and if you don't have a sword, sell your cloak and buy one" (Luke 22:36). This verse appears to justify the ownership of weapons designed to kill people. But please do not quote this verse out of context. Corey explains:

> The verse in total isolation certainly makes it appear that Jesus was a hypocrite by contradicting his previous teachings on nonviolence by telling his disciples to go out and buy swords if they didn't already have one. And, if that's all that Jesus said in that passage, they'd have a good case. While it wouldn't be a slam dunk on the Jesus and violence issue since he clearly stated in Matthew 5 that the children of God are nonviolent, it would show that Jesus was inconsistent on the issue and cast his entire teachings into doubt. However, the crucial flaw in the Luke 22:36 argument is the inconvenient existence of Luke 22:37, where Jesus goes onto explain why they needed to bring swords to his arrest. Jesus explains, as one will see plainly in the text, that there was an Old Testament prophesy stating the Messiah would be "counted among the lawless," and that he wanted to make sure this prophesy came to pass—thus why they needed to carry swords. Jesus interprets what he means right on the spot: he needed to fulfill the prophesy that he'd

[195] "Why Exodus 22:2 Doesn't Work to Justify Armed Self-Defense," January 15, 2016. Available at The Official Blog of Benjamin L. Corey at www.patheos.com.

> be arrested like a common criminal! How best to be a common criminal? Carry a sword. Carry a gun.
>
> The ultimate proof that Jesus wasn't promoting violence in self-defense is what we see happen just an hour or two later: Peter actually uses one of the swords to cut someone's ear off, and Jesus not only rebukes Peter for doing that, ("Put away your sword! Whoever lives by the sword will die by it!"), but he goes one step further in healing the ear of one of his own enemies who had come to arrest him.
>
> The verdict is in: there is absolutely, positively no possible way to use Luke 22:36 to support the use of violence unless you also contend that Luke 22:36 is the last verse in the book of Luke. This passage neither commands "sword ownership" nor endorses the use of violence.[196]

Obviously Christians who don't own guns might become martyrs. The word "martyr" scares us. But the word "martyr" didn't always scare Christians.[197] In the early Church, Christians declared that "the blood of the martyrs is the seed of the Church." When we become witnesses to nonviolence, others sit up and take notice. They wonder why. They become interested in the world's most nonviolent person—Jesus. They may even come to love and follow him.

Remember what St. Paul, an imitator of Jesus, says, "Don't hit back; discover beauty in everyone. If you've got it in you, get along with everybody. Don't insist on getting even; that's not for you to

---

196 "No, Jesus Didn't Command We Own Weapons," January 16, 2014. Available at The Official Blog of Benjamin L. Corey at www.patheos.com.

197 A Christian martyr is a person who is killed for following Jesus. In early church years, this often occurred through stoning, crucifixion, burning at the stake, or other forms of torture and capital punishment. The word "martyr" comes from the Greek word *martys,* which means "witness." At first, the term applied to Apostles. Once Christians started to undergo persecution, the term came to be applied to those who suffered hardships for their faith. Finally, it was restricted to those who had been killed for their faith. The early Christian period before Constantine I was the "Age of Martyrs."

do. 'I'll do the judging,' says God. 'I'll take care of it'" (Rom. 12:19). Again I ask, "Would Jesus shoot a bullet at someone?" If you cannot imagine Jesus using a gun and you are a follower of Jesus, how can you honestly justify owning a gun?

So please take this vow when visiting my home or church

- I will not bring my guns into Andy's home.[198]
- I will not bring my guns into the church Andy attends.
- I will not shoot Andy if he knocks on the door of my house at 1:00 a.m.
- I will keep my guns locked in a home cabinet so that they are not stolen or used without permission.
- I will keep my guns locked in a home cabinet so that someone doesn't use one of my weapons to commit suicide.[199]
- I will try to protect myself by not shooting myself.[200]
- I will encourage the passage of legislation that will reduce the number of killings in the United States by supporting laws that place a ban on the purchase of assault weapons and require background checks on all who wish to purchase guns.

---

198 The home is an even riskier place than the venues attacked by mass shooters. Gun-safety studies have found that a gun in the home is twenty-two times more likely to be used in a family homicide, suicide, or accident than to be used in self-defense. More than 1.5 million children under the age of eighteen live in homes with loaded, unsecured guns, leaving them sixteen times more likely to be killed than in safer homes, according to the Law Center to Prevent Gun Violence, a research group. It is hard to imagine how any politician who kisses babies on the campaign trail can fail to demand mandates and penalties to keep guns unloaded and locked up at home.

199 Margot Sanger-Katz, "Gun Deaths are Largely Suicides," *The New York Times*, October. 8, 2015.

200 Reports appear almost daily about gun owners shooting themselves. Here's a typical instance: "A long-time borough resident and attorney who runs a business selling firearms to law enforcement was taken to an area hospital early Friday after accidentally shooting himself." "Owner of gun shop accidentally shoots himself in Midland Park," *The Record*, October 16, 2015, available at http://www.northjersey.com/news/owner-of-gun-shop-accidentally-shoots-himself-in-midland-park-1.1434724.

- I will advocate the development of gun manufacturing that employs finger print technology and gunlocks.
- I will work for the passage of laws that will expand the Brady Bill, restore the assault weapons ban, improve our nation's care for Americans with mental illnesses, and work toward passing federal laws eliminating the "iron pipeline" of traffic in guns from states with weak laws to those with stronger laws. These proposals are some of the steps citizens should be discussing to reduce the intolerable bloodshed from guns.[201]
- I will vote responsibly to lessen gun violence.

What a Desert Elder once said

And then there's this story and conversation that is said to have taken place after Constantine:

> One of the Fathers asked Abba Sisoes, "If I am sitting in the desert and a barbarian comes to kill me and if I am stronger than he, shall I kill him?" The old man said to him, "No, leave him to God. In fact, whatever the trial is which comes to a man, let him say, "This has happened to me because of my sins," and if something good comes say, "It is through the providence of God."[202]

As a private US citizen and a Christian who does not carry a gun, I am blessed knowing that I am in good company with many like-minded Christians. I stand shoulder to shoulder with my unarmed brothers and sisters, especially those who today salute our

201 Editorial Board, *The New York Times*, "Despair Over Gun Deaths Is Not an Option," December 12, 2015.

202 *The Sayings of the Desert Fathers: The Alphabetical Collection*, ed. Benedicta Ward (Oxford: Cistercian Publications, 1984), 219.

nonviolent Lord in organizations like the Fellowship of Reconciliation and the Lutheran Peace Fellowship.[203]

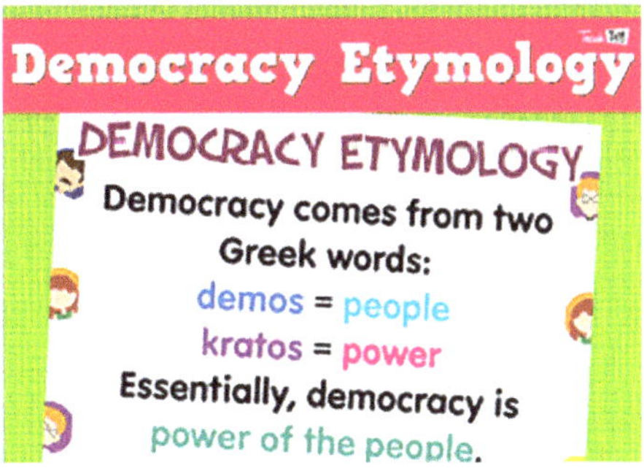

In 1998 I bought an old Chevy truck, and on its rear left bumper I posted a sticker proclaiming "Jesus was a Liberal." When someone in the family objected, I immediately ordered another which announced: "Jesus was a Conservative," posting it on the bumper's right side. Had I been more informed, I might also have posted one in the middle: "Jesus was a Socialist."[204] All three are available today. As always, it's sometimes difficult to be political without being divisive, defensive, and discordant. It's also equally difficult to be welcoming, friendly, and charitable with people with whom you politically disagree. Strangely, Jesus was able to be both loving and compassionate, disagreeable and judgmental. It's almost as though we have two views of Jesus. On the one hand, he loved tax-collectors, prostitutes, people with infectious diseases, foreigners, the poor, and strangers. He enjoyed wedding parties, often ate with the wealthy and was friendly with military soldiers. On the other hand, he could be judgmental, chastising, condemnatory, shaming his egotistical fellow Jews, especially the rich. Now that's some paradox. Being neither politically one-sided or totally for or against popular opinions, Jesus traveled in all

203 The Fellowship of Reconciliation (FOR <forusa.org>) has been working for peace, justice, and nonviolence since 1915; composed of people who recognize the essential unity of all creation, the FOR explores the power of love and truth for resolving human conflict. The Lutheran Peace Fellowship(LPF <lutheranpeace.org>) is an organization of Lutherans who work for peace and social justice issues. It includes members and supporters in all the Lutheran denominations and more than a few people from other faith traditions. As a nonprofit organization, LPF is supported largely by its members as well as a variety of grants and honoraria from workshops, events, and trainings.

204 See, example, Peter Dreier, "Jesus was a Socialist," *Huffington Post* (December 25, 2016); available at https://www.huffpost.com/entry/jesus-was-a-socialist_b_13854296. Many agree; many disagree.

neighborhoods. He even slipped into towns other Jews avoided. Urging a Third Way, he spoke to the crowds speaking in parables and said pointedly, "Turn the other cheek. Hand over your cloak. Go for two miles. Do not turn your back on one who wants to borrow. Don't be a doormat. Stand up for yourself. Help others. Go the extra mile. Live mercifully. Share what you have with others."

Within each of us, Jesus also opens up the real possibility of a Third Way. You don't have side with what Walter Wink calls a "Denomination System" characterized by unjust economic relations, oppressive political relations, biased race relations, patriarchal gender relations, hierarchical power relations, and the use of violence to maintain them all.[205] Nor do you need you to be a screaming liberal, a high-energy left-winger writing condemnatory letters to local newspapers. And you need not fall into despair when seeing what's happening politically in America or elsewhere. You can actually live a Third Way. You can realize that it's not the magnitude of a challenge that crushes the human spirit. You don't have to feel powerless as though standing up for time-honored democracy is futile. You can actually join up with thousands upon thousands of Third-Way Americans united across a spectrum of ideologies, creating what Frances Moore Lappi and Adam Eichen call a "canopy of hope" in *Daring Democracy*.[206] As an action-spirited contemplative, I urge you to join the millions of Americans who are leaving despair

Teddy Abrams
Conductor of The Louisville Orchestra

[205] Walter Wink, *The Powers That Be: Theology for a New Millennium* (Minneapolis, MN: Augsburg Press, 1998), 39-40.

[206] *Daring Democracy: Igniting Power, Meaning, and Connection for the America We Want* (Boston: Beacon Press, 2017) is a magnificent "third-way" political vision, written by two luminaries from different generations, who integrate an understanding about how it is that although the power of individuals is being undermined, we can indeed take steps--given that understanding--to turn things around."

behind as all of us push for and are achieving historic change. Let's be politically courageous in the daring fight for a Third Way in America!

Allow me to provide an example. As you might well remember, going to a large city's concert hall to hear music usually meant listening to well-dressed musicians playing classical music, maybe that of Brahms or Mozart. If that wasn't your gig, perhaps you went to a night club to be with jazz musicians or to a huge outdoor arena to hear soul music like that by Motown artists. You went to hear one or the other, not both or all three at the same time. There is now, however, a Third Way of enjoying Bach and Rock at the same time. When you visit Kentucky's Louisville Orchestra, you get to see and hear the Third Way. Teddy Abrams, age 32, is doing what most musical directors have never done; he's conducting two worlds on music simultaneously. When boxing champion Muhammad Ali died in 2016, classical pianist Abrams set up his keyboard and played for his city's local mourners. Then like a musical poet laureate, he wrote an opera about Louisville's famous citizen, "The Greatest." In it Teddy Abrams cast a local rapper and hip-hop artist Arthur Jecorey "1200 as Ali." Here's why, as Abrams tells us:

> A music director should, if they're going to be the music director of X orchestra, live in X, and care about the people of X, and become one of them," he said. "I often say it's just like a politician; if you wanna get elected, you better be out on the streets meeting people. And it's exactly the same thing here. What I try to do is go meet the actual people that you're going to make music for.[207]

And guess what! Attendance at the Orchestra's performances has increased 30%. Then, imagine this: Abrams also invites those who have never heard a symphony--newly arrived refugees from

---

[207] Excerpted from the transcript of "Teddy Abrams, the Louisville Orchestra's rock star," an episode on *CBS Sunday Morning* (May 26, 2019); available at https://www.cbsnews.com/news/teddy-abrams-conductor-of-the-louisville-orchestra/.

Central America!—to enjoy the music as he enjoys himself with them. That's the Third Way. The contemplatively political can follow suite. We can hold hands with people who label themselves Tea Party, Social Democrats, "No Labels,"[208] Republicans, supporters of the Coffee Party,[209] and Doctors without Borders.[210] Let's conclude with the wisdom of Richard Rohr:

> The contemplative stance is the Third Way. We stand in the middle, neither taking the world on from another power position nor denying it for fear of the pain it will bring. We hold the hardness of reality and the suffering of the world *until it transforms us,* knowing that we are both complicit in evil and can participate in wholeness and holiness. Once we can stand in that third spacious way, neither directly fighting or fleeing, we are in the place of grace out of which genuine newness can come. *This is where creativity and new forms of life and healing emerge.*[211]

If I were to put another sticker on the back end of an old Chevy Silverado, it would read "Live Simply so that Others Can Simply Live."

By the way, when he goes to work to conduct the Symphony Orchestra, Teddy Abrams rides a bicycle.

May the Way of Jesus encourage all!

---

208 No Labels is an American political organization whose mission is to combat partisan dysfunction in politics and "usher in a new era of focused problem solving in American politics." For more information, visit http://www.nolabels.org.

209 Coffee Party USA envisions a nation of diverse communities sharing a culture of informed public engagement that sustains a tradition where our solemn duty to vote is the currency of our democracy. Visit https://coffeepartyusa.com/ for more information.

210 Find out how to take action at https://www.doctorswithoutborders.org.

211 "The Third Way," *Daily Meditation* (Monday, June 4, 2018); available at https://cac.org/the-third-way-2018-06-04/.

For Further Consideration

Bacevich, Andrew J. *The Limits of Power: The End of American Exceptionalism.* New York: Metropolitan Books, 2008.

Booker, Cory. *United: Thoughts on Finding Common Ground and Advancing the Common Good.* New York: Ballantine Books, 2017.

Borg, Marcus J. *Conflict Holiness and Politics in the Teachings of Jesus.* Harrisburg, PA: Trinity Press International, 1984.

Chase, Kenneth R., and Alan Jacobs, eds. *Must Christianity Be Violent? Reflections on History, Practice, and Theology.* Grand Rapids, MI: Brazos Press, 2003.

DeBrabander, Firmin. *Do Guns Make Us Free? Democracy and the Armed Society.* New Haven, CT: Yale University Press, 2015.

Douglas, James W. *The Non-Violent Cross: A Theology of Revolution and Peace.* Eugene, OR: Wipf & Stock, 1968.

Drier, Peter. *The 100 Greatest Americans of the 20th Century: A Social Justice Hall of Fame.* New York: Nation Books, 2012.

Gabor, Thomas. *Confronting Violence in America.* Independent Publisher (Palgrave), 2016.

Hauerwas, Stanley, and Jean Vanier. *Living Gently in a Violent World: The Prophetic Witness of Weakness.* Downers Grove, IL: InterVarsity Press, 2008.

Hendricks, Obery M., Jr. *The Politics of Jesus: Rediscovering the True Revolutionary Nature of Jesus' Teachings and How They Have Been Corrupted.* New York: Doubleday, 2006.

Peace is the Way: Writings on Nonviolence from the Fellowship of Reconciliation, ed. Walter Wink. Maryknoll, NY: Orbis Books, 2000.

Wink, Walter. *Engaging the Powers: Discernment and Resistance in a World of Domination.* Minneapolis, MN: Fortress Press, 1992.

---. *Jesus and Nonviolence: A Third Way.* Minneapolis, MN: Fortress Press, 2003.

Chapter 13

THE PLEASURES OF LIVING CONTEMPLATIVELY

Happiness, true happiness, is an inner quality.
It is a state of mind.
If your mind is at peace, you are happy.
If your mind is at peace,
but you have nothing else, you can be happy.
If you have everything the world can give
—pleasure, possessions, power—
but lack peace of mind, you can never be happy.
—Dada Vaswani

In the sweetness of friendship let there be laughter,
and sharing of pleasures.
For in the dew of little things
the heart finds its morning and is refreshed.
—Khalil Gibran

Art is unquestionably one of the purest and highest elements in human happiness.
It trains the mind through the eye, and the eye through the mind. As the sun colors flowers, so does art color life.
—John Lubbock, *The Pleasures of Life*

Many of us pursue pleasure with such breathless haste that we hurry past it.
—Søren Kierkegaard

A pleasure is full grown only when it is remembered.
—C.S. Lewis, *Out of the Silent Planet*

A man without pleasure is a man without any idea what life is about.
—Michael Grant, *BZRK*

When God laughs at the soul and the soul laughs back at God,
the persons of the Trinity are begotten.
When the Father laughs at the Son and
the Son laughs back at the Father,
that laughter gives pleasure, that pleasure gives joy, that joy gives love,
and that love is the Holy Spirit.
—Meister Eckhart

Wine is like many of the fine experiences in life which take time and experience to extract their full pleasure and meaning.
—Douglas Preston, *Crimson Shore*

Being left-handed

I'm a leftie, and in the first half of my life it pleased me no end to find out in a college psychology course that left-handed people have historically produced an above-average quota of high achievers.[212] As a leftie, the right side of my bicameral

[212] More recently, in *Right-Hand, Left-Hand: The Origins of Asymmetry in Brains, Bodies, Atoms and Cultures* (London: Weidenfeld and Nicolson, 2002), Chris McManus reports that left-handers' brains are structured differently (in a way that increases their range of abilities) and the genes that determine left-handedness also govern development of the language centers of the brain:

If by intelligent you mean someone who performs better on IQ tests, the simple answer is no. Studies in the U.K., U.S. and Australia have revealed that left-handed people differ from right-handers by only one IQ point, which is not noteworthy.

Left-handedness is, however, much more common among individuals with severe learning difficulties, such as mental retardation. A slightly higher proportion of left-handers have dyslexia or a stutter. Other problems, such as a higher rate of accidents reported in left-handers, mostly result from a world designed for the convenience of right-handers, with many tools not made for left-handed use. Although some people claim that a higher percentage of left-handers are exceptionally bright, large research studies do not support this idea.

If by smarter you mean more talented in certain areas, left-handers may have an advantage. Left-handers' brains are structured differently from right-handers' in ways that can allow them to process language, spatial relations and emotions in more diverse and potentially creative ways. Also, a slightly larger number of left-handers than right-handers are especially gifted in music and math. A study of musicians in professional orchestras found a significantly greater proportion of talented left-handers, even among those who played instruments that seem designed for right-handers, such as violins. Similarly, studies of adolescents who took tests to assess mathematical giftedness found many more left-handers in the population. The fact that mathematicians are often musical may not be a coincidence.

For other talents and skills, the benefits of being left-handed are less clear. In one-on-one competitive sports, being in the minority can be a tactical advantage. For instance, most right-handed tennis players have little experience playing left-handers, whereas left-handers have plenty of experience playing right-handers. Sports arenas can also be asymmetric, which may give left-handers an advantage. In baseball, for instance, a left-handed hitter is closer to first base after striking the ball than a right-handed batter is.

Whatever the advantages, handedness seems to be genetic. With 10 percent of people preferring their left hand, there must be some selective advantage, or else the genes would probably not survive. (283–85)

brain influences my leftist tendencies toward "big picture" orientations, a strong imagination, love for symbols and images, gravitation toward religions and philosophy, risk taking, and intuitive knowledge. It's little wonder that I'm attracted to literature, the liberal arts, theology, music, photography, iconography, the theater, coffee houses, walks in the woods, and quiet places, "thin places" of the earth as the Celts call them.[213]

Lest, however, as a leftie I get too egotistical about such musings, Harvard economist Joshua Goodman reports that left-handed people earn 10–12 percent less over the course of their lives than right-handed people.[214] O, dear!

And so we have so many left-handed musicians! Hundreds of them! Thousands! Here are but a few of my favorites:

- Paul McCartney, singer, songwriter, and guitarist with the Beatles. He first tried playing right handed but made no progress. Then he saw a picture of Slim Whitman playing left handed and realized that it was necessary to reverse the guitar, pick with the left hand, and reverse the strings.
- Paavo Berglund, well-known Finnish left-handed conductor and violinist, often joined his orchestra players for chamber music just for fun. Due to the value of his violin collection, he did not want to change his instruments and so trained himself to play left handed on violins with a normal setup.
- Kermit the Frog, musician extraordinaire with the banjo! Many Muppets whose arms are controlled by rods play instruments left handed because most right-handed puppeteers control the puppets' heads with their right hands leaving their left hands for playing.

---

213 While much has been written about "thin places" (sometimes called "thin spaces"), Barbara Brown Taylor best describes them in one of her Epiphany sermons in *Home by Another Way* (Lanham, MD: Rowman and Littlefield, 1999), 57 ff.

214 Joshua Goodman, "The Wages of Sinistrality: Handedness, Brain Structure and Human Capital Accumulation," *Journal of Economic Perspectives* 28, no. 4, 2014: 193–212, available at http://j.mp/14jLoya.

And, wonder of wonders! There are many truly terrific pieces of music played only with the left hand. Spend some time listening to piano music played by these two notables:

- Paul Wittgenstein whose determination to pursue an international career as a concert pianist with only one arm has enriched the piano literature with many great works and has been an inspiration for later pianists in more or less the same situation. Do yourself a big favor and listen to his "Left to Play Solo." You may become a leftie yourself!
- Alexander Nikolayevich Scriabin (1871–1915), a Russian composer and pianist, one of the most innovative and controversial of early modern composers. The *Great Soviet Encyclopedia* says of him that "no composer has had more scorn heaped on him or greater love bestowed." Leo Tolstoy described Scriabin's music as "a sincere expression of genius." Scriabin had a major impact on the music world over time, influencing composers such as Igor Stravinsky and Sergei Prokofiev. His ten published sonatas for piano, which arguably provided the most consistent contribution to the genre since the time of Beethoven's set, have been increasingly championed. "Though of diminutive stature and with hands that could barely span an octave, Scriabin attacked the most difficult repertoire during his years at the conservatory; in 1891 he severely strained his right hand with excessive practicing. Forbidden by a doctor to play, he focused on his left hand and developed a formidable technique." If you wish to hear his left-hand masterpieces, you can't do better than enjoying his Prelude in C-sharp minor and Nocturne in D-flat, Op. 9, nos. 1 and 2. Enjoy!

Now for my favorite: Thelonius Monk! I first heard him play on old vinyl 78s when I was eighteen years old and in college in Fort Wayne, Indiana. Knowing little about music and nothing about jazz, when I listened to Monk, I was really impressed with the sound of his left-handed piano work. When I studied Koine Greek as a freshman, I listened to him continually. His jazz and my diving into Koine Greek were a nightclub rendezvous. Monk's way of playing is mostly based on the right hemisphere of the brain. As a consequence, his cognitive style is what many consider, "irrational, global and synthetic." Much like Koene (biblical, that is, unclassical) Greek, which Garry Wills nicely describes as "ungrammatical, "muddled," and undignified,"[215] Monk's stress on the use of the left hand gives us phrases characterized by "wrong" notes, harmonically off by a half tone so that the tension is increased and then left unresolved:

> He often plays two adjacent keys on the piano simultaneously, maximizing dissonance. He strikes the keys with his flat fingers (instead of bowing them). In particular moments of elation he shakes the keyboard with his powerful elbows. When he plays others' compositions, he displaces the tunes, then interprets them again, upsetting the structure by changing accents and using advances, delays, pauses and swing.
>
> Reflecting on Monk's music, critics have emphasized a sort of childlike quality and "primitivism." These definitions do not indicate deficiency in modernism, rather they mirror the originality of his "primordial" musical style, meaning that it seems to be strictly connected to the origin. Very often his tunes sound like children's chants while they are at play. They have the same free and reiterative musical pattern.[216]

In Biblical imagery, Monk played like a goat, on the wrong side of things and life. Like me. I think that unconsciously that's why I like him and still do.

---

215 *What Jesus Meant* (New York: Viking Penguin, 2006), xii, xiii.

216 Bud Powell, "Thelonious Monk and the 'Split Brain,'" n.d., available at http://www.jazzitalia.net/articoli/powellmonk_eng.asp#.WMAsibGZOi4.

It's little wonder, then, that annually I quietly celebrate Left-Handers Day on August 13!

Smoking my pipe

Holding my tobacco pipe in my left hand, too much have I loved smoking—from a very young age, something like thirteen or fourteen. Back in the early 1950s when I was shipped off to prep school at Concordia Collegiate Institute in Bronxville, New York, I began smoking unfiltered Camels (after forging a parental permission slip) and kept up the sucking and puffing for years. Increasingly addicted until I chain-smoked two packs a day in the late 1960s. Not a single label on any pack told to avoid smoking for health reasons.

One morning in my late twenties in Lafayette, Louisiana, I woke up with my chest in a state of rigor mortis, from neck to waist, as stiff as a sheet of drywall sheeting. Although I had seen pictures of smoke-damaged lungs, the color of rotten-tomato-purple, in a *Playboy* magazine, I paid no heed to the effects of smoking until that frightful Louisiana awakening. By 10:00 a.m., I stopped cold-turkey, never again to light up another cig, not another Marlboro, my brand of choice at that time.

But I didn't say a wholesale good-bye to tobacco. Not entirely. Working on a master's degree at the University of Southwestern Louisiana while serving as pastor of Trinity Lutheran Church, I allowed myself a number of achievement rewards for the likes of writing A+ papers, finishing a thesis, and passing final exams. After such accomplishments, I'd drive from Lafayette, Louisiana, to New Orleans, park somewhere in the French Quarter, and buy a medium-priced pipe and load up on half a pound of premium tobacco laced with Turkish latakia, blended with Virginia burleys and cavendish. And puff away. Enjoyably. On and on for another ten years until sometime in my early years at Eastern Kentucky University, I quit (I can't remember why) all tobaccos once and for all.

Or so I thought. After being self-enrolled in Tobacco Anonymous for twenty years, several years ago, while looking into a beautiful antique cherry box in which I had kept a few of Kris's things after he died in 1993, I found two of his pipes, one rather small, the other terribly good-looking and inviting. Taking the latter with me when June and I vacationed in Gatlinburg, Tennessee, I lucked upon a decent pipe shop and purchased (from a lady smoking a pipe!) three ounces of tobacco. Memories flooded back, and I felt especially privileged to puff on Kris's pipe. I bought a zip lighter, a tamper, and two dozen pipe cleaners. The first few days of my return were not entirely satisfactory. The weather was hot; my throat burned a bit. But once into the cool of fall of 2012, a daily pipeful became a pleasure indeed.

For several years now, I imagine myself blowing smoke rings as someone enjoying life with two of my favorite pipers—Carl Jung and C. S. Lewis. Inasmuch, however, as June doesn't keen up to the smell of incense no matter how liturgical or mundane (even though her father smoked Prince Albert tobacco), I restrict myself to savorings of "Edwards Supreme" or a more expensive "Balkan Sobbranie" on the back porch, in the workshop, or while driving around town with Mitzie. So once again, I'm hooked and frankly don't give a damn.

Well, actually I do give a damn. My personal physician, Dr. Lee Woodall (mentioned in chapter 7), smilingly approves of my pipe habit because, as we both know, numerous studies indicate that there are indeed health benefits from smoking a pipe, provided one puffs a bowlful just once a day.[217] Puffing so, I'm as happy as I used to be as a fourteen-year-old lighting up a Camel, only now I look a wee bit more distinguished with a Dunhill between my teeth. Or at least I think so. So begging your pardon, I'm off to lighting up a special blend that came my way yesterday. I'll light it in Kris's pipe. And lest you think I'm off to some nefarious business, don't forget: somebody famously once said, "No man ever committed a crime smoking a pipe."

217 See, for example, "Surprisingly, Smoking Tobacco from a Pipe May Have Health Benefits" at http://eattheplanet.org/surprisingly-smoking-tobacco-from-a-pipe-may-have-health-benefits/.

Enjoying fine wine and good beer

In my home there's generally a good bottle or two of wine on the shelf, some stout beer in the refrigerator, and a bottle of bourbon in the library.

More than once I've made some beer. One time my teetotaling wife June even helped me cap fifty or sixty bottles. Although I remember times in my younger days when I got the dry heaves from downing too much, lately I've been something of a conservative at the tap. Just to show you how conservative I am, let me share a story with you; I got it from my friend Betty Panick. Here it is, slightly edited:

> Andy walks into a bar in Dublin, orders three pints of Guinness and sits in the corner of the room, drinking a sip out of each pint in turn. When he had finished all three, He went back to the bar and ordered three more.
>
> The barman says, "You know a pint goes flat soon after I pull it. Your pint would taste better if you bought one at a time."
>
> Andy replies, "Well now, I have two brodders, one live in Arizona, and de odder in Indiana. And here I am in Dublin. When we all left home, we promised dat we'd drink dis way to remember de days we all drank togedder."
>
> The barman admits that this is a nice custom and says no more.
>
> Andy becomes a regular customer, and always drinks the same way. He orders three pints and drinks a sip out of each in turn, until they are finished.
>
> One day, he comes in and orders just two pints.
>
> All the other regulars in the bar notice! And they fall silent. When he goes back to the bar for the second round, the barman says, "I don't want

> to intrude on your grief but I wanted to offer my condolences on your great loss."
>
> Andy looks confused for a moment, then the penny drops, and he starts to laugh, "Oh no," Andy says, "Begorrah, everyone is fine! Tis me! I've quit drinking!"

Well, maybe in a joke, but not in life. I don't image that I'll stop sipping a good beer or a glass of dark red wine.

Or maybe at the end of the day: a little Jim Beam

Centering Prayer also helps me become less and less fearful of death. As best I can tell, I'm not afraid of death. I even now look forward to entering the cosmic world held in God's arms and One-ing. This doesn't mean I'm hurrying toward death, but I realize at that I am dying. I've lived my life expectancy; and, yes, there may be many more years ahead. But maybe not. In between the "here and now" and the "there and not yet," I find myself echoing what the late Phyllis Tickle, was reported to have said.[218] In an interview at her home with David Gibson, she pointed to her coffee mug filled with Postum (she had to forego caffeine) and told Gibson, "I am no

---

218 Religious News Service. "Author Phyllis Tickle faces death just as she enjoyed life: 'The dying is my next career." May 22, 2015. By the way, you can't beat Tickle when it comes to good, optimistic writing about the future of Christianity. Gibson nicely summarizes her contribution to Christianity's coming revolution this way:

In 2008, her landmark work, "The Great Emergence: How Christianity Is Changing and Why," she probed how a new and vibrant Christianity is recovering elements of the past and carrying them into a whole new future. That's a theme she continued to develop in a 2013 book, "The Age of the Spirit: How the Ghost of an Ancient Controversy Is Shaping the Church." She has yet more to say on that, cancer permitting. Taken together, Tickle's works combine the sprawling scope of historian Karen Armstrong with the fine-grained command of sociologist Robert Bellah and the rural sensibilities of poet Wendell Berry. Throw in a dash of Thomas Merton's sense and spirituality for good measure. "Tickle has earned her place as one of the modern spiritual masters of the late twentieth and early twenty-first centuries," her friend and occasional collaborator Jon Sweeney writes in the introduction to an upcoming selection of Tickle's writings in Orbis' Modern Spiritual Masters Series.

more afraid of dying than I am of, I don't know, drinking coffee." Good for Tickle. But there's more. She's also grateful—and so am I—that she can still drink a nightly whiskey. "Jack Daniels, of course!" she announced as a Tennessean. What a model of a saint! In fact, such a model that I'd taken Gibson's article and pasted it into a book my friend Mark Miller sent me several weeks ago: Michael P. Foley's *Drinking with the Saints: The Sinner's Guide to a Holy Happy Hour*.[219] Like Tickle, while falling upward, I'm in a blessed happy hour, so much so spiritually and physically that almost nightly, an hour or so after my Centering, I like a wee bit of bourbon whiskey. Or maybe better yet as a Kentuckian—a gin and tonic, done right with squeeze of lime. Or if the cabinet provides one—a good wine, maybe even a high-end twenty-dollar bottle. Surely my Lord and winebibber Jesus shares my delight; after all, he once served some several barrels of red so good that it flabbergasted the guests at a wedding in Cana: how good it tasted! Something like a well-aged bottle of Barone Ricasoli Castello di Brolio Chianti Classico.

Dear Phyllis, I lift tonight's glass of Fireball Cinnamon Whiskey to you. You have so blessed me with your writings and publications.[220]

As you might imagine, I appreciate Jesus's endorsement of our drinking good wine, among the many other ways he encouraged us to enjoy the beautiful wherever it may be found. Dr. John Gillespie, my Kentucky physician, once told me to drink at least two glasses of wine a day, and I've tried hard to keep up the regimen. Yes, I

---

219 (Washington, DC: Regnery History, 2005).

220 Among Phyllis Tickle's many books, I especially recommend *The Great Emergence: How Christianity Is Changing and Why* (Grand Rapids, MI: Baker, 2008); with Jon M. Sweeney, *The Age of the Spirit: How the Ghost of an Ancient Controversy Is Shaping the Church* (Grand Rapids, MI: Baker, 2014); and her seasonal three volumes for daily prayer (e.g., *The Divine Hours: Prayers for Summertime* [New York: Random House, 2000]). *The Divine Hours* is the first major literary and liturgical reworking of the sixth-century Benedictine Rule of fixed-hour prayer. This beautifully conceived and thoroughly modern three-volume guide will appeal to the theological novice as well as to the ecclesiastical sophisticate. Making primary use of the *Book of Common Prayer* and the writings of the Church Fathers, *The Divine Hours* is also a companion to the *New Jerusalem Bible*, from which it draws its Scripture readings. The trilogy blends prayer and praise in a way that, while extraordinarily fresh, respects and builds upon the ancient wisdom of Christianity.

enjoy drinking and sipping wine and its alcoholic cousins, beer and bourbon. While never having practiced the high art of vintology, several times I've made batches of homebrew, especially Dunkelweizen (double hopped). And after visiting the Jim Beam distillery in Kentucky upon returning home from a visit to Amy, Kevin, Mary Carol, Jackson, and Hayden, I discovered I like Red Stag, a cherry-flavored bourbon that's probably a girly whiskey. Who cares? More toward the macho, thanks to friend Bill Gates, I now know how to make a decent vodka martini.

Writing icons

I won't say too much (but I could) about my love for and fascination with icons. The joy of beholding them began years ago when in my four-volume prayer book, *For All the Saints: A Prayer Book For and By the Church*,[221] Frederick J. Schumacher introduced me to twelve of the church's most well-known icons, among them *The Icon of the Nativity*, *The Icon of the Pantocrator*, and *The Icon of the Descent of the Holy Spirit*. Schumacher's essays on each of the twelve grounded me into a lifelong appreciation not only of the Orthodox Church but also of its deeply imaginative iconic theology. Under the tutelage of several master iconographers, I was gifted with privilege of actually learning how to "write" an icon. My first attempt, *The Icon of the Annunciation*, still hangs on a wall in my library. Four other icons (*I am the Way*, *I am the Good Shepherd*, *I am the Resurrection*, and *I am the Gate*) made possible as a group

221 Comp. and ed. Frederick J. Schumacher with Dorothy A. Zelenko (Delhi, NY: American Lutheran Publicity Bureau, 1995).

effort under the direction of Debbie Hardegree, now hang within the sanctuary of my parish.

Loving icons, I give them places of honor in my study so that as I enter to read, write, and sit for centering prayer, I always see *The Icon of the Anastasis, Christ Pantocrator* from the Sinai Monastery of St. Catherine, and Andrei Rublev's *The Holy Trinity.*[222] It should not surprise you that I often visit Orthodox churches to gaze at such masterful works of Christian art.

Taking photographs

Ah, photography. Introduced to cameras and the darkroom when a freshman at Concordia Junior College in Ft. Wayne, Indiana, I learned how to operate the Speed Graphic and develop prints in a dank basement darkroom. Some of my prints eventually got into the yearbooks. Since then I've owned all

Celtic Quiet

[222] *The Icon of the Anastasis* depicts the most important event in the Eastern Orthodox Church year, the Resurrection. It will look strange to most Americans or Western Europeans because the iconic form of the Resurrection originally preferred in Eastern Orthodoxy is the event known in the West as the "Descent into Hell" or more colorfully, "The Harrowing of Hell."

The *Christ Pantocrator* of St. Catherine's Monastery at Sinai is one of the oldest Byzantine religious icons, dating from the sixth century AD. It is the earliest known version of the pantocrator style that still survives today and is regarded by historians and scholars to be one of the most important and recognizable works in the study of Byzantine art as well as Orthodox Christianity.

Andrei Rublev's most famous work and the most famous of all Russian icons, *The Trinity,* is also called *The Hospitality of Abraham*. The Trinity depicts the three angels who visited Abraham at the Oak of Mamre (Gen. 18:1–8), but the painting is full of symbolism and is interpreted as an icon of the Holy Trinity. At the time of Andrei Rublev, *the Holy Trinity* was the embodiment of spiritual unity, peace, harmony, mutual love, and humility. Little is known about The Trinity's history; art historians can only make suggestions based on few known facts. Even the authorship of Rublev is questioned sometimes. Various authors suggest different dates, such as 1408–25, 1422–23, or 1420–27. The official version states 1411 or 1425–27. The Trinity is currently held in the Tretyakov Gallery in Moscow.

sorts of cameras: twin-lens reflexes, thirty-five-millimeter Nikons, and most recently a Nikon D5200. While none of my photographs will take a prize at any showing, there is one, taken of a stone cottage as I was walking along the coast of North Ireland, that I especially like; I've titled it "Celtic Quiet" because it reminds me of the many places where I have been given the gift of union with all life. With memberships in camera clubs, some of my prints have been here and there in local exhibits. Nothing outstanding, but a few of which I'm enjoyably proud.[223]

Mentioning Ireland, I confess that I also like to travel with June. She and I have also visited Egypt, Greece, Italy, Turkey, England, Scotland, Wales, France, Germany, Honduras, Belize, Mexico, Canada, Panama, and many of the Caribbean islands. I would love to visit Sweden! In-between times, I've dabbled in making pottery in classes at Gordon State College, making birdhouses in my workshop, writing poetry (none of which was ever published), and learning to dance, among other brief preoccupations. But more than anything, I like to write. After all, as Mark Twain once said, "Writing is easy. All you have to do is cross out the wrong words."

Gardening

Finally, you should know that I feel no more at home with the world and God than when I'm on my knees in my flower and vegetable gardens. When living in Kansas in the 1970s, I did a good bit of organic gardening in the backyard. Collecting chicken shit and manures wherever I could find such stuff in and around Winfield, God let me produce a rather attractive veggie garden (at least I thought so). Now some thirty years later, I'm once again on my knees in Barnesville, Georgia.

Thank you, Great Gardener God, for introducing me to James Mays, surely Barnesville's gardener valedictorian! After driving past

[223] For those interested in using cameras as a contemplative resource, I heartily recommend Dirk Devries' *Contemplative Vision: Photography as a Spiritual Practice* (New York: Church Publishing, 2019).

James's magnificent gardens on Houston Street many times, I finally stopped one day to chat with him, and we became friends. In his mid=fifties, James now calls me "Pop" and June "Mom," so close has our friendship become. When I was unlearned and unable to tend to amending the soil, James has made it rich with a variety of manures. He has shown me how to plant tomatoes that grow up to six feet tall with ripe red fruit, how to mound up asparagus with black mulch so that daily cutting is possible, and how to maintain a garden that's the envy of neighbors. James is my "University Professor of Gardening," and I try to be a good student. "Thanks, Dr. Mays, for all you have given to me!"

Just being

More than anything, I enjoy simply being alive. I don't fear death and even look forward to it as best I can. I live without anxieties, work at attentiveness, am reasonably aware of political situations, able to wake up, take naps, eat blueberries, drink wine, take a shower, and go to the bathroom. When I consider how able I am to move about in my eighth decade, I know I'm blessed more than most men my age. I still enjoy reading my Greek New Testament. I look forward to receiving mail and e-mail. Sure, I have my aches and pains, a minor surgery now and then, and a keen awareness that I may not live out the day. I have been blessed with reasonably good health. My teeth are still with me; my blood pressure is okay, and I'm not burdened with too much extra weight. Maybe that's due to eating lots of fruits and vegetables, no longer eating meat like a Neanderthal, and avoiding processed sugars as much as possible. Whatever the reason—good genes, a reasonably stress-less way of living, or whatever—I know that I'm fortunate, fortunate as the Hebrew poet says:

You got me when I was an unformed youth, God, and taught me everything I know.
Now I'm telling the world your wonders;I'll
keep at it until I'm old and gray.
(Psalm 71.17-18)

Chapter 14

A SECOND NAÏVETÉ

In my next life I want to live my life backwards.
You start out dead and get that out of the way.
Then you wake up in an old people's home feeling better every day.
You get kicked out for being too healthy, go collect your pension,
and then when you start work, you get a gold watch
and a party on your first day.
You work for 40 years until you're young enough to enjoy your retirement.
You party, drink alcohol, and are generally promiscuous,
then you are ready for high school.
You then go to primary school, you become a kid, you play.
You have no responsibilities, you become a baby until you are born.
And then you spend your last 9 months floating
in luxurious spa-like conditions
with central heating and room service on tap,
larger quarters every day and then Voila!
You finish off as an orgasm!
—Woody Allen

Going back

Wendell Berry, the first living writer to be inducted into the Kentucky Writers Hall of Fame,[224] tells us in his Sabbath Poems that "there is no going back":

"No Going Back"
No, no, there is no going back.
Less and less you are
that possibility you were.
More and more you have become
those lives and deaths
that have belonged to you.
You have become a sort of grave
containing much that was
and is no more in time, beloved
then, now, and always.
And so you have become a sort of tree
standing over the grave.
Now more than ever you can be
generous toward each day
that comes, young, to disappear
forever, and yet remain
unaging in the mind.
Every day you have less reason
not to give yourself away.

At first blush you'd think that "No Going Back" says it all. But that's not true. You and I can go back, but not as we might have first

224 Wendell E. Berry (born August 5, 1934) is an American novelist, poet, environmental activist, cultural critic, and farmer. A prolific author, he has written many novels, short stories, poems, and essays. He is an elected member of the Fellowship of Southern Writers, a recipient of the National Humanities Medal, and the Jefferson Lecturer for 2012. He is also a 2013 Fellow of the American Academy of Arts and Sciences. Berry was named the recipient of the 2013 Richard C. Holbrooke Distinguished Achievement Award. On January 28, 2015, he became the first living writer to be inducted into the Kentucky Writers Hall of Fame.

imagined. We do indeed go back—only not as we go forward. It's not like driving to the grocery store and returning home. When you grow older and begin to retrace your steps, your way back in time is often accompanied with remembered grief and disappointment. Returning, we relive and "become those lives and deaths that have belonged" to us. Instead of becoming more as we return, Berry reminds us that we become less. Losing a loved one, losing a kneecap, we also lose the many memories of that husband, wife, child, that kneecap. They linger on like photographs "unaging in the mind." More and more we sense a gradual emptiness as we age, learning how to become a "tree standing over a grave." Aging and returning over our lives, we find life teaching us lots of lettings go, how to become less and less, often even to the point of "every day having less reason /not to give [ourselves] away." The end starts to arrive, and we are taught how to make a one hundred and eighty degree U-turn, returning to our beginnings. For me, it means that I'm learning to return to the beginnings of my life as I described them in in chapter 1.

A second naïveté

Going back to the beginnings of my life, when I was utterly with God and with my mother in her womb, is a return, a second birthing, Thomas Traherne[225] so beautifully describes:

225 In 1637, Thomas Traherne, the son of a shoemaker, was born in Hereford, England. He received his education from the University of Oxford and was ordained as an Anglican clergyman in 1660. Traherne first served in a parish near Credenhill and later became the chaplain to Sir Orlando Bridgeman, Lord Keeper of the Great Seal.

In his lifetime, Traherne published only one work, *Roman Forgeries* (1673), and very little else is known of his biography., his most important prose work, was published posthumously in 1675. His Thanksgivings appeared anonymously in 1699 as *A Serious and Pathetical Contemplation of the Mercies of God.* Traherne is often considered as the last of the metaphysical poets, which included such major figures as John Donne, George Herbert, and Henry Vaughn.

The majority of Traherne's poetry remained unknown until 1896, when two of his manuscripts were discovered by chance in a London bookstall. *Poetical Works* was first published in 1903; it was followed in 1908 by *Centuries of Meditations.* In 1910, a manuscript found in the British Museum was published as Traherne's *Poems of Felicity.* More of his work continued to come to light over the course of

The Return

To infancy, O Lord, again I come,
That I my manhood may improve:
My early tutor is the womb;
I still my cradle love.
'Tis strange that I should wisest be,
When least I could an error see.

Till I gain strength against temptation, I
Perceive it safest to abide
An infant still; and therefore fly
(A lowly state may hide
A man from danger) to the womb,
That I may yet new-born become.

My God, Thy bounty then did ravish me!
Before I learned to be poor,
I always did Thy riches see,
And thankfully adore:
Thy glory and Thy goodness were
My sweet companions all the year.

---

the twentieth century. As late as 1967, a poetry manuscript attributed to Traherne was discovered in a refuse dump near Lancashire by a man in search of spare auto parts. The manuscript was published as *Commentaries of Heaven: The Poems in 1989*. Much of his work to this date remains unpublished.

Traherne's great theme is the visionary innocence of childhood, and in this respect, he has been compared with William Blake and Walt Whitman. His style, too, bears resemblance to these authors in its incantatory rush, repetitions, and disregard for the rules of standard English. His poems, such as the often-anthologized "Shadows in the Water," suggest that adults have lost the joy of childhood, and with it an understanding of the divine nature of creation. In his writing, Traherne sought to reclaim this joy in the world. Thomas Traherne died on September 27, 1674, and was buried in Teddington under the reading desk in the church where he had served. (From the Academy of American Poets. Available at https://www.poets.org/poetsorg/poet/thomas-traherne.)

In the first chapter, I shared my beginnings, my births: one from Mom and second "from above," from God. Such was the time of my first "naïveté" (the word "naïveté" deriving from the Latin *navitus*, "by birth," "original") when as a baby I lived innocent and naïve. One'd with God in my mother's womb, warm and content, I knew no thoughts. I was the infant described in Psalm 131: "Like a baby content in its mother's arms, my soul was a baby content." I was *tabula rasa*, a blank slate, with God.

I'm often reminded of my baby beginnings because my eighty-year-old high chair still sits in a corner of my home, near the breakfast table. Ever since I left that antique high chair eight decades ago, Jesus has been telling me, "Andy, unless you turn around and become like a little child, you will never enter the kingdom of heaven." Today I'm listening to Jesus and learning to become like a little child, a toddler. Sitting in that high chair I was already within God and God was within me. Returning to that womb, that chair in centering and mystical prayer, I'm letting go of life's accumulations and returning in unitive consciousness to who I was in the first months and years of my life. I need to live within that reality, that innocence, the unitive consciousness with an ever-growing loss of binary thinking, a life of this and that.

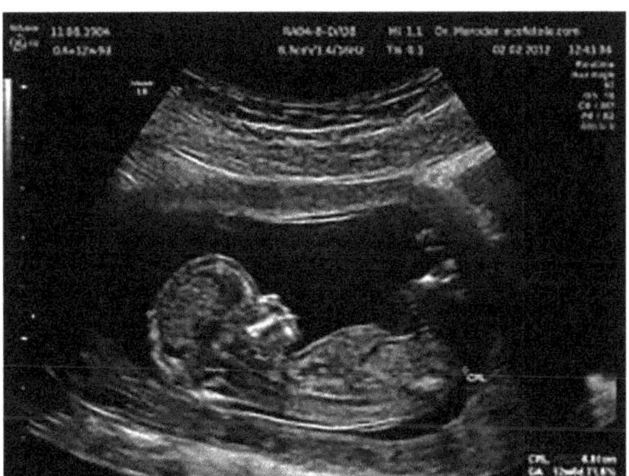

Buddhist wisdom teachers within their own tradition remind us of this reality with their question: "When you're not thinking of anything good and anything bad, at that moment, what is your original face?" Paraphrasing the question, a wisdom teacher might ask, "Before you learned to think about things and make judgments, who were you and what were you like?" However one responds to that question, the answer must somehow imply an awareness of unitive consciousness. The answer needs to imply the absence of dualistic thinking or one's wonderful original naïveté. Recently my granddaughter Audrey sent me an ultrasound image of her little girl fetus resting within her womb. It was a picture of her daughter's first naïveté. Simplicity itself, oneness with God. All of us in our beginnings were one with the Divine. Buddhists call such unitive realization our Buddha nature. Such a reality, Buddhists tell us, is always with us. Christians use the word "God" for the Great Presence. God has always been with us, one with us.

No one less than Meister Eckhart reminds us that "God is at home; it's we who have gone out for a walk." We all started taking that figurative walk shortly after we're born. Learning how to develop and have egos, we entered our cultural system. In my case, I went on a journey with an inherited identity from my parents, church, community, and schools. First, I learned how to read some English, German, and Latin. Later some Greek and Hebrew. I got an education, earned a PhD, got married several times, left the church, returned again, and let friends introduce me to the practice of letting-go as I entered the second half of my life. My letting-go practice has given me opportunities to realize that "in my end is my beginning," as T. S. Eliot succinctly puts it.[226] What he means is that all of us eventually go full circle. We return to our naïveté.

Some call such a return a "second simplicity." We need to take Jesus seriously when one time his grown-up disciples came to him and asked, "Who is to be the greatest in the kingdom of heaven?" Be shocked at what happens in this teaching moment:

> Jesus called a child over and had the child stand near him. Then he said: "I promise you this. If you don't change and become like a child, you will never get into the kingdom of heaven. But if you are as humble as this child, you are the greatest in the kingdom of heaven. And when you welcome one of these children because of me, you welcome me." (Matt. 18:2–5, CEV)

---

[226] T. S. Eliot, "East Coker," *Collected Poems, 1909-1962* (New York: Harcourt, Brace & Company), 190.

Jesus says it this way in Eugene Peterson's *The Message*:

> "I'm telling you, once and for all, that unless you return to square one and start over like children, you're not even going to get a look at the kingdom, let alone get in. Whoever becomes simple and elemental again, like this child, will rank high in God's kingdom. What's more, when you receive the childlike on my account, it's the same as receiving me." (Matt. 18:3–5)

Then in the very next chapter, when the disciples try to stop people from bringing their children to Jesus for prayer and blessing, presumably because Jesus has more important things to do than hang out with kids, Jesus tells the disciples to knock it off. "Let the little children come to me and stop keeping them away. For the kingdom of heaven belongs to people like these" (14).

Late in my life I want to become a child so that I can hear Jesus say, "Come here, little one!" I want Jesus to pick me up and hold me in his lap. Although I have a picture of me sitting in my toddler's high chair when I was only one-and-a-half-years old, I really don't remember what it was like to be a toddler. But let me guess. I was wide-eyed and open to all of life. I had very few pre-conceptions about the people I saw around me. I loved Mommy and Daddy. I liked learning how to walk and talk. I laughed a lot. I liked somebody reading to me. I enjoyed music, food, naps, and a good night's sleep. Here is how Thomas R. Kelly (1893-1941), a Quaker missionary, describes such second simplicity that is the goal of mature adulthood:

> The last fruit of holy obedience is the simplicity of the trusting child, the simplicity of the children of God.

> It is the simplicity which lies beyond complexity. It is the naiveté which is the yonder side of sophistication. It is the beginning of spiritual maturity, which comes after the awkward age of religious busyness for the Kingdom of God—yet how many are caught, and arrested in development, within this adolescent development of the soul's growth! The mark of this simplified life is radiant joy. . . . Knowing sorrow to the depths it does not agonize and fret and strain, but in serene, unhurried calm it walks in time with the joy and assurance of Eternity. Knowing fully the complexity of men's problems it cuts through to the Love of God and ever cleaves to Him. . . . It binds all obedient souls together in the fellowship of humility and simple adoration of Him who is all in all.
>
> This amazing simplification comes when we "center down," when life is lived with singleness of eye, from a holy Center where the breath and stillness of Eternity are heavy upon us and we are wholly yielded to Him. Some of you know this holy, recreating Center of eternal peace and joy and live in it day and night. Some of you may see it over the margin and wistfully long to slip into that amazing Center where the soul is at home with God. Be very faithful to that wistful longing. It is the Eternal Goodness calling you to return Home, to feed upon green pastures and walk beside still waters and live in the peace of the Shepherd's presence. It is the life *beyond* fevered strain. We are called beyond strain, to peace and power and joy and love and thorough abandonment of self. We are called to put our hands trustingly in His hand and walk the holy way, in no anxiety assuredly resting in Him.[227]

[227] Qtd. Richard Rohr in his *Daily Meditation*, "Simplicity," posted on October 3, 2016; available at https://cac.org/truth-is-one-2016-10-03/.

Jesus says that we all would do well to go back to our beginnings, to being children. We are to see life like little toddlers. We are to unload ourselves of our culture's materialistic mentality and supervision. For some it may be a time of nakedness, innocence, and poverty—both spiritually and materialistically. Perhaps a single- or two-bedroom one-thousand-square-foot home will do as well as a *Better Homes and Garden* mansion. Maybe better. Perhaps less doctrinaire certitude about what's what. Perhaps wonderment in seeing the world again for the first time. The gift of grace and freedom.

The difference between our second and first naivetes

There's a huge difference between first and second naivetes. Our first naivetes are pre-critical; that is, within them, we tend to believe nearly everything, indeed too much. In our first naivetes we enjoy well-being; we're largely unaware of oppression and life's incongruities. Appreciating community, in one's first naivete, one is protectively unaware of hurt. Clothed in our first naivetes, we can afford to be uncritical because nearly everything makes good sense. But then comes growing up and out, and almost inevitably we move to criticism, to seeing things and issues differently. We become aware of a self (with a small "s") in conflict, of others in dishonest interestedness, and of God clothed often lashing out in enmity, harsh judgments, and exclusions. This critical dimension of our pilgrimage discovers the slippage between appearance and reality in our social arrangements, slippage poorly covered by ideology and inadequate theologies. In sharp contrast, as Nick Nowalk observes, the second naivete is decidedly post-critical, not pre-critical:

> The second naivete has been through the pit and is now prepared to 'hope all things' (1 Cor. 13:7). But now hope is after the pit. It now knows that finally things have been reduced and need be reduced no more. It knows that our experience is demystified as it

> must be. But it knows that even in a world demystified and reduced, grace intrudes and God makes all things new. The ones who give thanks and sing genuinely new songs must be naive or they would not bother to sing songs and to give thanks. But it is a praise in which the anguish of disorientation is not forgotten, removed, or absent.... The song celebrative of reorientation is a movement out of the disorientation marked by lament...The song of celebration is a new song sung at the appearance of a new reality, new creation, new harmony, new reliability (Pss. 33:3; 40:3; 96:1; 98:1; 144:9; 149:1; Isa. 42:10; Rev. 14:3). Its style and rhetoric must speak of the quality of surprise and newness that are appropriate to such new reality...It is the experience that the world has a new coherence, that the devastating hopelessness of the lament is not finally appropriate for the way life is.[228]

Living within a second naivete doesn't mean that we are uneducated, stupid, or lacking wisdom; it simply means that after our first orientation to life we have experienced the gift of disorientation, and by God's grace we've eventually entered a wonderful reorientation. The Domination System no longer necessarily controls the way we perceive Reality. After a good many labor pains, newly delivered and within a second naivete, we now breathe deeply and sing lustfully, fully aware of who we are, where we have been, and where we are today.

Life within a child's naivete

Having long admired Frederick Buechner, especially his sermons written with the sensibility of a poet, the cadence of a consummate

[228] "Sing a New Song: The Difference between First Naivete and Second Naivete," posted on his blog, *The Strange Triumph of the Lamb* (October 7, 2015); available at https://strangetriumph.wordpress.com/2015/10/07/sing-a-new-song-the-difference-between-first-naivete-and-second-naivete/.

storyteller, and the conviction that God is compassionate beyond all comprehension, I appreciate how Buechner wonderfully tells us what it's like to live child-like with our Abba Father:

> A child knows how to accept a gift. He does not worry about losing his dignity or becoming indebted if he accepts it. His conscience does not bother him because the gift is free and he has not earned it and therefore really has no right to it. He just takes it, with joy. In fact, if it is something that he wants very much, he may even ask for it. And lastly, a child knows how to trust. It is late at night and very dark and there is the sound of sirens as his father wakes him. He does not explain anything but just takes him by the hand and gets him up, and the child is scared out of his wits and has no idea what is going on, but he takes his father's hand anyway and lets his father lead him wherever he chooses into the darkness.[229]

Within the mystic Presence of God, that's exactly how we all want to live within our second naivetes.

With humility

The gift of contemplative prayer helps us in our journey as we empty ourselves of egotistical thinking and behaviors. Such a journey has everything to do with humility. As Carmen Butcher notes, "A good dictionary will tell us that humility has several different meanings: The first is "the quality of being humble," which makes me

[229] *The Magnificent* Defeat (New York: HarperCollins, 1966), 135.

look up humble: "not proud or arrogant, modest"; the second definition listed for humility is "having a feeling of insignificance, inferiority," and the third is "being courteously respectful."[230] But Butcher also tells us that we need more than a dictionary to know how the goodness of humility may genuinely take root in one's life. Humility is not to be defined as a feeling of insignificance or inferiority. Nor is humility a lack of faith in our unworthiness; "it's not self-hatred of any sort." It's not telling yourself that you not smart. Such thoughts are useless when it comes to being humble. Humility is rather complete rest in Christ. It's becoming empty in order to be full of Christ. As Butcher repeatedly emphasizes, humility is one's willingness to be taught, to be open, to remain vulnerable, to be like Jesus. To help us understand, Butcher tells us this story about her son, John:

> He is eight. When he was four, I would say to him, "John, you sure are handsome."
>
> He would answer without hesitation, "I know." And then he was off to play or to be kind to his sister or to offer to help me take the clothes out of the dryer or to give me a hug, his admission forgotten.
>
> I would marvel. I would contemplate why he could say that with such confidence and with such a lack of self-consciousness. In my friendship with God I have long longed to have such a combination of confidence and un-self-consciousness as my son has in the love my husband and I have for him.
>
> John can answer in that simple but profound statement, "I know," because he feels completely loved. He totally trusts his father and me. He feels safe in the knowledge that he is part of (yes, imperfect but) a very caring family.

[230] What is Humility?" *Carmen's Blog* (January 29, 2010); available at http://www.carmenbutcher.com/wordpress/?p=812

> So humility is accepting love. It is considering life from another person's perspective. Humility is embracing that I am one member of God's global, non-exclusive family.
>
> Humility is not bitterly grimacing and putting up the neon "CLOSED" sign on my heart. It is accepting moment by moment that God loves me and being kind to my own self. It is also reaching out through my own pain as God nudges me, to love others. It is also not accepting abuse but respecting my self and having healthy boundaries because God loves me.
>
> .... Whenever I consider how important humility is and how much I have to learn about it, I realize that humility is the foundation of everything good in this world and that humility is another way of pronouncing the word *love.*

May all of us learn to live within such a combination of confidence and un-self-consciousness, "another way of pronouncing the word *love.*"

Even as we fall down

Yes, now and then we may fall down. Again and again. Ursula Fleming reminds us that "we are born, so they say, with only two natural fears: fear of falling and fear of loud noises."[231] On June 16, 2015, this note found its way into my journal:

[231] Ursula Fleming (1930–92) was an English psychotherapist, Lay Dominican, and author. Educated at Crichton Royal Hospital in Dumfries in south west Scotland, she began developing pain-control techniques, as she wanted to be a concert pianist and wanted to control her nerves. Her attempts to find a cure for her unsteady hands led her to find a technique, which she used to treat thousands of patients, and led

> At 6:30 this morning as I was going out of the front door of the house to water the side garden of day lilies, my right leg gave out and I fell down, landing on the stone steps. It was a surprise, and I landed safely, cushioning myself with both hands as I toppled. It's not the first time. Six weeks ago, the same thing happened in the bedroom. Somewhat concerned, two days later I talked things over with Dr. Lee Woodall, my physician. He recommended that we investigate things by my having a look at my spinal column with an MRI scan. Sure enough, a week later the report indicated moderate degeneration of some discs that protect my leg nerves. I took a few pain-relievers and decided to lose some weight. So far I've let go of ten pounds and feeling better. When I fell again this morning, I was glad to know that at least an extra ten of me didn't hit the stone steps.

For those of us who are getting older, falling to the ground is not easily forgotten. I certainly don't relish anticipating the next time I hit the floor with my legs up and my bottom down. I much prefer the stability of sitting comfortably in my Windsor or the strength to stand up straight and tall (well, as tall as my five feet eight inches will allow). But fall I must. It's part of life, a big part. Falling, however defined, is our enmeshment in life's gravity. We're all sitting, standing,

---

to her follow a career in alternative medicine. Her technique, known as the Fleming Method, relies on relaxed concentration to overcome pain.

One of the cofounders of The Eckhart Society, she has also been influential in promoting the mystical understandings of medieval theologian Meister Eckhart. The society website states:

The impact of Ursula's work has been enormous. There is now a veritable industry of publications about Eckhart, both books and articles in scholarly journals. Eckhart is becoming ever more widely known. Lutheran Dag Hammarskjöld, the former Secretary General of the United Nations, always had Eckhart's works by his bedside. The Meister Eckhart Gesellschaft was established in Germany in 2004. Each year there are many doctoral theses published on Eckhart in different languages, and the constant demand for back issues of The Eckhart Review are proof if more were needed of Ursula's success in helping to rehabilitate the Meister.

walking, running, jumping, and lying down within the gravitas, the weight and heaviness of life.

Just as Mr. and Mrs. Humanity (Adam and Eve) are said to have "fallen" into sin,[232] so too I have fallen and will continue to fall in lots of ways, sin included. So when I "fall" like Adam, I like to remember what one Desert Father is reported to have said:

> A monk asked Abba Sisoes, "What am I to do since I have fallen?" The Abba replied, "Get up." "I did get up, but I fell again," the monk told him. "Get up again," said the Abba. "I did, but I must admit that I fell once again. So what should I do?" "Never fall down without getting up," the Abba concluded.[233]

What this story doesn't say is that we don't get up from this kind of falling without help. When we fall like Adam, God is our helper, our picker-upper. Nobody gets up by himself or herself. God gets down on his knees, puts his arms under our bruised and hurting lives, and lifts us up.

My online friend Kayla McClurg[234] has regularly sent me Daily Words postings on inward/outward, which again and again I have

---

232 How we are to interpret the "fall of Adam and Eve" is, of course, much discussed among Christians. *Four Views on the Historical Adam*, ed. Ardel B. Caneday, Matthew Barrett, and Stanley N. Gundry (Grand Rapids, MI: Zondervan, 2013) provides an excellent overview of the interpretive options.

233 "Saint Sisoes the Great (+ 429)," Mystagogy Resource Center (July 6, 2009), available at http://www.johnsanidopoulos.com/2009/07/sisoes-great-and-contemplation-of-death.html

234 Kayla has been on the staff at The Church of the Saviour in Washington, DC, for over sixteen years. She grew up on a farm in Iowa and was an English teacher and church lay leader in Iowa and Oklahoma. She volunteered one summer in Harlem and fell in love with New York, returning a year later to live in a community of homeless women, children, and nuns called Providence House. She also taught college classes inside Sing Sing and Bedford Hills prisons.

When she arrived in DC, Kayla worked part-time at the Potter's House, where she became friends with Gordon Cosby and started to work with him and Bill Branner, his long-time associate. Today she continues to minister/administer, welcome visitors, edit, and write. In 2006, Kayla started facilitating inward/outward.

found insightful and helpful in living a Christian life. On March 6, 2017, while I was editing this book, Kayla sent her readers this observation by Leonardo Boff, a Brazilian theologian and writer, known for his active support for the rights of the poor and excluded:

Falling is not just a physical accident. Falling means recognizing freely and sincerely the limits of our strength in the face of situations that are beyond us and force us to submit. Falling shows our human frailty. It reveals the fragile clay of which we are made, showing us that we are neither omnipotent nor invulnerable. Confronted with such a fall, we may nurture a spirit of revolt…Or we may nurture a spirit of resignation…There is a third possibility, however. We can nurture the spirit of humility. While calmly accepting our fall, we may still trust in God, whose strength comes to reinvigorate our weakness, and get up again with renewed courage.

Then to my surprise Kayla appended this note:

> Starting today, and for some undetermined length of time, I will need to suspend inward/outward due to having contracted pneumonia, complicated by a chronic heart condition and an overflow of ungrieved losses and exhaustion. This quote was already lined up before I knew that perhaps the Spirit had chosen it particularly for me. Oh, but I do see it now—I am the one falling; I am the fragile clay.
>
> Thank you for your faithful reading, sharing, and posting in the past, and remember that all of the earlier Daily Words, and more, can be found again and again at www.inwardoutward.org. Keep digging for your own life's truth. It's closer than you might think, in every falling, getting up moment.—peace, Kayla[235]

A long-time member of the Potter's House Church, Kayla serves as resident manager of Andrew's House, the guesthouse for out-of-town friends visiting the church. She loves to help people explore the community.

[235] Inward/outward, March 6, 2017, available at http://inwardoutward.org.

Someday, perhaps soon, I will—one way or another—send out a similar note to my family and friends.

Falling upward

As much downward, however, as I will surely fall, I will not simply only, or just fall down. Kayla and I will also "fall upward." That paradoxical truth telling came to me several years ago when I opened up Richard Rohr's *Falling Upward: A Spirituality for the Two Halves of Life*. That book so impressed me that a year later, I arranged for our Centering Prayer group to spend an entire weekend listening to Rohr at the Calvin Center, a nearby wooded retreat campus where we immersed ourselves in *Falling Upward*.

While this is not the place to write an extensive review of Rohr's book (I'll do better by convincing you to read it), let me give you one reviewer's summary:

> Most of us are stuck in the first part of our spiritual life, the part that is about creating the structures and the container for who we will be when we start living for others, start pouring ourselves out like Christ did.
>
> Rohr's imagery and references may be too universal for many readers. If you can't get past this because of your own religious fundamentalism (not necessarily a bad thing, btw), just skip it. But his insights into what makes us tick, and then what SHOULD make us tick when we finally get to the "second half of our spiritual life," are more than worth navigating his multi-religious musings. (For the record, [Rohr] is a Catholic priest and a Franciscan, so though he borrows thoughts from all religious and philosophical traditions, he is firmly planted in Christianity.) His style reminds me a bit, by the way, of Dallas Willard, and I'm surprised Willard never gets mentioned here.

> How much did I like this book, as a 47-year old who is wrestling with his own thoughts on how to engage my "second half"? I'll simply put it this way. After finishing this book, I immediately began a second read (it's not long, but is very dense) and plan to take many copious notes and process the content very very carefully.[236]

Take those two "veries" seriously.

More emptyful sitting

As I continue to practice centering prayer always in the morning and often in the evening, I experience no letup in struggling with my shadow self. It is always with me. But when I breathe deeply and quietly in the presence of God, silently murmuring "Abba" and whispering God's name with the promptings of the Holy Spirit, the struggle subsides and I am released slowly and often ushered into the One-ing. I begin to know what St. Paul means when he says:

> If God himself has taken up residence in your life, you can hardly be thinking more of yourself than of him. Anyone, of course, who has not welcomed this invisible but clearly present God, the Spirit of Christ, won't know what we're talking about. But for you who welcome him, in whom he dwells—even though you still experience all the limitations of sin—you yourself experience life on God's terms. It stands to reason, doesn't it, that if the alive-and-present God who raised Jesus from the dead moves into your life, he'll do the same thing in you that he did in Jesus, bringing you alive to himself? When God lives and

[236] Posted on March 24, 2011, by P. Hamm of Maineville, Ohio, and available as a five-star review on amazon.com.

> breathes in you (and he does, as surely as he did in Jesus), you are delivered from that dead life. With his Spirit living in you, your body will be as alive as Christ's! (Rom. 8:9–11)

It's little wonder that, as Jesus recommends, I slip daily into some sort of closet and pray secretly to Abba Father. Perhaps it's on the back porch at five in the morning before the dawn arrives. Perhaps in the workshop in the late afternoon after using the table saw. Perhaps by the vegetable garden, somewhere, anywhere where it's reasonably quiet. Or if waiting for a plane departure, in a noisy airport.

Yes, sometimes it's boring and unsettling. I get fidgety and at times uncomfortable. It's then, however, that again I hear St. Paul whispering in my ear, again when he wrote:

> The moment we get tired in the waiting, God's Spirit is right alongside helping us along. If we don't know how or what to pray, it doesn't matter. He does our praying in and for us, making prayer out of our wordless sighs, our aching groans. He knows us far better than we know ourselves, knows our pregnant condition, and keeps us present before God. That's why we can be so sure that every detail in our lives of love for God is worked into something good. (8:26–28)

As boundaries are perforated and borders between me and people and trees and the backfires of a mile-away logging trucks become less bothersome, I find myself not so much alone as with and among everything. Even that backfires.

Centering Prayer has given me great peace even within a noisy world, a world filled with conflicts, political bushwhacking, and abrasive arguments even among Christians.

Luther and his apple tree

Martin Luther's love for the ordinary at the end of his day is impressive and heart-warming. Tradition has it that when someone asked Luther what he would do to if he knew the end was coming tomorrow, he replied, "If I knew that tomorrow was the end of the world, I would plant an apple tree today!" Biblically an apple symbolizes liberality, felicity, peace, and salvation. Fruits of all kinds were considered evidence of God's creational kindness, symbols of God's goodness. Concerning Israel, Moses sings that Yahweh found his people in the wilderness, "in an empty, windswept wasteland"; he threw his arms around Israel, lavishing attention on his beloved, guarding her as "the apple of his eye" (Deut. 32:10). No wonder the Psalmist later cries out, "Keep me as the apple of your eye; hide me in the shadow of your wings" (Ps. 17:8). Elsewhere he declares, "You shall eat the fruit of the labor of your hands; you shall be happy, and it shall go well with you" (128:2). In Psalm 1 the righteous man who delights in and meditates on the Word of God is "like a tree planted by the rivers of water, that brings forth fruit in its season." On the eve of the end—whether of the world or himself—Luther plants his apple tree, anticipating his garden to be nurtured in God's love.

Near the end of life: ordinary living

In *After the Ecstasy, the Laundry: How the Heart Grows Wise on the Spiritual Path*, Jack Kornfield tells us that the centered heart is a gift that allows us to live in the messy business of life with grace and stability. To which Richard Rohr says, "Amen." In *Falling Upward*, Rohr unpacks the paradox of a "bright sadness":

> There is a gravitas in the second half of life, but it is now held up by a much deeper lightness, or "okayness." Our mature years are characterized by a kind of bright sadness and a sober happiness, if that makes any sense. I am just grabbing for words to

> describe many wonderful older people. If you have met them, you know for yourself, and will find your own words. There is still a darkness in the second half of life—in fact maybe even more. But there is now a changed capacity to hold it creatively and with less anxiety.[237]

Jimmy and Rosalynn Carter are two such wonderful older people. His one-term presidency is remembered for the events that overwhelmed it: inflation, energy crisis, war in Afghanistan, and hostages in Iran. After one term in office, voters strongly rejected Jimmy Carter's honest but gloomy outlook in favor of Ronald Reagan's telegenic optimism. Things are different now. Having given himself to the welfare of the world,[238] Jimmy told us on August 20,

---

[237] Rohr, *Falling Upward*, 117.

[238] The following accurately describes Carter's life after losing to Ronald Reagan in 1981:

> Despite a largely unsuccessful one-term presidency, Jimmy Carter later rehabilitated his reputation through his humanitarian efforts after leaving the White House. He is now widely considered one of the greatest ex-presidents in American history. He has worked extensively with Habitat for Humanity and founded the Carter Presidential Center to promote human rights and alleviate suffering across the globe. In particular, Carter has worked effectively as an ex-president to develop community-based health care systems in Africa and Latin America, to oversee elections in fledgling democracies and to promote peace in the Middle East. In 2002, Jimmy Carter received the Nobel Peace Prize "for his decades of untiring effort to find peaceful solutions to international conflicts, to advance democracy and human rights, and to promote economic and social development." Carter has also written many books in the years since his presidency, including several memoirs, *Our Endangered Values: America's Moral* Crisis (2006) and *Palestine: Peace Not Apartheid* (2007).
>
> Jimmy Carter will not go down in history as one of America's most effective presidents. However, because of his tireless work both before and since his presidency in support of equality, human rights, and the alleviation of human suffering, Carter will go down as one of the nation's great social activists. Delivering his Nobel Lecture in 2002, Carter concluded with words that can be seen as both his life mission and his call to action for future generations. "The bond of our common humanity is stronger than the divisiveness of our fears and prejudices," he said. "God gives us the capacity for choice. We can choose to alleviate suffering. We can choose to work together for peace. We can make these changes—and we must." Taken from http://www.biography.com/people/jimmy-carter-9240013#taking-office.

2015, "I'm perfectly at ease with whatever comes. Now I feel it's in the hands of God."

That's how I feel. Many years ago while studying John Milton and reading his poetry under the tutelage of David Shelly Berkley, my dissertation director, I read and memorized Milton's Sonnet XVI ("On His Blindness"):

When I consider how my light is spent,
Ere half my days in this dark world and wide,
And that one talent which is death to hide
Lodged with me useless, though my soul more bent

To serve therewith my Maker, and present
My true account, lest He returning chide;
"Doth God exact day-labor, light denied?"
I fondly ask. But Patience, to prevent

That murmur, soon replies, "God doth not need
Either man's work or His own gifts. Who best
Bear His mild yoke, they serve Him best. His state
Is kingly: thousands at His bidding speed,
And post o'er land and ocean without rest;
They also serve who only stand and wait.

Allow the still-resident English professor in me to share my reading of this beautiful Petrarchan sonnet.[239] The back story to understanding the poem that John Milton's eyesight began to fail in 1644.[240] Sometime around 1652, about halfway through life at age forty-four, Milton really wonders how his life has been *spent* in a double sense: how he has lived so far and what it now means to live without the gift of sight. While writing his sonnet, he refers us to a

---

239 The rhyme scheme (ABBA, ABBA, CDE, and CDE) was popularized by the Italian priest Petrarch (1304–74).

240 By 1652 Milton was totally blind. Remarkably, he wrote his greatest works, *Paradise Lost* and *Paradise Regained*, after he became totally blind.

little story Jesus once told (known today as the Parable of the Talents) about an employer who gave his workers monies (talents) they should invest during his absence.[241] Here's my telling of the story from St. Matthew's Greek text (25.14-30):

> An employer went off on an extended trip. He called his workers together and delegated responsibilities. To one he gave five thousand dollars, to another two thousand, to a third one thousand, depending on their abilities. Then he left. Right off, the first servant went to work and doubled his master's investment. The second did the same. But the man with the single thousand dug a hole and carefully buried his master's money.
>
> After a long absence, the employer came back and requested an accounting as to how things went. The one given five thousand dollars showed him how he had doubled his investment. His master commended him: "Good work! You did your job well. From now on be my partner." The worker with the two thousand showed how he also had doubled his master's investment. His master commended him: "Terrific! You did your job well. From now on you too will be my partner." The employee given one thousand said, "Sir, I know you have high standards and hate careless ways, that you demand the best and make no allowances for error. I was afraid I might disappoint you, so I found a good hiding place and secured your money. Here it is, safe and sound down to the last cent." His employer was furious. "That's a terrible way to live! It's criminal to live cautiously like that! If you knew I was after the best, why did you

[241] The employer distributes the money in talents, a unit of weight used in ancient times to establish the value of gold, silver, or any other medium used as money. Thus, a Roman might pay ten talents of gold for military supplies or seven talents of silver for a quantity of food.

> do less than the least? The least you could have done would have been to invest the sum with the bankers, where at least I would have gotten a little interest. Take the thousand and give it to the one who risked the most. And get rid of this "play-it-safe" who won't go out on a limb. Throw him out into utter darkness."

The whole point of the story is that Jesus also wants us to take risks. The first two workers did not play it safe and took risks. And they doubled their resources. Jesus congratulates them, urging us to take similar risks. We are not to be afraid of disappointing him. We are to invest our lives in ways that may be dangerous. Like Jesus we can love our enemies, let go of our need for safety, put away our swords, and dare to be unpopular by the prevailing cultural standards. We can befriend outsiders, march for justice, and speak truth to powers. Even when those powers are in the church (and they are there) or in local, state, and national governments (they are really there!). That's what Jesus did. He did not play it safe. He did not put his life's resources in a backyard box-in-a-hole under some grass. We are to be partners with Jesus. We are not to play it safe and bury our God-given resources into whatever Cayman Islands our society thinks a good investment. We are to enter our futures, however they may unfold, in the security of God's grace. Just like Jesus did.

That's what Milton did. And he got himself into a lot of trouble.[242] But in midlife, reduced in talents, and blind as a bat, he wonders about his life in God's presence. He's frustrated because his disability prevents from serving God as well as he desires to. "Fondly" (that is, "foolishly") he asks, "Will God demand a full day's labor from a blind man?" Someone personified as Patience replies that

---

[242] Barbara K. Lewalski's *The Life of John Milton: A Critical Biography* (Malden, MA: Blackwell Publishers, 2000) is by far the best narrative rehearsal and evaluation of Milton as a proto-Libertarian, dissenter, and radical Christian. In her detailed account of his life and career, Lewalski provides a close analysis of his prose and poetry, focusing on the development of his ideas and his art. She shows how Milton, even as a young poet, constructed himself as new kind of author, commanding astonishing resources of learning and artistry to develop a radical politics, reformist poetics, and an inherently revolutionary prophetic voice.

God needs nothing from Milton. What God values is Milton's ability to bear God's "mild yoke," to tolerate whatever God asks faithfully and without complaint. After all, as the famous last line sums it up, "They also serve who only stand and wait."

Milton stood and waited for three more decades while I in my eighth-decade "sit and wait" in my emptyful chair. Like Milton, I don't have to do anything but risk investing all my life in God's goodwill and grace whatever "mild yoke" I experience. What might that mild yoke feel like?

A loss of labels and a bucket list

While I stand, sit, and wait, I too may want to unburden myself a bit. Perhaps I'll peel off some of the labels I've once enjoyed. The little polo emblem on the shirt. The model and make of the car. And how about those abbreviations before and after my name? How about a strike-through over PhD? May I unload some clothes and books? And what about editing my obituary so it will read like what'll look like the little brass plate engraved with "Andrew Harnack, 1937—whatever"? Maybe I'll get to die unobserved. Wouldn't that be something?

Yet as I sit and wait progressively emptyful, I confess I have a bucket list near my chair. After visiting the Jimmy Carter Center in Atlanta a while back, I came to realize that Jimmy had a bucket list a mile long. And he has lived some ninety years! He has taken his bucket list all over the world.

My bucket list is short. First, with respect to books, with I want my *Last Will and Testament* to indicate that I bequeath all my library books to the Lutheran Theological Center in Atlanta, Georgia, knowing that the Center will do what's best for their survival and usefulness. Second, regarding my property, I want to make sure that Article 6 of my Last Will and Testament, reads as follows:

> I hereby give, devise and bequeath all the rest, remainder and balance of my property, both real, personal and mixed, tangible and intangible, and wherever located to Grace Missions, Inc. to be used on behalf of and for the benefit of the girl's orphanage in the country of Haiti, which is known as CHEZ MOI ORPHANGE, IN MEMORY OF MY LATE SON Krister Martin Harnack and my late daughter CHELSEA CARROLL HARNACK.

With those two items taken care of, I want to read about and take in much more of the spirituality described by the so-called Rhineland Mystics into my life. So with a stack of books on lampstand next to my chair and bed, I hope to read more deeply in Meister Eckhart, following the example of Ursula Fleming as the Eckhart Society tells us:

> She never pretended to be an Eckhart scholar, but no human being influenced her more profoundly than did Meister Eckhart—not even Marco Pallis, and that is saying quite a lot. When, in her teens, she abandoned her Catholic religion, intending to become a Buddhist, she turned for spiritual guidance to Pallis—mountaineer, musician and philosopher as well as a Buddhist himself—but he told her: "Go back to the religion of your birth. Go back to the Sacraments. And read Eckhart." When, having done what her spiritual guide told her, she said to him: "I like Eckhart but I only understand fragments of what he is saying," Marco Pallis replied: "Don't try to understand him. Just go on reading him."[243]

243 Available at http://www.eckhartsociety.org/eckhart/his-teachings.

Eckhart's "Wayless Way"

While reading Eckhart, as Christopher Malcolm Knauf tells us, we find lots of mystical insights to last a lifetime:[244]

> The consensus among scholars seems to be that, while Eckhart tolerates whatever might be expedient for progress in the spiritual life, particularly for beginners, he sees such things as temporary crutches at best. This is not to say that he has no counsel for the spiritual seeker, just that it is less distinct and prescriptive than that offered, for example, in the "Jesus Prayer" of the desert fathers, the Exercises of St Ignatius or the Practices of St Teresa of Avila.
>
> Eckhart prescribes no special techniques, practices, penances or pilgrimages, insisting that "whoever seeks God in a special way gets the way and misses God who lies hidden in it." It is for this reason that his spirituality is often referred to as a "wayless way." More than any particular method of contemplation, Eckhart's "way" consists primarily of an inner attitude or orientation that is at once theocentric, contemplative and this-worldly. The fundamental orientation of Eckhart's way is theocentric; its "true north" is God. The goal of the spiritual life is simply to "have God." The person with such an inner desire or appetite for God will in Eckhart's thinking also be temperamentally and morally equipped for "the way," which is not for the "natural, undisciplined man, for he is entirely remote from, and totally ignorant of this birth."
>
> The orientation of the spiritual seeker is, then, necessarily also contemplative, involving a disciplined

244 What follows is largely taken from "Meister Eckhart and the 'Wayless Way,'" available at https://lifeisthismoment.com2014/05/19/meister-eckhart-and-the-wayless-way/.

attention of the intellect upon its Divine object, "quite collected and turned entirely inward, not running out through the five senses into the multiplicity of creatures." Through this "collected" inwardness of contemplation, the "bare mind," one is able to achieve the radical "detachment" from "multiplicity" and "creatures" that is the prerequisite of the birth and the chief activity of Eckhart's spirituality. This will ultimately include a detachment even from the ideas and images we use to give form to the formless One, the theological concepts with which we are clothed nakedly in the great "Is-ness." The I AM. We must detach from the "imagined God" that vanishes when the idea vanishes and be satisfied only with the "essential God."

The third aspect of this orientation is a radical this-worldliness whereby the God whom we seek is apprehended "equally in all things and all places." For Eckhart the contemplative life is fully consonant with the active and involved life, for God is in one's ordinary life and it is there that he must be found. The best place to find God, says Eckhart, is "where we left him." Whoever and wherever I am, the "way" for me must begin in the world of my own experience. I was asked, "Some people shun all company and always want to be alone; their peace depends on such emptiness, and on being in church. Was that the best thing?" And I said, "No!" Now see why. He who is in a right state, is always in a right state wherever he is, and with everybody...He has only God, thinks only of God, and all things are for him nothing but God.[245]

[245] See Appendix C for the full text of Knauf's essay.

Having read a good bit of Eckhart, I think Pallis and Knauf give us good advice. In fact, I'm eager to pursue and experience the "wayless" path leading deeper and deeper into the endless cave of God's Presence. Joel F. Harrington maps its unmarked trails in *Dangerous Mystic: Meister Eckhart's Path to the God Within*, a wonderful book.[246] I also want to read more of Eckhart's students--Henry Suso and John Tauler--along with Mechthild of Magdeburg, Christina Ebner, and Nicholas of Cusa. Lord, let me live a long time.

If it happens that the last years of my life must be lived alone, I want to live in a very small place, preferably somewhere near a woodsy area or in a beautiful valley. One of my friends, Catherine Campbell lives in such a tiny (and I mean tiny!) home, just twelve feet by twelve feet or 144 square feet. I don't think I can do that. I do well imagine I can do with something no larger than 900 square feet. Maybe it will have a small tool shed nearby. And if that's not available then, I'll go for a one-bedroom apartment somewhere, maybe one available at St. George's Court in Griffin, Georgia. And if worse comes to worst, then a cardboard box in some alley may have to do. Well, not really. Perhaps a church pew will be just what I need.

I want to "write" at least one more icon, hoping it will be one that tells the story of Jesus welcoming children into his lap and life.

I want to visit *Chez Moi* in Haiti at least once a year.

Finally, I want my cremains to be buried in the columbarium garden at St. John Lutheran Church in Griffin, Georgia.[247] Then I want to see all of you in heaven, the Great Oneness.

---

246 (New York: Penguin Press, 2018).

247 A columbarian garden is usually a church enclosure in which cremated ashes are poured directly into the ground, and covered by grass or a ground-cover vine; these ashes are commingled with other ashes and with soil, in a tangible symbol of the communion of saints. In memorial gardens, there is usually a plaque somewhere nearby on which the names and dates can be inscribed. It is common to install a fountain in the memorial garden, which symbolizes our baptism in living water and is often comforting to the bereaved. It is also common to have some benches, so people can sit and meditate. For more information about such enclosures, visit "What are columbaria and memorial gardens?" at http://download.elca.org/ELCAResource Repository/What_are_columbaria_and_memorial_gardens.pdf.

If after reading these last pages of *An Emptyful Chair*, you are even remotely interested in reading more about meditation, contemplative practice, and entrance into the mystical Presence, go to your library and obtain, perhaps by interlibrary loan, one or more of the following books. Of if you are like me, an inveterate marker-upper of books with a pencil or pen, go to amazon.com and purchase a cheap, used copies of book that seem provocative and interesting.

Your personal practice in an emptyful chair will, of course, be the best of all books.

For Further Reading

Bauerschmidt, Fredereick. *Why the Mystics Matter Now*. Notre Dame, IN: Sorin Books, 2003.

Campolo, Tony, and Mary Albert Darling. *The God of Intimacy and Action: Reconnecting Ancient Practices, Evangelism, and Justice.* San Francisco, CA: Jossey-Bass, 2007.

Cole, David. *The Mystic Path of Meditation: Beginning a Christ-Centered Journey*. Vestal, NY: Anamchara Books, 2013.

Fanning, Steven. *Mystics of the Christian Tradition*. London: Routledge, 2001.

Fox, Matthew, ed. *Christian Mystics: 365 Readings and Meditations.* Novato, CA: New World Library, 2011.

Griffin, Emilie. *Wonderful and Dark Is This Road: Discovering the Mystic Path*. Brewster, MA: Paraclete Press, 2004.

Happold, F. C. *Mysticism: A Study and Anthology*. New York: Penguin, 1970.

Harmless, William. *Mystics*. Oxford: Oxford University Press, 2008.

Harrington, Joel F. *Dangerous Mystic: Meister Eckhart's Path to the God Within*. New York: Penguin Press, 2018.

Hollywood, Amy, and Patricia Z. Beckman, eds. *The Cambridge Companion to Christian Mysticism*. New York: Cambridge University Press, 2012.

Johnston, William. *Mystical Theology: The Science of Love*. Maryknoll, NY: Orbis, 2000.

King, Ursala. *Christian Mystics: The Spiritual Heart of the Christian Tradition*. New York: Simon & Schuster, 1998.

Kruschwitz, Robert, ed. *Mysticism: The Christian Reflection Project*. Institute for Faith and Learning. Waco, Texas: The Center for Christian Ethics, 2005.

Marion, Jim. *Putting on the Mind of Christ: The Inner Work of Christian Spirituality*. Charlottesville, VA: Hampton Road, 2011.

McColman, Carl. *Answering the Contemplative Call*. Charlottesville, VA: Hampton Roads Publishing, 2015.

———. *The Big Book of Christian Mysticism: The Essential Guide to Contemplative Spirituality*. Charlottesville, VA: Hampton Roads Publishing, 2010.

———. *Christian Mystics: 108 Seers, Saints, and Sages*. Charlottesville, VA: Hampton Roads Publishing, 2016.

McGinn, Bernard. *The Essential Writings of Christian Mysticism*. New York: Random House, 2006.

Meister Eckhart. *The Complete Mystical Works of Meister Eckhart*, trans. Maurice O'C Walshe. New York: Cross Road Publishing, 2009.

Rohr, Richard. *Essential Teachings on Love*. Maryknoll, NY: Orbis Books, 2018.

______. *Everything Belongs: The Gift of Contemplative Prayer*. New York: Crossroad Publishing, 1999.

______. *Just This: Prompts and Practices for Contemplation*. London: SPCK, 2018.

———. *The Naked Now: Learning to See as the Mystics Do*. New York: Crossroad Publishing, 2015.

———. *What the Mystics Know: Seven Pathways to Your Deeper Self*. New York: Crossroad Publishing, 2015.

Ryrie, Alexander. *Silent Waiting: The Biblical Roots of Contemplative Spirituality*. Norwich, Norfolk, 1999.

Smith, Amos. *Be Still and Listen: Experience the Presence of God in Your Life*. Brewster, MA: Paraclete P, 2018.

Tuoti, Frank X. *Why Not Be a Mystic?* New York: Crossroad, 1995.

Underhill, Evelyn. *Mysticism: A Study in the Nature and Development of Spiritual Consciousness*. Mineola, NY: Dover, 2002.

Vincent, Ken R. T. *The Golden Thread: God's Promise of Universal Salvation*. Lincoln, NE: iUniverse, 2005.

Wolpert, Daniel. *Creating a Life with God: The Call of Ancient Prayer Practices*. Nashville, TN: Upper Room Books, 2003.

Appendix A

THE METHOD OF CENTERING PRAYER[248]

Be still and know that I am God.
—-Psalm 46.10

Contemplative Prayer

We may think of prayer as thoughts or feelings expressed in words. But this is only one expression. In the Christian tradition contemplative prayer is considered to be the pure gift of God. It is the opening of mind and heart--our whole being--to God, the Ultimate Mystery, beyond thoughts, words, and emotions. rough grace we open our awareness to God whom we know by faith is within us, closer than breathing, closer than thinking, closer than choosing, closer than consciousness itself.

248 Available at https://www.contemplativeoutreach.org/sites/default/files/private/method_cp_eng-2016-06_0.pdf

Centering Prayer

Centering Prayer is a method designed to facilitate the development of contemplative prayer by preparing our faculties to receive this gift. It presents ancient Christian wisdom teachings in an updated form. Centering Prayer is not meant to replace other kinds of prayer; rather it casts a new light and depth of meaning on them. It is at the same time a relationship with God and a discipline to foster that relationship. is method of prayer is a movement beyond conversation with Christ to communion with him.

Theological Background

The source of Centering Prayer, as in all methods leading to contemplative prayer, is the indwelling Trinity: Father, Son, and Holy Spirit. e focus of Centering Prayer is the deepening of our relationship with the living Christ. It tends to build communities of faith and bond the members together in mutual friendship and love.

The Root of Centering Prayer

Listening to the word of God in Scripture *(Lectio Divina)* is a traditional way of cultivating friendship with Christ. It is a way of listening to the texts of Scripture as if we were in conversation with Christ and he were suggesting the topics of conversation. e daily encounter with Christ and reflection on his word leads beyond mere acquaintanceship to an attitude of friendship, trust, and love. Conversation simplies and gives way to communing. Gregory the Great (6th century) in summarizing the Christian contemplative tradition expressed it as "resting in God." is was the classical meaning of contemplative prayer in the Christian tradition for the first sixteen centuries.

The Guidelines

1. Choose a sacred word as the symbol of your intention to consent to God's presence and action within.
2. Sitting comfortably and with eyes closed, settle briefly and silently introduce the sacred word as the symbol of your consent to God's presence and action within.
3. When engaged with your thoughts, return ever-so-gently to the sacred word.
4. At the end of the prayer period, remain in silence with eyes closed for a couple of minutes.

Centering Prayer Guidelines

I. Choose a sacred word as the symbol of your intention to consent to God's presence and action within.

- The sacred word expresses our intention to consent to God's presence and action within.
- The sacred word is chosen during a brief period of prayer to the Holy Spirit. Use a word of one or two syllables, such as: *God, Jesus, Abba, Father, Mother, Mary, Amen.* Other possibilities include: *Love, Listen, Peace, Mercy, Let Go, Silence, Stillness, Faith, Trust.*
- Instead of a sacred word, a simple inward glance toward the Divine Presence, or noticing one's breath may be more suitable for some persons. The same guidelines apply to these symbols as to the sacred word.
- The sacred word is sacred not because of its inherent meaning, but because of the meaning we give it as the expression of our intention to consent.
- Having chosen a sacred word, we do not change it during the prayer period because that would be engaging thoughts.

II. Sitting comfortably and with eyes closed, settle brie y and silently introduce the sacred word as the symbol of your consent to God's presence and action within.

- "Sitting comfortably" means relatively comfortably so as not to encourage sleep during the time of prayer.
- Whatever sitting position we choose, we keep the back straight.
- We close our eyes as a symbol of letting go of what is going on around and within us.
- We introduce the sacred word inwardly as gently as laying a feather on a piece of absorbent cotton.
- If we fall sleep, we simply continue the prayer upon awakening.

III. When engaged with your thoughts, return ever-so-gently to the sacred word.

- "Thoughts" is an umbrella term for every perception, including body sensations, sense perceptions, feelings, images, memories, plans, reflections, concepts, commentaries, and spiritual experiences.
- Thoughts are an inevitable, integral and normal part of Centering Prayer.
- By "returning ever-so-gently to the sacred word" a minimum of e ort is indicated. is is the only activity we initiate during the time of Centering Prayer.
- During the course of Centering Prayer, the sacred word may become vague or disappear.

IV. At the end of the prayer period, remain in silence with eyes closed for a couple of minutes.

- The additional two minutes enables us to bring the atmosphere of silence into everyday life.
- If this prayer is done in a group, the leader may slowly recite a prayer, such as the Lord's Prayer, while the others listen.

Some Practical Points

1. The minimum time for this prayer is 20 minutes. Two periods are recommended each day, one first thing in the morning and the other in the afternoon or early evening. With practice the time may be extended to 30 minutes or longer.
2. The end of the prayer period can be indicated by a timer which does not have an audible tick or loud sound when it goes off. There is a free Centering Prayer mobile app timer available.
3. Possible physical symptoms during the prayer:

    - We may notice slight pains, itches, or twitches in various parts of the body or a generalized sense of restlessness. ese are usually due to the untying of emotional knots in the body.
    - We may notice heaviness or lightness in our extremities. is is usually due to a deep level of spiritual attentiveness.
    - In all cases we pay no attention and ever-so-gently return to the sacred word.

4. The principal fruits of Centering Prayer are experienced in daily life and not during the prayer period.
5. Centering Prayer familiarizes us with God's first language which is SILENCE.

Points for Further Development

1. During the prayer period, various kinds of thoughts may arise:

    - Ordinary wanderings of the imagination or memory.
    - Thoughts and feelings that give rise to attractions or aversions.
    - Insights and psychological breakthroughs.

- Self-reflections such as, "How am I doing?" or, " This peace is just great!"
- Thoughts and feelings that arise from the unloading of the unconscious.
- When engaged with any of these thoughts return ever-so-gently to the sacred word.

2. During this prayer we avoid analyzing our experience, harboring expectations, or aiming at some specific goal such as:

   - Repeating the sacred word continuously.
   - Having no thoughts.
   - Making the mind a blank.
   - Feeling peaceful or consoled.
   - Achieving a spiritual experience.

Ways to Deepen Our Relationship with God

1. Practice two 20-30 minute periods of Centering Prayer daily.
2. Listen to the Word of God in Scripture and study *Open Mind, Open Heart.*
3. Visit our website to access various online resources, practices, courses and groups.
4. Join a weekly Centering Prayer Group.

   - It encourages the members of the group to persevere in their individual practices.
   - It provides an opportunity for further input on a regular basis through multi-media resources and discussion.
   - It offers an opportunity to support and share the spiritual journey.

What Centering Prayer Is and Is Not

- It is not a technique but a way of cultivating a deeper relationship with God.
- It is not a relaxation exercise but it may be quite refreshing.
- It is not a form of self-hypnosis but a way to quiet the mind while maintaining its alertness.
- It is not a charismatic gi but a path of transformation.
- It is not a para-psychological experience but an exercise of faith, hope and selfless love.
- It is not limited to the "felt" presence of God but is rather a deepening of faith in God's abiding presence.
- It is not reflective or spontaneous prayer, but simply resting in God beyond thoughts, words, and emotions.

Appendix B

A WEEK WITH RICHARD ROHR'S "UNKNOWING"[249]

Beyond Comprehension

My thoughts are not your thoughts,
my ways are not your ways. . . .
As high as the heavens are above the earth,
my ways are beyond your ways,
and my thoughts are beyond your thoughts.
—Isaiah 55:8-9

We cannot comprehend the work of God from beginning to end.
—*My* Ecclesiastes 3:11

Within his Judaic tradition, Jesus was formed by the passage above from Isaiah which teaches humility before the mystery of God.

[249] I have been subscribing to Richard Rohr's Daily Meditations for many years. This appendix provides you with a week's sample of his daily meditations which arrive about 2:00 a.m. every morning. You may subscribe to Richard Rohr's Daily Meditations at www.cac.org.

When we presume we know fully, we can be very arrogant and goal-oriented. When we know we don't know fully, we are much more concerned about practical, loving behavior. Those who know God are humble about their knowledge of God; those who don't really know God, often speak in platitudes and certainties (about which they are not really certain).

When we speak of God and things transcendent, all we can do is use metaphors, approximations, and pointers. No language is adequate to describe the Holy. As an early portrait of Saint John of the Cross illustrates, we must place a hushing finger over our lips to remind ourselves that God is finally unspeakable and ineffable. Or, like the Jews, we may even refuse to pronounce the name YHWH.

All our words, beliefs, and rituals are merely "fingers pointing to the moon." They are never 100% right or perfect. This is the necessary and good poverty of all spiritual language. Remember, Jesus never said, "You must be right!" or even that it was important to be right. He largely talked about being honest and humble (which is probably our only available form of rightness).

Such admitted poverty in words should keep us humble, curious, and searching for God. Yet the ego doesn't like such uncertainty. So, it's not surprising that the history of the three monotheistic religions, in their first few thousand years, has largely been the proclaiming of absolutes and dogmas. In fact, we usually focus on areas where we can feel a sense of order and control—things like finances, clothing, edifices, roles, offices, and who has the authority. In my experience, I observe that *the people who find God are usually those who are very serious about their quest and their questions.* It is said that asking good questions is a sign of intelligence. But Western culture has spent centuries admiring and promoting people who supposedly have all the answers—which, too often, they have read or heard from someone else.As Rainer Maria Rilke (1875-1926) wrote in his *Letters to a Young Poet*:

I want to ask you, as clearly as I can, to bear with patience all that is unresolved in your heart, and try to love the questions themselves. . . . For everything must be lived. Live the questions now, perhaps then, someday, you will gradually, without noticing, live into the answer.[250]

Recovering Our Balance

Can you find out the depths of God?
Or find out the perfection of the Almighty?
It is higher than the heavens; so what can you do?
It is deeper than Sheol; so what can you know?
It is longer than the earth and broader than the sea.
—Job 11:7-9

The Bible, in its entirety, finds a balance between knowing and not-knowing, between using particular and carefully chosen words and having humility about words, even though the ensuing traditions have not often found that same balance. "Churchianity," by its very definition, needs to speak with absolutes and certainties. It feels its job is to make absolute truth claims and feels very fragile when it cannot. Then, we followers think we must be certain about things we are not really certain of at all (which is the beginning of the loss of *faith*)! This is a similar predicament that politicians experience, needing to project an image of self-assurance and confidence, even though we all know they're faking it just like the rest of us. As Marcus Borg (1942-2015) and others suggest in *The Emerging Christian Way*, absolute correctness is the largely impossible task institutional Christianity has taken upon itse[251] Organized religion is now crumbling beneath this impossible and false goal, it seems to me.

I understand the individual ego's and the institution's structural need for clarity, some basic order, and identity, especially to get us started when we are young. Religion then needs a key to unlock itself from itself—but from the inside, which many call

[250] Rainer Maria Rilke, *A Year with Rilke: Daily Readings from the Best of Rainer Maria Rilke,* trans. Joanna Macy and Anita Barrows (HarperOne: 2009), 49.

[251] See *The Emerging Christian Way: Thoughts, Stories, and Wisdom for a Faith of Transformation*, ed. Michael Schwartzentruber (CopperHouse: 2006).

the mystical or contemplative tradition. Most successful reforms come from using one's own internal resources to self-correct. The words "mystery," "mystical," and "mutter" all come from the Indo-European root word *muein,* which means to "hush or close the lips." We must start with humble, patient, wordless unknowing, sincere curiosity, or what many call "beginner's mind." Only then are we truly teachable. Otherwise, we only hear whatever confirms our present understanding.

Without such humility, religion has cried "wolf" too many times in history and later been proven wrong. Observe earlier authoritative Church statements on democracy, war, torture, slavery, women, treatment of Jews, revolutions, liturgical forms, the "Doctrine of Discovery" of the New World, the Latin language, and the earth-centered universe—to name just a few big ones. If we had balanced our "knowing" with some honest not-knowing, we would never have made such egregious mistakes. We could always prove whatever we wanted by twisting one line of Scripture. The biblical text was not allowed to change us as much as many Christians have used it to exclude and judge other people.

Darkness and Light

Darkness is not dark for you,
and night shines as the day.
Darkness and light are but one.
—Psalm 139:12

Perhaps the most universal way to name the two spiritual traditions of knowing and not-knowing is *light* and *darkness.* The formal theological terms are *kataphatic* or "affirmative" way—employing words, concepts, and images—and *apophatic* or "negative" way—moving beyond words and ideas into silence and beyond-rational knowing. I believe both ways are good and necessary, and together they create a magnificent form of higher consciousness called biblical faith.

The *apophatic* way, however, has been largely underused, undertaught, and underdeveloped since the Protestant Reformation and the Enlightenment. In fact, Westerners became ashamed of our "not-knowing" and tried to fight our battles rationally. For several centuries, Christianity in the West has been in a defensive mode, a siege mentality where not-knowing and the mystical tradition are considered too risky.

If we are going to talk about light, then we must also talk about darkness, because they only have meaning in relation to one another. In much of the world's art, the sun and the moon are pictured together as sacred symbols. The solar light gives glaring brightness but paradoxically creates defined shadows. Patriarchal religions usually preferred "sun" gods and the worship of fire, light, and order. While order and clarity are good, they also give us an arrogance about that very order and clarity. The very sun that illuminates also blinds, dehydrates, and kills when we get too much of it.

Lunar light is much more subtle, filtered, and indirect, and in that sense, more clarifying and not so quickly conclusive. Note that when God first divided light from darkness, God did *not* call it "good" (Genesis 1:3). At the very beginning of the Bible we are warned that we cannot totally separate light from darkness, or the two have no meaning. The whole of Creation exists inside of one full cycle: "Evening came and morning came and it was the first day" (Genesis 1:5). Separating them is apparently not good!

All things on earth are a mixture of darkness and light. When we idolize things as totally good or condemn otherness as totally bad, we get ourselves in trouble. Jesus simplifies this task by saying: "God alone is good" (Mark 10:18). Even the good things of this world are still subject to imperfection, wounding, and decay. I find it very hard to admit, but often tragedies produce much good fruit and good people.

Jesus is a "lunar" teacher, patient with darkness and slow growth. He says, "The seed is sprouting and growing but we do not know how" (Mark 4:27). He even shockingly says to let the good and bad seeds grow together until the harvest (Matthew 13:30). He seems to be willing to live with non-perfection, surely representing the cosmic patience and freedom of God, who is Infinite Love and Life that finally fills all the gaps. When you are God and you know you will ultimately "win"—because Love will always win—you do not have to nail everything down along the way. You can work happily and even effectively with "mustard seeds" (Mark 4:31) and with "the good and bad alike" sitting at the same table (Matthew 22:10).

Ascent and Descent

When it says, "He went up,"
it must mean that he first went down
to the deepest levels of the earth . . .
to fill all things.
—Ephesians 4:9-10

Philosophies and religions are either Ascenders, pointing us *upward* (toward the One, the Eternal, and the Absolute) or they are Descenders, pointing us *downward* (toward the sacred within the many, the momentary, the mystery, and the earth), seldom both at the same time. Yet that's what we need.

Metaphors of darkness, descent, and unknowing are found throughout the Bible: caves, clouds, the Exodus, exile, the belly of the whale, wilderness, and desert. Within Scripture we also see a spirituality of light, ascent, and knowing which is represented by mountaintop images, especially Sinai, Horeb, Tabor, and the Mount of the Beatitudes. "The pillar of flame by night and the pillar of cloud by day" (Exodus 13:21-22) are both good guides, but not one without the other!

Jesus himself points us both upward and downward at the same time. He fully rests in a trustworthy Absolute, his anchored self, made in the image and likeness of God. This is his only real knowing or *ascent*. From there, he is free to dive into a fully incarnate and diverse world—as it is. He can love this ordinary and broken world, honor and protect its diversity and complexity, and critique all false absolutes and idolatries at the same time. This is Jesus' *descent* into the world of earthiness.

We have both knowing and not-knowing, ascent and descent, beautifully integrated in two companion pieces in the Scriptures: Moses on Mount Sinai and Jesus on the Mount of Transfiguration. When Moses is on Sinai, God is somehow manifest in thick darkness (Exodus 20:9). "You saw no shape on that day at Horeb" (Deuteronomy 4:15). Moses "sees" and "hears" to some degree, yet YHWH does not allow Moses to see God's "glory" or "face." The most that Moses can see is, humorously, YHWH's backside (see Exodus 33:18-23).

In the parallel story of Jesus on the Mount of Transfiguration (Luke 9:28-36; Mark 9:2-8; Matthew 17:1-9), there is first dazzling light yet a cloud soon over-shadows the whole scene. The epiphany is both light and darkness, knowability and unknowability, disclosure and non-disclosure. Jesus then deliberately walks with the disciples back down the mountain, onto the plain and desert of everyday life, and out of this enlightening, but also dangerously ego-inflating experience.

Honeymoon experiences cannot be sustained. We must always return to the ordinary. Jesus tells the disciples who witnessed his transfiguration, "Don't talk about it!" (Matthew 17:9). Jesus knew that talking too soon would only weaken the experience. Silence seems necessary to preserve the sacred and the mysterious, just as in sexual intimacy.

Spirit always desires to incarnate itself. Matter always wants to be God. The Christ Mystery is uniquely saying that we *can* have it both ways—the enlightenment of Spirit balanced out by the density and opaqueness of matter. Maybe that is the essence of the human condition.

Listening and Learning

Human history is in a time of great flux, of great cultural and spiritual change. The psyche doesn't know what to do with so much information. I am told that if you take all of the information that human beings had up until 1900 and call that one unit, that unit now doubles every ten years. No wonder there's so much anxiety, confusion, and mistaking fact for fiction and fiction for fact!

In light of today's information overload, people are looking for a few clear certitudes by which to define themselves. We see various forms of fundamentalism in many religious leaders when it serves their cultural or political worldview. We surely see it at the lowest levels of religion—Christianity as well as Judaism, Islam, and secular fundamentalism, too—where God is used to justify violence, hatred, prejudice, and whatever is "my" way of doing things.

The fundamentalist mind likes answers and explanations so much that it remains willfully ignorant about how history arrived at those explanations or how self-serving they usually are. *Satisfying untruth is more pleasing to us than unsatisfying truth,* and Big Truth is invariably unsatisfying—at least to the small self.

Great spirituality, on the other hand, seeks a creative balance between opposites. As Jesuit William Johnston writes, "Faith is that breakthrough into that deep realm of the soul which accepts paradox with humility."[252] When you go to one side or the other too much, you find yourself either overly righteous or overly skeptical and cynical. There must be a healthy middle, as we try to hold both the necessary light and darkness.

We cannot settle today's confusion by pretending to have absolute and certain answers. But we must not give up seeking truth, observing reality from all its angles. We settle human confusion not by falsely pretending to settle all the dust, but by teaching people an *honest and humble process for learning and listening,* which we call contemplation. Then people come to wisdom in a calm and compassionate way. There will not be the knee jerk overreactions that we have in so many on both Left and Right today.

The Judeo-Christian tradition was not supposed to be a top-down affair, but an organic meeting between an Inner Knower (the Indwelling Holy Spirit) accessed by prayer and experience; and the Outer Knower, which we would call Scripture (Holy Writings) and

[252] William Johnston, *Christian Zen* (Fordham University Press: 1997), 63.

Tradition (all the ancestors). This is a calm and wonderfully healing way to know full Reality.

Prayer Beyond Words

The two paths of knowing and not-knowing are primarily taught through prayer itself! No wonder all spiritual teachers emphasize prayer so much.

In Jesus' teaching and example, we may first notice the prayer of words in the Our Father and his encouragement to "ask" and "knock" (Matthew 7:7). From these and Jesus' prayer at the Last Supper, Christians have developed various forms of social, public, and liturgical prayer, often centering around intercession, gratitude, and worship.

But Jesus also taught prayer beyond words: "praying in secret" (Matthew 6:5-6), "not babbling on as the Gentiles do" (Matthew 6:7), or his predawn, lonely prayer (Mark 1:35), because "your Father knows what you need even before you ask" (Matthew 6:8). These all point toward what many today call contemplation—openness to and union with God's presence; resting in God more than actively seeking to fully know or understand.

Given Jesus' clear model and instruction, it seems strange that wordy prayer took over in the monastic Office, in the Eucharistic liturgy, and in formulaic prayer like the Catholic rosary and Protestant memorizations. It's all the more important that these be balanced by prayer beyond words.

Much of Buddhism's attraction for so many people today is that Buddhism is absolutely honest about the theology of darkness—about our inability to know. It is much more humble than the monotheistic religions are about the possibilities of words and formulas. Judaism, Christianity, and Islam took a great risk in relying on words.

In the Christian tradition this "Word became flesh" (John 1:14), but we didn't want flesh. We didn't want an embodied relationship with God. Instead we wanted words with which we could proclaim certainties and answers. The price the three "religions of the book" have paid for a certain idolatry of words is that they became the least tolerant of the world's religions. Both Buddhism and Hinduism tend to be much more accepting of others than we are.

At their lower levels, the three monotheistic religions insist on absolute truth claims *in forms of words,* whereas Jesus' truth claim was his person (John 14:6), his presence (John 6:35), his ability to participate in God's perfect love (John 17:21-22). Emphasizing perfect agreement on words and forms (which is never going to happen anyway!), instead of inviting people into an experience of the Formless Presence, has caused much of the violence of human history. Jesus gives us *his risen presence* as "the way, the truth, and the life." At that level, there is not much to fight about, and in fact fighting becomes uninteresting and counter-productive to the message. Presence is known by presence from the other side. It is always *subject to subject knowing*, never subject to object.

Appendix C

CHRISTOPHER MALCOLM KNAUF, "MEISTER ECKHART AND THE 'WAYLESS WAY'"[253]

What might a medieval German mystic offer spiritual seekers today? This essay is a personal reflection on the teachings of the fourteenth-century Dominican philosopher and theologian, Meister Eckhart, who offers a deeply refreshing perspective on human spirituality, particularly for those like me who have long thirsted for a draught more satisfying than that on offer from many Christian pulpits. I present this reflection not as an Eckhart expert, but as one seeker to another. It is admittedly a long piece, and the Meister's teachings are challenging, but I trust you find it an edifying read. References and a bibliography are included for those readers who might like to explore the subject further.

I first encountered Meister Eckhart through his *aphorisms*, pithy and usually paradoxical snippets quoted in 'popular' writing on spirituality and in recent years even 'posted' as 'memes' on social media. This led to some serious reading, the work of scholars such as Bernard McGinn, Richard Woods and Oliver Davies, and finally the Meister's writings themselves. What initially attracted me to Eckhart

[253] https://lifeisthismoment.com/2014/05/19/meister-eckhart-and-the-wayless-way/

was not only his ideas, which are the primary focus of this essay, but also the way he expressed his ideas. A renowned preacher, much of what comes down to us of his work are transcripts of sermons and talks he delivered in the vernacular, Middle High German. His vernacular sermons, full of rich and unusual metaphors, irony, paradox, puns and word-plays, bear witness as much to homiletic and literary genius as to spiritual insight. And while, modern scholars suggest, it was quite possibly more Eckhart's 'difficult' mode of expression than his theology that brought him to the attention of the Inquisition and ultimately led to his censure,[1] it seems to me that his extraordinary influence among spiritual seekers of his own day and his continuing currency in ours is due in part to his way with words.

Historical context

Johannes Eckhart von Hochheim was born into a family of the lower German aristocracy around 1260 in the mountain village of Tambach in Saxony.[2] References in Eckhart's works to hearing lectures of Albertus Magnus (1205-1280), the mentor of Thomas Aquinas, suggest that Eckhart must have entered the Order of Preachers (Dominicans) and begun his studies at Cologne some time before 1280. He was appointed to the University of Paris in 1294 where he lectured on Lombard's *Sentences* and received the coveted title of *Meister* (Master). His teaching, though widely influential, was controversial in some circles, leading in 1329—the year after his death—to aspects of his doctrine being condemned as heretically unorthodox.

Eckhart's teaching in a nutshell

In keeping with the Christian 'mystical' tradition[3] in which he stood Eckhart's teaching emphasizes the direct experience of the Divine by the individual through contemplation. For Eckhart, however, God is not 'out there' somewhere beyond us but rather already-always present within the 'silent middle' of the human soul.

The problem is that human consciousness of this inner divine presence is hindered by our manifold habitual and intractable 'attachments'. The way to experience the union with God that is the birthright and potential of every person is to strip away these attachments. Where Eckhart differs from other monastic, ascetic and even sacramental teachers that might share his desire for beatific union with God is in his insistence that our methods for achieving this ascent of the soul are themselves attachments that, no matter how helpful, must also in the end be stripped away. Eckhart goes so far as to suggest that even all our cherished 'images' or ideas of God must ultimately be recognized as attachments and transcended in pursuit of the 'God beyond God'.

The God beyond God

Meister Eckhart's teaching is radically *theocentric*; it begins and ends with God, although not the 'God' of the theologians but the 'Godhead', the One, the Divine unity that is 'prior' even to the Trinity of Father, Son and Holy Spirit. At this fundamental level Eckhart's God is ineffable, empty and formless, unlike anything or anyone. God's nature, he says in German Sermon (DW) 53, is 'unspeakable', and in language reminiscent of the anonymous English mystical classic, *The Cloud of Unknowing*, he says, 'the hidden darkness of the eternal light of the eternal Godhead is unknown and shall never be known.'[4] The Godhead is 'unspeakable', 'hidden' and 'unknown' precisely because 'He is pure nothing: he is neither this nor that. If you think of anything he might be, he is not that!'[5] The Godhead is not 'a being', does not 'have being', does not 'exist' as such, but is rather 'pure being itself'. In an early Latin work Eckhart asserts, in an intentional reversal of Thomas's ontotheological formula 'God is existence' (*Deus est esse*), that 'existence is God'(*esse est deus*).[6] The 'isness' of all that exists is God.

In the vernacular sermons Eckhart employs the metaphor of the *ground* (Middle High German *grunt*) to connote this innermost depth of the divine reality.[7] The Godhead at its *ground* is utterly One;

'simple' and undifferentiated, and therefore 'impersonal' in the sense of an absolute absence of relations. The ground is also utterly passive and at rest, nothing but pure possibility, 'the unmoving precondition of all activity' as McGinn puts it.[8] The crux and arguably most controversial aspect of Eckhart's mysticism is that this very divine *ground* is also 'the innermost of the (human) soul'.[9] As Eckhart says in numerous places: 'God's ground is my ground and my ground is God's ground.'[10] In the ground the divide between the divine and the human does not hold, for there is there no distinction, no creator and creature, only 'the One'. From the human perspective the ground, which is 'by nature receptive to nothing save only the divine essence, without mediation',[11] is thus the 'interface', the 'place' where the identity of the human person is fused with God's identity. The goal of the spiritual life is to penetrate to this inner ground and so to realize our true identity as God's 'image and likeness', to participate in the eternal movement of grace that Eckhart characterizes as the 'birth of God in the soul'.

Why do we pray, why do we fast, why do we do all our works, why are we baptized, why (most important of all) did God become man? I would answer, in order that God may be born in the soul and the soul be born in God. For that reason all the scriptures were written, for that reason God created the world.[12]

The 'birth of the Son of God in the soul'

Thus, in Eckhart's Christology the reason for the Incarnation (indeed, for the Creation) is that human beings might come to a realization or conscious awareness of themselves as the 'image and likeness of God', bringing forth or 'giving birth' to the Son of God within their innermost soul. This is a Christology, suggests Matthew Fox, in which Christ is understand not as Redeemer but as Reminder: 'Christ came to remind us of our blessed and divine origins as images and likenesses of God in a grace-filled universe. The purpose of his coming is *more our divinization than our redemption* from sin and guilt.'[13]

How is this brought about, this 'divinization', this penetration to the 'ground' and 'birth of God in the soul'? While Eckhart does refer to methods and practices, he seems to give far less weight to the 'birth' as the achievement of human effort than as the product of divine grace. The human role in the process, one of humble cooperation with grace, is clearly secondary. In Eckhart's theology the divine life or 'light', a favoured symbol borrowed from the Fourth Gospel, emanates naturally, necessarily and irresistibly from the Godhead. 'In this birth God pours forth His light in such a way that its richness floods the very ground and essence of the soul until it overflows into its powers, even to the outer person.'[14] This is how, through the agency and movement of the Trinity, God both creates the world out of nothing and enters the world as Son. 'I sometimes mention two springs,' says Eckhart, 'the one, where grace wells up, is where the Father bears forth his only-begotten Son … the other is where creatures flow out from God.'[15] Importantly for Eckhart, the creation is not a past event but a continuous activity, such that 'God is creating the whole world now in this instant.'[16] In the same way the Father's bearing forth his Son is not limited to the one-off historical event of the birth of Jesus but occurs in the 'eternal Now' of the *ground* and is, from the perspective of time, a continuously present and manifold event. Thus, although there is only one 'only-begotten Son', the one Son is born over and over in the many, for we are the 'same son as the Son of God.'[17]

Of the birth of the Son of God in the soul Eckhart once famously asked on behalf of us all: 'What does it avail me that this birth is always happening, if it does not happen in me?'[18] The implication here is that for all the Divine outpouring of grace that makes the birth possible, something else is required to bring the event from the realm of 'pure possibility' to actuality within the individual in time. There must be in the individual a response to grace that is an opening up to God through a turning inward, a journey 'into the silent land' as Martin Laird has called it,[19] into the 'vast and silent terrain'[20] that is the *ground* of the soul. What, then, must one do to undertake this inner journey?

Eckhart's spirituality: the 'Wayless Way'

The consensus among scholars seems to be that, while Eckhart tolerates whatever might be expedient for progress in the spiritual life, particularly for beginners, he sees such things as temporary crutches at best. This is not to say that he has no counsel for the spiritual seeker, just that it is less distinct and prescriptive than that offered, for example, in the 'Jesus Prayer' of the desert fathers, the Exercises of St Ignatius or the Practices of St Teresa of Avila. Eckhart prescribes no special techniques, practices, penances or pilgrimages, insisting that 'whoever seeks God in a special way gets the way and misses God who lies hidden in it.'[21] It is for this reason that his spirituality is often referred to as a 'wayless way'.

More than any particular method of contemplation Eckhart's 'way' consists primarily of an inner attitude or *orientation* that is at once *theocentric*, *contemplative* and *this-worldly*. The fundamental orientation of Eckhart's way is *theocentric*; its 'true north' is God. The goal of the spiritual life is simply to 'have God.' The person with such an inner desire or appetite for God will in Eckhart's thinking also be temperamentally and morally equipped for 'the way', which is not for the 'natural, undisciplined man, for he is entirely remote from, and totally ignorant of this birth.'[22]

The orientation of the spiritual seeker is, then, necessarily also *contemplative*, involving a disciplined attention of the intellect upon its Divine object, 'quite collected and turned entirely inward, not running out through the five senses into the multiplicity of creatures'.[23] Through this 'collected' inwardness of contemplation, the 'bare mind', one is able to achieve the radical 'detachment' from 'multiplicity' and 'creatures' that is the prerequisite of the birth and the chief activity of Eckhart's spirituality. This will ultimately include a detachment even from the ideas and images we use to give form to the formless One, the theological concepts with which we clothe naked 'isness'. We must detach from the 'imagined God' that vanishes when the idea vanishes and be satisfied only with the 'essential God'.[24]

The third aspect of this orientation is a radical *this-worldliness* whereby the God whom we seek is apprehended 'equally in all things and all places'.[25] For Eckhart the contemplative life is fully consonant with the active and involved life, for God is *in* one's ordinary life and it is there that he must be found. The best place to find God, says Eckhart, is 'where we left him.' Whoever and wherever I am, the 'way' for me must begin in the world of my own experience.

I was asked, 'Some people shun all company and always want to be alone; their peace depends on it, and on being in church. Was that the best thing?' And I said, 'No!' Now see why. He who is in a right state, is always in a right state wherever he is, and with everybody … He has only God, thinks only of God, and all things are for him nothing but God.[26]

Questions

I turn now to two questions that emerge from my reading of Eckhart's teachings. The first involves the apparent dissonance between Eckhart's demand for 'detachment' from the 'multiplicity' of the material, historical and social world in which we live and his call to find the one God 'equally in all things'. The second is a question I can hear Nietzsche, and even Dewey and James, asking of the Dominican Master and concerns the possibility of annexing Eckhart's demanding theological metaphysics from the more pragmatic aspects of his 'wayless way'.

First, is there, as Richard Woods alleges, 'an inescapable bias in Eckhart's teaching' against the material creation?[27] Does Eckhart ultimately drive a dualistic wedge between the interior God and the exterior world? If this is indeed the case Eckhart's teaching would seem to run counter to recent welcome advances in 'Creation Spirituality' and the call for a greater awareness of 'embodiment' in our spiritual practices. I suspect that Eckhart's response to this question would focus on his understanding of God, the ground and the soul, which are practically indistinguishable. God, he would begin, *as* the 'isness of all things' is indivisible from that which flows eternally from him. In his creating God graces to every 'creature' its being, its goodness, and its truth and to disrespect or denigrate the 'creature' would be to dishonor He who is in the creature as its most fundamental reality, its 'isness'. I can also hear Eckhart suggesting that the soul, in its deepest ground, its most noble part, is the sole locus of the capacity to see the Divine 'isness' in all things, all activities and all places. It is within the soul's silent ground that God himself knows himself as he is in himself, and within all things. There is, then, no dissonance between the silent 'detached' interiority of Eckhart's spirituality and the exterior world.

In a sense my second question emerges from the answer to the first. If the problem of the divide between God and the material world is solved by reminding ourselves that for Eckhart God is no-thing other than the 'isness' of all things, is it necessary to retain his Neoplatonist metaphysics or his Alexandrian theology at all? Why not replace 'Godhead' with 'isness' at the outset? If in our quest for the transformed consciousness that Eckhart has called 'the birth of God in the soul' we must ultimately detach from all our 'images' of 'God' to apprehend the 'God beyond God' that is the pure, formless 'isness' of all things, why do we need theological language at all? Is it not a mere hindrance?

This question is much more serious than the first, and I suspect that this is why, at least intuitively, many Christians feel as uncomfortable with Eckhart as did the Avignon Papacy. I rather imagine that Eckhart, however, would be unperturbed by it and, with a quiet nod to Nietzsche, would simply repeat his mantra, that one is most likely to find God 'where he left him'. In other words, one's own cultural world will inevitably furnish the perspective from which, if one is lucky, one penetrates beyond the banality of everyday perceptions and cultivates an awareness of the One formless 'isness' that underlies everything. If this means abandoning the metaphysics and egoic constructs for the naked experience of my true self, then so be it.

Such an imagined answer might, of course, misrepresent the devout Dominican terribly. He may be as horrified at the prospect of a redundant theology as many twenty-first century Christians. But I suspect not. I rather think that Eckhart would turn this very question back on me and I conclude my discussion by considering my own place in the trajectory of Christian contemplative practice and my response to Eckhart. A brief autobiographical excursus will set up the context.

Having grown up in a Christian home and given myself in the first two decades of my adult life to professional Christian ministry I experienced a personal crisis in the 1990s that led ultimately to my abandoning my faith and identifying for much of the next decade as an atheist. My atheism was not of the angry, militant kind, but was nonetheless well considered, for I had studied theology and philosophy to postgraduate level. It was also, it seemed, quite irreversible. Then, after reading a book by Eckhart Tolle,[28] I began to meditate in the very simple and unstructured way that Tolle advocated. Very soon I began experiencing fleeting 'flashes' of heightened awareness and decided there was something in this. The thought struck me one day that what I was experiencing in meditation was actually what I had sought (and rarely found) my entire life as a Christian believer. It also struck me that Tolle's teaching, although not at all religious, resonated with much of what I had once deeply appreciated in the Christian scriptures. Tentatively at first, I returned to those scriptures and then to the church, albeit now as a Catholic 'convert'. There I discovered the ancient contemplative tradition and Meister Eckhart, who, I soon realized, had been a significant Western source for Eckhart Tolle, whose thought seems to resonate most clearly with Buddhism.

And so the question that Meister Eckhart's teaching puts to me at this stage in my spiritual journey is this: if I had discovered in Eckhart Tolle's 'secular spirituality' a practical means of connecting with the underlying 'isness' that is the deepest truth of my own existence, why did I return to the Christian metaphysical framework that I not only once abandoned but still do not 'believe' in a literal sense? Does this indicate, to use Meister Eckhart's term, some recalcitrant and pathological 'attachment' to 'God' that serves only to cloud my vision of the truth 'beyond God'?

I'm not sure whether there is a definitive answer to that question. What I do know is that my spiritual quest and my spiritual practice is deeply nourished and powerfully energised by the elegant conceptual framework and simple call to inner silence that Christian thinkers like Meister Eckhart have left us. Eckhart's 'way' is, despite it's mystical language, still the simple 'way' to the Father that Jesus shows us in himself. I know also that if and when I need to let go of anything, it will become clear. For now I hold it lightly in soft hands.

Notes

[1] '…when read in the context of Eckhart's deeply apophatic theology, many of the seemingly heretical statements appear more orthodox, and even *illustrative of the apophatic impetus that underlies Eckhart's mystical discourse.*' (Nelstrop, L. 2009: 216.) Italics mine.

[2] See McGinn, B. 2001: 2-19.

[3] (James, 1952: 371-420). Some writers use 'mysticism' almost interchangeably with 'contemplation', but whether all contemplative thinkers were 'mystics' in the sense that Meister Eckhart, Marguerite Porete and Julian of Norwich were for example is questionable.

[4] Meister Eckhart, Pr. 51 (Walshe No. 83, p254)

[5] Meister Eckhart, Pr. 23 (Walshe No. 54, p287)

[6] Maurer, A. 1974: 77-105

[7] McGinn suggests that *ground* is indeed the 'master metaphor' of Eckhart's mysticism and that because there is no direct equivalent for this simple but 'semantically rich' German word in scholastic Latin this key concept is actually only found in the vernacular works. (2001: 38-39).

[8] McGinn, B. 2001: 81.

[9] McGinn, B. 2001: 41

[10] Meister Eckhart, Pr. 5b (Walshe No. 13b, p109)

[11] Meister Eckhart Pr. 101 (Walshe, No. 1, p31)

[12] Meister Eckhart, Pr. 38 (Walshe No. 29, p177)

[13] Fox, M. 1981: p218-219. Italics mine.

[14] Meister Eckhart, Pr. 102 (Walshe, No. 2, p40)

[15] Meister Eckhart, Pr. 38 (Walshe, No. 29, p181)

[16] Meister Eckhart, Pr. 30 (Walshe, No. 18, p133)

[17] Tobin, F. 1986: p115.

[18] Meister Eckhart, Pr. 101 (Walshe, No. 1, p29)

[19] Laird, M. 2006.

[20] McGinn, B. 2001: 48.

[21] Meister Eckhart, Pr. 5b (Walshe No. 13b, 110)

[22] Meister Eckhart Pr. 101 (Walshe, No. 1, p30)

[23] Meister Eckhart Pr. 101 (Walshe, No. 1, p30)

[24] Meister Eckhart, *Talks of Instruction*, No. 6. (Walshe, p491)

[25] Meister Eckhart DW Pr. 68 (Walshe, No. 69, p353

[26] Meister Eckhart, *Talks of Instruction*, No. 6. (Walshe, p490)

[27] Woods, R. 2011.

[28] Tolle, E. 2005.

Suggested readings

Fleming, Ursula. *Meister Eckhart: the man from whom God nothing hid.* Edited by Ursula Fleming. Springfield, Illinois: Templegate Publishers, 1988.

Fox, Matthew. *Western Spirituality: historical roots, ecumenical routes.* Edited by Matthew Fox. Santa Fe, New Mexico: Bear & Company, 1981.

James, William. *The Varieties of Religious Experience: A Study in Human Nature: Being the Gifford lectures on Natural Religion Delivered at Edinburgh 1901-1902.*London: Burne and Oates, 1952.

Laird, Martin. *Into The Silent Land: A Guide to the Christian Practice of Contemplation.* New York: Oxford University Press, 2006.

Maurer, Armand. A. *Meister Eckhart: Parisian Questions and Prologues.* Toronto: PIMS, 1974.

McGinn, Bernard. *The Mystical Thought of Meister Eckhart: the man from whom God hid nothing.* New York: The Crossroad Publishing Company, 2001.

Nelstrop, Louise. "Mysticism and heresy." In *Christian Mysticism: An introduction to Contemporary Theoretical Approaches*, by Nelstrop, Louise with Magill, Kevin, and Onishi, Bradley. B. 203-221. Surrey: Ashgate Publishing Limited, 2009.

Tobin, Frank. *Meister Eckhart: Thought and language.* Philadelphia: University of Pennsylvania Press, 1986.

Tolle, Eckhart. *A New Earth: Awakening to Your Life's Purpose.* London: Penguin, 2005.

Walshe, Maurice O'C. *The Complete Mystical Works of Meister Eckhart.* New York: Crossroads Herder, 2008.

Woods, Richard. *Meister Eckhart: Master of Mystics.* New York: Continuum International Publishing Group, 2011.

Andy asks that upon reading An Emptyful Chair,

you submit a review on

www.amazon.com's website

where you can share your thoughts.

CPSIA information can be obtained
at www.ICGtesting.com
Printed in the USA
BVHW021115120719
553192BV00036B/389/P

9 781950 955268